Leadership:

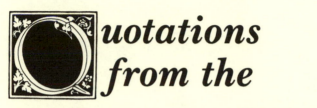 *uotations from the Military Tradition*

Leadership:

Quotations from the Military Tradition

Robert A. Fitton

editor

Westview Press
Boulder • San Francisco • Oxford_____

Copyright © 1990 by Westview Press, Inc.

Published in 1990 in the United States of America by Westview Press, Inc., 5500 Central Avenue, Boulder, Colorado 80301, and in the United Kingdom by Westview Press, 36 Lonsdale Road, Summertown, Oxford OX2 7EW

Library of Congress Cataloging-in-Publication Data
Leadership: quotations from the military tradition / Robert A.
Fitton, editor.
    p.   cm.
  ISBN 0-8133-7867-2
    1. Command of troops—Quotations, maxims, etc.   2. Leadership—
Quotations, maxims, etc.   I. Fitton, Robert A.
UB210.L396   1990
355.3′3041—dc20   90-34115
                                                                                          CIP

Printed and bound in the United States of America

The paper used in this publication meets the requirements
of the American National Standard for Permanence of Paper
for Printed Library Materials Z39.48-1984.

10   9   8   7   6   5   4   3   2

*In memory of my father,
who instilled in me the
appreciation for traditional values*

*And dedicated to the many
military professionals with whom
I have been privileged to serve*

It is a good thing for an uneducated man to read books of quotations.

—Sir Winston Churchill
My Early Life, 1930

Contents

Part One
Quotations

Part Two
Readings on Leadership

Foreword

Leadership is many things to many people. Its basic intellectual underpinnings are a matter of debate. Is it art or science? Is it inherited, or must it be learned? Is it the same in industry and business as it is in military matters? Why are some people better at it than others? Why, even after so much has been written and taught about it, are there so many daily examples of failed leadership?

Leadership, at its core, is the process of taking finite resources and organizing and directing those resources toward finite goals. Inevitably, the most precious, least expendable, and hardest to manage of those resources is people. Thus, leadership is the art of running things—of enabling people to accomplish tasks.

There are two primary reasons leaders fail: a lack of understanding of what leadership is and a lack of knowledge of how to lead. All too frequently, both types of failure reflect an inability to understand or cope with people.

Military leadership is particularly intriguing. Among other challenges, it must cope with one of humanity's most pervasive problems—the conquest of fear. Fear—apprehension in the face of the unknown—is a phenomenon observed and experienced daily; fear of being wounded or of dying in battle is manifestly its ultimate and most difficult form. All leadership challenges therefore are elevated to a new apogee in the demanding work of the profession of arms. Surely it is for this reason that so many people, with and without direct and personal knowledge of the matter, have issued pronouncements about war— about battle and the nature and scope of its challenge—especially its challenge to leadership. This book is a fascinating collection of some of the more pithy of those pronouncements.

The military profession lays substantial store by the study of leadership; it is one of the essential professional skills, and as such its study, practice, refinement, contemplation, and improvement are closely woven into the fabric of military behavior, career development, and advancement. Not every good leader rises to the top; nor do the less successful leaders fall by the wayside as soon and as often as they should. But almost without exception, leadership is a subject military professionals study all their lives. That is why many of the most enduring and quotable pronouncements on the subject are those of military men.

Leadership styles vary with personalities and to some extent with the circumstances in which leadership must be applied. However, when all is said and done, wars are won by the courage of soldiers, the excellence of the leadership they have been provided, and the quality of the training undertaken by soldiers and leaders in their units before battles begin. Therein is the total leadership concept—leadership of people by other people who have trained themselves to overcome their own fear and who know almost instinctively how to help others overcome their fear under the most adverse circumstances imaginable. It also includes the organizational cohesion of highly trained, highly motivated soldiers, all bent on the accomplishment of their most demanding tasks. To the extent that this well-selected compendium of leader observations provides grist for the intellectual mill that inevitably must continue to grind on the subject, it is a most worthwhile contribution to this complex and controversial subject. Not only military leaders, but leaders from all walks of life, will benefit from the wisdom of these quotations.

Donn A. Starry
General, U.S. Army (Retired)

Preface

The purpose of this book of leadership quotations is to distill and bring together some of the most memorable thoughts, words, and concepts concerning leadership from the military tradition. It began several years ago as an effort to capture those tried and true phrases that I could recollect in part but whose exact wording or specific attribution I had unfortunately forgotten all too soon. What evolved was a collage of concepts, thoughts, and philosophies using military leadership as the central focus.

The basic premise is simple—traditional values that are essential to good leadership underlie each quotation. Leaders must thoroughly understand and continually demonstrate those values their profession demands and then be able to foster the development of those values in their subordinates. Military values are unique because the military profession often demands personal and organizational sacrifices during trying circumstances. The essence of enduring professional military values is captured and articulated in the thoughts and words of great leaders.

Military leadership is demanding and challenging. There are no magic formulas. Personalities differ, situations vary, and conditions change; however, I have been told by some wise old leaders that watching and talking with great leaders are some of the best ways to learn about military leadership. Unfortunately, opportunities for personal exposure to great leaders are limited. Yet, opportunities to learn and better understand the personal philosophies of great leaders can be extensive through the study of historical accounts, autobiographies, memoirs, writings, and quotations.

The quotations included here cover a broad spectrum of authors and topics related to military leadership. Most are thought provoking;

a few are provocative. The majority of authors represented are great military leaders, statesmen, or philosophers, but also included are pertinent thoughts by corporate leaders, scholars, poets, and writers. International in scope, this book covers a vast period of time—from ancient to contemporary. It also includes material on leadership that is often sought but at times difficult to locate, such as the cadet prayers of the military service academies.

Some of the topics are unique to military leaders, yet the broad concepts addressed are applicable to leaders of any profession. After all, the modern study of leadership can trace its lineage to the study of human experiences during World War II. This book should be of special value to students of military history and past military leaders as well as to military professionals seeking to better understand their profession and to refine their personal philosophy of leadership. It can serve as a reference source for researchers, writers, and speakers or as a source for personal introspection and reflection.

The quotations are arranged in a concise, easily accessible format. They can be located through either the chapter headings in the Table of Contents or the Index of Authors. The quotations in each chapter are listed alphabetically by author, with the exception of those at the beginning of the Military Leadership chapter. The latter, which provide Army definitions of military leadership, are arranged chronologically to highlight the evolution of the concept of military leadership. The index lists specific topic areas for each author, which will allow the reader to review all of an author's included contributions or simply to seek that author's thoughts on a particular topic. Scattered throughout the book are quotations attributed to perhaps the singularly most prolific (and at times most profound) author—*Anonymous.*

The quotations were derived from many sources, and a conscientious effort was made to properly ascribe the authorship and source of the quotations. As my "library" of quotations expanded, I began to specify the sources in greater detail. Quotations from the Bible are from the King James Version. Quotations originally appearing in a foreign language appear with an English translation. Dates generally indicate when the major work was written or first published. It can be noted that in many cases the military rank of an author varies in entries and in the index. With the quotations, I cited the rank of the author at the time a statement was made; in the index, I listed the highest military rank that person attained. Posthumous publication dates occasionally occur.

I recognize that the delineation of quotations into one subject area versus another can be challenged. Certainly some quotations could appropriately apply to several subject headings; however, to avoid repetition, quotations are correlated to what I consider to be the most pertinent subject heading. I included quotations under particular topic headings based on the thoughts I feel the quotations convey and not merely on the mention of specific key words.

This book is by no means exhaustive or all-inclusive but rather provides a starting point for thoughts on leadership. It is the culmination of the initial phase of what I see as a dynamic, evolving project. If you feel that your favorite leadership quotation has been overlooked or that a specific quotation should appear under a different topic area, please write to me in care of Westview Press.

Finally, this book offers an opportunity to remember that although leadership is learned through practice rather than by teaching, leadership skills can be enhanced through personal study and reflection. It is my hope that this book will be of value to soldiers and civilians alike. I believe everyone will be able to find several old and many new favorites within these pages.

Robert A. Fitton
Lieutenant Colonel, U.S. Army

Acknowledgments

I am deeply grateful to the Colonel's Lady, my lovely wife, Mary Alice, and our two beautiful daughters, Tracy and Jennifer, for their understanding, patience, and unwavering support, without which I certainly could not have devoted the necessary time and effort to complete this project.

I am indebted to Colonel (U.S. Army, Retired) John D. Beasley III, who provided me with the impetus to compile quotations on military leadership, and to Colonel Christopher C. Shoemaker for his expert advice, support, and counsel.

I must also thank my editors at Westview Press, Peter Kracht and Beverly LeSuer, and my copy editor, Linda Cetrulo. Finally, I owe more than can be expressed to a host of unnamed others who offered encouragement, helped research data, and answered many troublesome inquiries.

R.A.F.

PART ONE

Quotations

Ability

Man for man one division is as good as another. They vary only in the skill and leadership of their commanders.

General Omar N. Bradley

The commander's success will be measured more by his ability to lead than by his adherence to fixed notions.

General Dwight D. Eisenhower

To be great is to be misunderstood.

Ralph Waldo Emerson
Essays: First Series, "Self Reliance," 1841

Everyone must row with the oars he has.

English proverb

The same man cannot well be skilled in everything; each has his special excellence.

Euripides
Rhesus, circa 450 B.C.

Most do violence to their natural aptitude, and thus attain superiority in nothing.

Baltasar Gracián Y Morales
The Art of Wordly Wisdom, 1647

3

God obligeth no man to more than he hath given him ability to perform.

Koran

The majority of men are more capable of great actions than of good ones.

Michel Eyquem de Montaigne
Essays, "Of Anger," 1588

The acid test of an officer who aspires to high command is his ability to be able to grasp quickly the essentials of a military problem, to decide rapidly what he will do, to make it quite clear to all concerned what he intends to achieve and how he will do it, and then to see that his subordinate commanders get on with the job.

Field Marshal Bernard L. Montgomery
Memoirs of Field Marshal the Viscount Montgomery of Alamein, 1958

Our vanity desires that what we do best should be considered what is hardest for us.

Friedrich Wilhelm Nietzsche
Beyond Good and Evil, 1886

A general's ability lies in judging the best moment for attack and in knowing how to prepare for it.

Ardant du Picq
Battle Studies, 1880

Skills vary with the man. We must tread a straight path and strive by that which is born in us.

Pindar
Òdes, circa fifth century B.C.

Do what you can, with what you have, where you are.

Theodore Roosevelt

The general must know how to get his men their rations and every other kind of stores needed for war. He must have imagination to originate plans—practical sense and energy to carry them through. He must be: observant, untiring, shrewd, kindly and cruel, simple and crafty, a watchman and a robber, lavish and miserly, generous and stingy, rash and conservative. All these and many other qualities both natural and acquired he must have. He should also, as a matter of course, know his tactics; for a disorderly mob is no more an army than a heap of building materials is a house.

Socrates

The skillful general conducts his army just as though he were leading a single man by the hand.

Sun-Tzu
The Art of War, circa fourth century B.C.

I rate the skillful tactician above the skillful strategist, especially him who plays the bad cards well.

Field Marshal Sir Archibald P. Wavell
Soldiers and Soldiering, 1953

Adversity

Better be wise by the misfortunes of others than by your own.

Aesop
Fables, "The Lion, the Ass, and the Fox Hunting,"
circa sixth century B.C.

When the going gets tough, the tough get going.

Anonymous
(Slogan in U.S. Military Academy gymnasium)

Education is an ornament in prosperity and a refuge in adversity.

Aristotle

The beauty of the soul shines out when a man bears with composure
one heavy mischance after another, not because he does not feel them,
but because he is a man of high and heroic temper.

Aristotle
Nicomachean Ethics, circa 340 B.C.

Prosperity doth best discover vice, but adversity doth best discover
virtue.

Sir Francis Bacon

In war, as in life, it is often necessary, when some cherished scheme has failed, to take up the best alternative open, and if so, it is folly not to work for it with all your might.

Sir Winston Churchill

Never complain and never explain.

Benjamin Disraeli

Little things affect little minds.

Benjamin Disraeli
Sybil, 1845

It is difficulties that show what men are.

Epictetus
Discourses, circa A.D. 100

In prosperity it is very easy to find a friend, but in adversity it is the most difficult of all things.

Epictetus
Fragment, circa A.D. 100

Es bildet ein Talent sich in der stille, sich ein Charakter in dem strom der Welt.
[A talent is formed in stillness, a character in the world's torrent.]
Johann Wolfgang von Goethe
Torquato Tasso, 1790

Life, misfortunes, isolation, abandonment, poverty, are battlefields which have their heroes; obscure heroes, sometimes greater than the illustrious heroes.

Victor Hugo
Les Misérables, 1862

Nothing gives one person so much advantage over another as to remain always cool and unruffled under all circumstances.

Thomas Jefferson

Great crises produce great men and great deeds of courage.
John F. Kennedy
Profiles in Courage, 1956

Where the willingness is great, the difficulties cannot be great.
Niccolò di Bernardo Machiavelli
The Prince, 1513

Campaigns and battles are nothing but a long series of difficulties to be overcome. The lack of equipment, the lack of food, the lack of this or that are only excuses; the real leader displays his quality in his triumphs over adversity, however great it may be.
General George C. Marshall
Address to first Officer Candidate Class
at Fort Benning, Georgia, 18 September 1941

An extraordinary situation requires extraordinary resolution. The more obstinate the resistance of an armed body, the more chances it will have of being succored or of forcing a passage. How many things apparently impossible have nevertheless been performed by resolute men who had no alternative but death!
Napoleon Bonaparte
Maxims, LXVII, 1831

That which does not kill me makes me stronger.
Friedrich Wilhelm Nietzsche
Twilight of the Idols, 1888

Publĭca virtūtĭs permălĕ facta via est.
[The road to valor is builded by adversity.]
Ovid
Trista, circa A.D. 10

No pain, no palm; no thorn, no throne; no gall, no glory; no cross, no crown.
William Penn
No Cross, No Crown, 1669

Anyone can hold the helm when the sea is calm.
Publilius Syrus
Moral Sayings, circa first century B.C.

Learn to see in another's calamity the ills which you should avoid.

Publilius Syrus
Moral Sayings, circa first century B.C.

Miseries seem light to a soldier if the chief who imposes hardships on him also volunteers to share them.

Comte de Ségur

Fire is the test of gold; adversity of strong men.

Seneca
De Prōvǐdentǐa, A.D. 64

Sweet are the uses of adversity;
Which, like the toad, ugly and venomous,
Wears yet a precious jewel in his head.

William Shakespeare
As You Like It, Act II, Scene i, 1600

While the battles the British fight may differ in the widest possible ways, they have invariably two common characteristics—they are always fought uphill and always at the juncture of two or more map sheets.

Field Marshal Sir William Slim
Unofficial History, 1959

You're all right as long as you're winners; I'm a hell of a general when I'm winning, anybody is, but it's when you're not winning—and I have not always been winning, if you had been a British general at the start of a war you'd know that—it is then that the real test of leadership is made.

Field Marshal Sir William Slim
Speech to U.S. Army Command
and General Staff College, 8 April 1952

There is no success without hardship.

Sophocles
Electra, circa 415 B.C.

He is the best sailor who can steer within fewest points of the wind, and exact a motive power out of the greatest obstacles.

Henry David Thoreau
A Week on the Concord and Merrimack Rivers, 1849

If you can't stand the heat, get out of the kitchen.

Harry S. Truman
Mr. Citizen, 1960

When things are going badly in battle the best tonic is to take one's mind off one's own troubles by considering what a rotten time one's opponent must be having.

Field Marshal Sir Archibald P. Wavell
Other Men's Flowers, 1944

Advice

Advice is like castor oil—easy enough to give, but difficult to take.

Anonymous

Have marked respect for the older captains, consult them frequently, show them friendship and confidence. Be the support, the friend, the father of the young officers; love the old sergeants and soldiers; speak to them often and always with good will, even seek their advice from time to time.

Marshal de Belle-Isle
Letter to his son

Hear counsel, and receive instruction, that thou mayest be wise in thy latter end.

Bible, Proverbs 19:20

Every purpose is established by counsel; and with good advice make war.

Bible, Proverbs 20:18

If it moves, salute it. If it doesn't move, pick it up. If you can't pick it up, paint it.

British Army proverb

Advice is seldom welcome; and those who want it the most always like it the least.

Earl of Chesterfield
Letter to his son, 29 January 1748

We are all wise for other people, none for himself.

Ralph Waldo Emerson
Journals, 1834

Everybody knows good counsel except him that has need of it.

German proverb

Many receive advice, few profit by it.

Publilius Syrus
Moral Sayings, circa first century B.C.

We may give advice, but we cannot inspire conduct.

François, Duc de La Rochefoucauld
Maximes, 1665

Nothing is given so profusely as advice.

François, Duc de La Rochefoucauld
Reflections, 1678

Be not afraid of greatness. Some are born great, some achieve greatness, and some have greatness thrust upon them.

William Shakespeare
Twelfth Night, Act II, Scene v, 1600

In giving advice seek to help, not to please, your friend.

Solon of Athens

No enemy is worse than bad advice.

Sophocles
Electra, circa 415 B.C.

Ambition

To take a soldier without ambition is to pull off his spurs.

Sir Francis Bacon
Essays, "Of Ambition," 1625

It is not the going out of port, but the coming in, that determines the success of a voyage.

Henry Ward Beecher
Proverbs from Plymouth Pulpit, 1887

By their fruits ye shall know them.

Bible, Matthew 7:20

What shall it profit a man, if he shall gain the whole world, and lose his own soul?

Bible, Mark 8:36

Ah, but a man's reach should exceed his grasp.
Or what's a heaven for?

Robert Browning
Men and Women, "Andrea Del Sarto," 1855

If you aspire to the highest place, it is no disgrace to stop at the second, or even the third, place.

Marcus Tullius Cicero
On Oratory, circa 55 B.C.

All ambitions are lawful except those which climb upward on the miseries or credulities of mankind.

Joseph Conrad
A Personal Record, 1912

Every man believes that he has a greater possibility.

Ralph Waldo Emerson
Essays: First Series, "Circles," 1841

First say to yourself what you would be; and then do what you have to do.

Epictetus
Discourses, circa A.D. 100

If you aim at nothing, you will surely hit it.

Lieutenant General Robert H. Forman

Who begins too much accomplishes little.

German proverb

Ai en aristeuein.
[Always to be the best.]

Greek motto

The way to be nothing is to do nothing.

Edgar W. Howe

A man's worth is no greater than the worth of his ambitions.

Marcus Aurelius Antoninus
Meditations, circa 170

Mighty rivers can easily be leaped at their source.

Publilius Syrus
Moral Sayings, circa first century B.C.

Ambition, the soldier's virtue.

William Shakespeare
Antony and Cleopatra, Act III, Scene i, 1607

Nothing is done. Everything in the world remains to be done or done over.

Lincoln Steffens

In the long run men hit only what they aim at. Therefore, though they should fail immediately, they had better aim at something high.

Henry David Thoreau
Walden, 1854

Attributes

Any complex activity, if it is to be carried on with any degree of virtuosity, calls for appropriate gifts of intellect and temperment. If they are outstanding and reveal themselves in exceptional achievement, their possessor is called a "genius."

Karl von Clausewitz
On War, 1832

No man was ever a great soldier without the most generous virtues of the soul, and the most distinguished powers of the intellect. The former are independence, self-reliance, ambition within proper bounds; that sort of physical courage which not only does not know fear, but which is not even conscious that there is such a thing as courage; that greater moral quality which can hold the lives of tens of thousands of men and the destinies of a great country or cause patiently, intelligently, and unflinchingly in his grasp; powers of endurance which cannot be overtaxed; the conscious habit of ruling men and of commanding their love and admiration, coupled with the ability to stir their enthusiasm to the yielding of their last ounce of effort. The latter comprise [a] business capacity of the very highest order, essential to the care of his troops; keen perceptions, which even in extraordinary circumstances or sudden emergencies are not to be led astray; the ability to think as quickly and accurately in the turmoil of battle as in the quiet of the bureau; the power to foresee to its ultimate conclusion the result of a strategic or tactical manoeuvre; the capacity to gauge the efforts of men and of masses of men; the many-sidedness which can respond to the demands of every detail of the battle-field, while never losing sight of the one object aimed at; the mental strength which weakens not under the tax of hours and days of unequalled strain.

Colonel Theodore A. Dodge
Great Captains, 1889

Humility must always be the portion of any man who receives acclaim earned in the blood of his followers and the sacrifices of his friends.

General Dwight D. Eisenhower
Address at Guildhall, London, 12 July 1945

These, then, are the three pillars of generalship—courage, creative intelligence, and physical fitness; the attributes of youth rather than of middle age.

Major-General J.F.C. Fuller
Generalship: Its Diseases and Their Cure, 1936

Imperturbable calm in the Commander is essential above all things.

General Sir Ian Hamilton
Dispatch from Gallipoli to Lord Kitchener,
12 May 1915

The young American responds quickly and readily to the exhibition of qualities of leadership on the part of his officers. Some of these qualities are industry, energy, initiative, determination, enthusiasm, firmness, kindness, justness, self-control, unselfishness, honor, and courage.

General John A. Lejeune
Reminiscences of a Marine, 1930

At the head of an army, nothing is more becoming than simplicity.

Napoleon Bonaparte
Political Aphorisms, 1848

It is rare and difficult to find in one man all the qualities necessary to a great general. That which is most desirable and which immediately sets a man apart is that his intelligence or talent be in equilibrium with his character or courage. If his courage is superior, a general heedlessly undertakes things beyond his conception; while, on the

17

contrary, if his character or courage is inferior to his intelligence, he does not dare carry out his conceptions.

Napoleon Bonaparte
Maxims, LXXXI, 1831

War is a very simple thing, and the determining characteristics are self-confidence, speed and audacity. None of these things can ever be perfect, but they can be good.

General George S. Patton, Jr.
War as I Knew It, 1947

The first of all qualities is *COURAGE.* Without this the others are of little value, since they cannot be used. The second is *INTELLIGENCE,* which must be strong and fertile in expedients. The third is *HEALTH.*

Marshal Comte de Maurice Saxe
Mes Rêveries, 1732

It is the merit of a general to impart good news, and to conceal the bad.

Sophocles

I want to tell you something about the military mind. It is a mind which seeks to anticipate and prepare for every eventuality.

Robert T. Stevens

I've made the points that leaders under pressure must keep themselves absolutely clean morally (the relativism of the social sciences will never do). They must lead by example, must be able to implant high-mindedness in their followers, must have competence beyond status, and must have earned their followers respect by demonstrating integrity.

Vice Admiral James Bond Stockdale
Military Ethics,
"Machiavelli, Management, and Moral Leadership," 1987

Neither bars nor stars make an officer. An individual becomes an officer only when he develops those inner qualities of honesty, self-sacrifice, and attention to duty that are always inherent to real leadership.

General Samuel D. Sturgis, Jr.

By command I mean the general's qualities of wisdom, sincerity, humanity, courage, and strictness.

Sun-Tzu
The Art of War, circa fourth century B.C.

I studied the lives of great men and famous women, and I found that the men and women who got to the top were those who did the jobs they had in hand, with everything they had of energy and enthusiasm and hard work.

Harry S. Truman

Competency and moral responsibility thus merge as the defining characteristic of the professional soldier, particularly in his role as combat commander.

Lieutenant Colonel Paul R. Viotti

What are the qualities of the good soldier, by the development of which we make the man war-worthy—fit for any war? . . . The following four—in whatever order you place them—pretty well cover the field: discipline, physical fitness, technical skill in the use of his weapons, battle-craft.

Field Marshal Sir Archibald P. Wavell
Lecture at the Royal United Service Institution,
15 February 1933

A general may succeed for some time in persuading his superiors that he is a good commander: he will never persuade his army that he is a good commander unless he has the real qualities of one.

Field Marshal Sir Archibald P. Wavell
"Lees Knowles Lectures,"
Trinity College, Cambridge, 1939

The many and contrasted qualities that a general must have rightly gives an impression of the great field of activity that generalship covers and the variety of the situations in which it has to deal, and the need for adaptability in the make-up of a general.

Field Marshal Sir Archibald P. Wavell
Generals and Generalship, 1939

What I hold to be the first essential of a general [is] the quality of robustness, the ability to stand the shocks of war.

Field Marshal Sir Archibald P. Wavell
"Lees Knowles Lectures,"
Trinity College, Cambridge, 1939

Authority

All power tends to corrupt; absolute power corrupts absolutely.
John Emerich E. Dalberg-Acton
Letter to Mandell Creighton, 5 April 1887

Law is a regulation in accord with reason, issued by a lawful superior, for the common good.
Saint Thomas Aquinas

Authority is never without hate.
Euripides
Ion, circa 421 B.C.

The sole advantage of power is that you can do more good.
Baltasar Gracián Y Morales
The Art of Wordly Wisdom, 1647

Lawful and settled authority is very seldom resisted when it is well employed.
Samuel Johnson
The Rambler, 1750

Delegation of authority is one of the most important functions of a leader, and he should delegate authority to the maximum degree possible with regard to the capabilities of his people. Once he has established policy, goals, and priorities, the leader accomplishes his objectives by pushing authority right down to the bottom. Doing so trains people to use their initiative; not doing so stifles creativity and lowers morale.

Admiral Thomas H. Moorer
Quoted in Karel Montor et al.,
Naval Leadership: Voices of Experience, 1987

The commander must try, above all, to establish personal and comradely contact with his men, but without giving away an inch of his authority.

Field Marshal Erwin Rommel

Top military people are much like successful business men. They are interested, receptive to new ideas, and, most of all, hold a strong belief in the authority of the civilian.

Robert T. Stevens

Strange as it sounds, great leaders gain authority by giving it away.

Vice Admiral James Bond Stockdale
Military Ethics, 1987

Boldness, Audacity

Ask, and it shall be given you; seek, and ye shall find; knock, and it shall be opened unto you.

Bible, Matthew 7:7

Never forget that no military leader has ever become great without audacity.

Karl von Clausewitz
Principles of War, 1812

Be audacious and cunning in your plans, firm and persevering in their execution, determined to find a glorious end.

Karl von Clausewitz
On War, 1832

It is even better to act quickly and err than to hesitate until the time of action is past.

Karl von Clausewitz
On War, 1832

The higher up the chain of command, the greater is the need for boldness to be supported by a reflective mind, so that boldness does not degenerate into purposeless bursts of blind passion.

Karl von Clausewitz
On War, 1832

On no account should we overlook the moral effect of a rapid, running assault. It hardens the advancing soldier against danger, while the stationary soldier loses his presence of mind.

Karl von Clausewitz
On War, 1832

Boldness, without the rules of propriety, becomes insubordination.

Confucius
Analects, circa 500 B.C.

Men of principle are sure to be bold, but those who are bold may not always be men of principle.

Confucius
Analects, circa 500 B.C.

Fighting when there is no hope of victory is not mad; it is the deepest wisdom, beyond the comprehension of timorous leaders who look into the book and decide all is lost. It is wisdom because courage achieves the impossible. Boldness driven by energy knows no barrier. War cannot be fought without sore loss. But any sacrifice today is small loss compared to a nation enslaved tomorrow.

Lieutenant Commander Ernest N. Eller

Fortune favors the audacious.

Desiderius Erasmus
Adagia, 1508

The bold are helpless without cleverness.

Euripides

Damn the torpedoes! Full speed ahead.

Admiral David G. Farragut
Battle of Mobile Bay, 5 August 1864

Whatever you can do, or dream you can, begin it. Boldness has genius, power, and magic in it.

Johann Wolfgang von Goethe

He who seizes the right moment,
Is the right man.

Johann Wolfgang von Goethe
Faust: Part I, 1808

When the situation is obscure, attack.

Attributed to General Heinz Guderian

It is the bold man who every time does best.

Homer
Odyssey, circa 700 B.C.

To move swiftly, strike aggressively is the secret of a successful war.

General Thomas J. "Stonewall" Jackson

Rommel's Maxim: "A maximum of caution, combined with supreme dash at the right moment."

B. H. Liddell Hart
The Rommel Papers, 1953

There is no security on this earth; there is only opportunity.

General Douglas MacArthur

My conclusion is, then, that, as fortune is variable and men fixed in their ways, men will prosper as long as they are in tune with the times and will fail when they are not. However, I will say that in my opinion it is better to be bold than cautious, for fortune is a woman and whoever wishes to win her must importune and beat her, and we may observe that she is more frequently won by this sort than by those who proceed more deliberately.

Niccolò di Bernardo Machiavelli
The Prince, 1513

Impetuosity and audacity often achieve what ordinary means fail to achieve.

Niccolò di Bernardo Machiavelli
Discorsi, 1531

Warfare today is a thing of swift movement—of rapid concentrations. It requires the building up of enormous fire power against successive objectives with breath-taking speed. It is not a game for the unimaginative plodder.

General George C. Marshall
Selected Speeches and Statements of General of the Army George C. Marshall, edited by Major H. A. DeWeerd, 1945

A general should show boldness, strike a decided blow, and maneuver upon the flank of his enemy. The victory is in his hands.

Napoleon Bonaparte
Maxims, XXV, 1831

With audacity one can undertake anything, but not do everything.

Napoleon Bonaparte

In war nothing is impossible, providing you use audacity.

General George S. Patton, Jr.
War as I Knew It, 1947

Audacity augments courage; hesitation, fear.

Publilius Syrus
Moral Sayings, circa first century B.C.

There are occasions in which daring and risky operations, boldly executed, can pay great dividends.

General Matthew B. Ridgway
Soldier: The Memoirs of Matthew B. Ridgway, 1956

Rapidity is the essence of war; take advantage of the enemy's unreadiness, make your way by unexpected routes, and attack unguarded spots.

Sun-Tzu
The Art of War, circa fourth century B.C.

God favors the bold and strong of heart.

General Alexander A. Vandegrift

Novelty and surprise throw an enemy into consternation; but common incidents have no effect.

Vegetius
Dē Re Mīlitāri, Book III, 378

Fortune sides with him who dares.

Virgil
Aeneid, 19 B.C.

A bold general may be lucky, but no general can be lucky unless he is bold. The general who allows himself to be bound and hampered by regulations is unlikely to win a battle.

Field Marshal Sir Archibald P. Wavell
"Lees Knowles Lectures,"
Trinity College, Cambridge, 1939

Caring

Instead of pointing a finger, hold out a hand.

Anonymous

And as ye would that men should do to you, do ye also to them likewise.

Bible, Luke 6:31

There are those who contend that the best strategist is the commander most distantly removed from his troops. . . . The strategist . . . cannot be infected by compassion for his troops. . . . But because war is as much a conflict of passion as it is of force, no commander can become a strategist until first he knows his men. Far from being a handicap to command, compassion is the measure of it. For unless one values the lives of his soldiers and is tormented by their ordeals, he is unfit to command.

General Omar N. Bradley

He who receives a benefit should never forget it; he who bestows should never remember it.

Pierre Charron

I am distrustful of a commander who points with pride to the number of casualties his unit has taken in battle. When the men brag about the few casualties their unit has taken in taking tough objectives, their commander is made.

General Bruce C. Clarke

What you do not want done to yourself, do not do to others.
Confucius
Analects, circa 500 B.C.

If you wish to be loved by your soldiers, do not lead them to slaughter.
. . . When you seem to be most prodigal of the soldier's blood, you
spare it, however, by supporting your attacks well and by pushing them
with the greatest vigor to prevent time from augmenting your losses.
Frederick the Great
Instructions for His Generals, 1747

Treat people as if they were what they ought to be and you help them
to become what they are capable of being.
Johann Wolfgang von Goethe

You've got to love your soldiers . . . some you have to love them more
than others.
General William J. Livsey

Coupled with self-control, consideration and thoughtfulness will carry
a man far. Men will warm toward a leader when they come to believe
that all the energy he stored up by living somewhat within himself is
at their service. But when they feel that this is not the case, and that
his reserve is simply the outward sign of a spiritual miserliness and
concentration on purely personal goals, no amount of restraint will
ever win their favor.
Brigadier General S.L.A. Marshall
The Armed Forces Officer, 1950

The people you're responsible for have got to know you care about
their well-being. This has more to do with the success of an organization
than anything else.
Lieutenant General James H. Merryman

Second to honesty and courage of purpose, I would place an unselfish
attitude as the greatest attribute of a leader. . . . Place the care and
protection of the men first; share their hardships without complaint
and when the real test comes you will find that they possess a genuine
respect and admiration for you. To do otherwise means failure at the

29

crucial moment when the support of your men is essential to the success of the battle.

General Alexander M. Patch

There are only three routes to strategic distinction for a company—constant innovation, superior service, and superior quality. All of those come from an all-hands effort. None of them can be mandated. The biggest mistake managers make is forgetting that excellence comes from people who care, not from a good reporting system or other system of control.

Tom Peters
Supervisory Management, February 1984

I remember a bitter joke that went the rounds of the Army soon after World War I. . . . At a staff meeting before a big attack some fire-eating division commander tapped at a little dot on the map with his riding crop and said: "I'd give ten thousand men to take that hill." There was a moment of silence, and then from the back of the room, where stood the battalion commanders whose men would have to go against the hill, there came an ironic voice: "Generous son-of-a-bitch, isn't he?"

General Matthew B. Ridgway
Soldier: The Memoirs of Matthew B. Ridgway, 1956

A commander must have far more concern for the welfare of his men than he has for his own safety. After all, the same dignity attaches to the mission given a single soldier as to the duties of the commanding general. The execution of the soldier's mission is just as vitally important, because it is the sum total of all those small individual missions, properly executed, which produces the results of the big unit. All lives are equal on the battlefield, and a dead rifleman is as great a loss, in the sight of God, as a dead general.

General Matthew B. Ridgway
Soldier: The Memoirs of Matthew B. Ridgway, 1956

A subtle approach to the affection of our men is an interest in their families. Ask any soldier about his wife and children, he is delighted to tell his story and is greatly flattered by the interest which his commander shows. An occasional letter from an officer to a member of a soldier's family—describing the good work which the son is doing in the Army—will reverberate through the entire command, and the officer will make a lifelong friend of the soldier in question.

General Maxwell D. Taylor

A reflective reading of history will show that no man ever rose to military greatness who could not convince his troops that he put them first, above all else.

General Maxwell D. Taylor

The work of impressing upon the soldier the fact that his officers are interested in his welfare should start from the first day when he joins his unit and be continuous thereafter.

General Maxwell D. Taylor

If his behavior shows that in all things the enlisted man comes first, he will receive loyal, uncomplaining service from his men, without the grumbling and 'bitching' which are the merited lot of the selfish officer.

General Maxwell D. Taylor
The Field Artillery Journal, January/February 1947

What you should hope that your recruits will hear is that the "old man" . . . keeps a sharp lookout for the comforts of his men, that he is genuinely interested in the unit's recreational life, and that he is warmly understanding of the men's personal problems.

General Maxwell D. Taylor
The Field Artillery Journal, January/February 1947

The commander must show by his behavior that the "old man" is always on the job, that he sees that the rations come up in time, that the mail is never delivered late, and that he is always looking for better conditions so as to improve the lot of his men. If on all sides there is this common tie of service—of the commander serving his men, of the men serving the commander—this will be a unit truly formidable in battle.

General Maxwell D. Taylor
Speech to Citadel cadets, 21 January 1956

For people are only too glad to obey the man who they believe takes wiser thoughts for their interests than they themselves do.

Xenophon
Cyropaedia, circa 360 B.C.

You have to care.

Major General Melvin Zais

I enjoin you to be ever alert to the pitfalls of too much authority. For the very junior leader beware that you do not fall into the category of the little man with the little job and the big head. In essence, be considerate. Treat your subordinates right and they will literally die for you.

Major General Melvin Zais, 1969

Character

Character is made by what you stand for; reputation by what you fall for.

Anonymous

Character consists of what you do on the third and fourth tries.

Anonymous

Be careful not to strut your humility.

Anonymous

Practice makes perfect, so be careful what you practice.

Anonymous

A good name is better than precious ointment.

Bible, Ecclesiastes 6:1

A good name *is* rather to be chosen than great riches, *and* loving favour rather than silver and gold.

Bible, Proverbs 22:1

A wounded reputation is seldom cured.

Henry George Bohn
Handbook of Proverbs, 1855

An honest man's word is as good as his bond.

Miguel de Cervantes
Don Quixote, 1615

A good name is better than riches.

Miguel de Cervantes
Don Quixote, 1615

The wise man is informed in what is right. The inferior man is informed in what will pay.

Confucius

A man's action is only a picture book of his creed.

Ralph Waldo Emerson

The force of character is cumulative.

Ralph Waldo Emerson
Essays: First Series, "Self-Reliance," 1841

Don't *say* things. What you *are* stands over you the while, and thunders so that I cannot hear what you say to the contrary.

Ralph Waldo Emerson
Letters and Social Aims: Social Aims, 1876

A man of character in peace is a man of courage in war. Character is a habit. The daily choice of right and wrong. It is a moral quality which grows to maturity in peace and is not suddenly developed in war.

General Sir James Glover
Parameters,
"A Soldier and His Conscience," September 1973

A man's character is his fate.

Heraclitus
Fragment 119, circa 500 B.C.

In matters of principle, stand like a rock; in matters of taste, swim with the current.

Thomas Jefferson

God grant that men of principle shall be our principal men.

Thomas Jefferson

The real character of sea officers cannot be masked from each other.

Lord Admiral John Jervis, Earl of St. Vincent

The union of wise theory with great character will constitute the great captain.

Baron Henri de Jomini
Précis de l'Art de la Guerre, 1838

Every man has three characters—that which he exhibits, that which he has, and that which he thinks he has.

Alphonse Karr

No intellectual brilliance and no technical capacity will be enough to qualify one for military leadership unless it is combined with qualities of character that inspire other men to give forth their best effort in a common cause.

Melvin R. Laird

A different habit, with worse effect, was the way that ambitious officers, when they came in sight of promotion to the general's list, would decide that they would bottle up their thoughts and ideas, as a safety precaution, until they reached the top and could put these ideas into practice. Unfortunately, the usual result, after years of such self-repression for the sake of their ambition, was that when the bottle was eventually uncorked the contents had evaporated.

B. H. Liddell Hart
As quoted by Josiah Bunting in *Worldview,*
"The Conscience of a Soldier," December 1973

Character is like a tree and reputation like its shadow. The shadow is what we think of it; the tree is the real thing.

Abraham Lincoln

The measure of a man's real character is what he would do if he knew he never would be found out.

Lord Thomas Babington Macaulay

A man should *BE* upright, not be *KEPT* upright.

Marcus Aurelius Antoninus
Meditations, circa A.D. 170

Waste no time arguing what a good man should be. Be one.

Marcus Aurelius Antoninus
Meditations, circa A.D. 170

Today war, total war, is not a succession of mere episodes in a day or a week. It is a long drawn out and intricately planned business and the longer it continues the heavier are the demands on the character of the men engaged in it.

General George C. Marshall
Selected Speeches and Statements of General of the Army
George C. Marshall, edited by Major H. A. DeWeerd, 1945

The traditional esteem of the average citizen for the military officer is a major ingredient, indeed a prerequisite, of the national security. The Armed Services have recognized this since the time of Valley Forge. That is why there is such extreme emphasis on the imperative of personal honor in the military officer: not only the future of our arms but the well-being of our people depend upon a constant reaffirmation and strengthening of public faith in the virtue and trustworthiness of the officer body. Should that faith flag and finally fail, the citizenry would be reluctant to commit its young people to any military endeavor, however grave the emergency. The works of goodwill by which leaders of our military seek to win the trust and approval of the people are in that direct sense a preservative of our American freedoms. By the same reasoning, high character in the military office is a safeguard of the character of the Nation. Anything less than exemplary conduct is therefore unworthy of the commission.

Brigadier General S.L.A. Marshall
The Armed Forces Officer, 1950

Conscience is the inner voice that warns us that someone may be looking.

Henry Louis Mencken
A Book of Burlesques, "Sententiae," 1920

A man's reputation is the opinion people have of him; his character is what he really is.

Jack Miner

Character is what you are in the dark.

Dwight L. Moody
Selected Sermons, "Character," 1881

A man of character becomes a man of courage in war.

Lord Charles Moran
The Anatomy of Courage, 1967

Character is much easier kept than recovered.

Thomas Paine
The American Crisis, 19 April 1783

The foundation of leadership is character.

General Alexander M. Patch

A good reputation is more valuable than money.

Publilius Syrus
Maxims, circa first century B.C.

God looks at the clean hands, not the full ones.

Publilius Syrus
Moral Sayings, circa first century B.C.

Character is the bedrock on which the whole edifice of leadership rests. It is the prime element for which every profession, every corporation, every industry searches in evaluating a member of its organization. With it, the full worth of an individual can be developed. Without it—particularly in the military profession—failure in peace, disaster in war, or, at best, mediocrity in both will result.

General Matthew B. Ridgway

A sound body is good; a sound mind is better; but a strong and clean character is better than either.

Theodore Roosevelt
Address at Groton, Massachusetts, 24 May 1904

The first test of a truly great man is his humility.

John Ruskin
Modern Painters, 1860

Men should be what they seem.

William Shakespeare
Othello, Act III, Scene iii, 1605

humility

[General Stilwell] did not believe in long speeches on occasions of promotion on the principle that "the higher a monkey climbs a pole, the more you see of his behind."

Attributed to General Joseph W. Stilwell
Quoted in *Stilwell and the American Experience in China, 1911–1945,*
by Barbara Tuchman, 1971

Professional competence is more than a display of book knowledge or of the results of military schooling. It requires the display of qualities of character which reflect inner strength and justified confidence in one's self.

General Maxwell D. Taylor

Even with the gifts of human understanding and of professional competence arising from careful training, our military leader will not be complete without the third attribute of greatness; namely, character— character which reflects inner strength and justified confidence in oneself.

General Maxwell D. Taylor
Speech to Citadel cadets, 21 January 1956

I hope I shall always possess firmness and virtue enough to maintain what I consider the most enviable of all titles, the character of an "Honest Man."

General George Washington

Cohesion

Union gives strength.

Aesop

When one treats people with benevolence, justice, and righteousness, and reposes confidence in them, the Army will be united in mind and all will be happy to serve their leaders.

Chang Yu

Do not split TOE units to perform tasks by details. Assign the tasks to squads, platoons, etc. This develops leaders, improves morale, and solidifies units. Jobs then have training value instead of being chores.

General Bruce C. Clarke

An army that maintains its cohesion under the most murderous fire; that cannot be shaken by imaginary fears and resists well-founded ones with all its might; that, proud of its victories, will not lose the strength to obey orders and its respect and trust for its officers even in defeat; whose physical power, like the muscles of an athlete, has been steeled by training in privation and effort; a force that regards such efforts as a means to victory rather than a curse on its cause; that is mindful of all these duties and qualities by nature of the single powerful idea of the honor of its arms—such an army is imbued with the true military spirit.

Karl von Clausewitz
On War, 1832

The only force that unites men is conscience, a varying capacity in most of them to put the interests of other people before their own.

Lionel Curtis
Quoted in S.L.A. Marshall's *Armed Forces Officer,* 1950

Teamwork is of utmost importance. The welding of troops together into a coordinated fighting unit leads all other training. But it isn't the whole of training. The soldier as a single fighter must be thought of right on through to battle and till our war is won.

Lieutenant Colonel Joseph I. Greene
The Infantry Journal Reader, 1942

There is strength in the union even of very sorry men.

Homer
The Iliad, Book XIII, circa 700 B.C.

I hold it to be one of the simplest truths of war that the thing which enables an infantry soldier to keep going with his weapons is the near presence or the presumed presence of a comrade.

Brigadier General S.L.A. Marshall
Men Against Fire, 1947

It is my belief that a system of man-to-man control on the battlefield is our great need in tactics and that it is fully attainable. This is not a metaphysical problem. It can be attacked by rather simple methods, once the factors of the problem are understood.

Brigadier General S.L.A. Marshall
Men Against Fire, 1947

The relationships within our Army should be based upon intimate understanding between officers and men rather than upon familiarity between them, on self-respect rather than on fear, and above all, on a close uniting comradeship.

Brigadier General S.L.A. Marshall
Men Against Fire, 1947

When men, working together, successfully attain to a high standard of orderliness, deportment, and response to each other, they develop the cohesive strength that will carry them through any great crisis.

Brigadier General S.L.A. Marshall
The Armed Forces Officer, 1950

We trained hard—but it seemed that every time we were beginning to form into teams, we would be reorganized. I was to learn later in life that we tend to meet any new situation by reorganization, and a wonderful method it can be for creating the illusion of progress while producing confusion, inefficiency and demoralization.

Petronius Arbiter
Sătӯricon, circa A.D. 50

If one does not wish bonds broken, one should make them elastic and thereby strengthen them.

Ardant du Picq

A wise organization insures that the personnel of combat groups changes as little as possible, so that comrades in peace time maneuvers shall be comrades in war.

Ardant du Picq
Battle Studies, 1880

Unity and confidence cannot be improvised. They alone can create that mutual trust, that feeling of force which gives courage and daring.

Ardant du Picq
Battle Studies, 1880

Combat requires to-day, in order to give the best results, a moral cohesion, a unity more binding than at any other time.

Ardant du Picq
Battle Studies, 1880

Pride exists only among people who know each other well, who have esprit de corps, and company spirit. There is a necessity for an organization that renders unity possible by creating the real individuality of the company.

Ardant du Picq
Battle Studies, 1880

41

In the beginning man battled against man, each one for himself, like a beast that hunts to kill, yet flees from that which would kill him. But now prescriptions of discipline and tactics insure unity between leader and soldier, between the men themselves.

Ardant du Picq
Battle Studies, 1880

The dominant feeling of the battlefield is loneliness.

Field Marshal Sir William Slim
Speech to the officers of the 10th Indian Infantry Division,
June 1941

In the Burma Campaign, very often owing to shortage of air transport, a lot of my troops, my forward formations, had to be on half rations. Whenever they went on half rations I used to put my own headquarters on half rations. It was a bit theatrical, I admit, but it did remind the young staff officers with healthy appetites what it is like to be hungry, and it perhaps put a little more ginger in getting the supplies forward.

Field Marshal Sir William Slim
Speech to U.S. Army Command and General Staff College,
8 April 1952

The Spartans on their side spoke their words of encouragement to each other man to man, singing their war songs, and calling on their comrades, as brave men, to remember what each knew so well, realizing that the long discipline of action is a more effective safeguard than hurried speeches, however well they may be delivered.

Thucydides
History of the Peloponnesian War, circa 404 B.C.

Commander's Intent

For if the trumpet give an uncertain sound, who shall prepare himself to the battle?

Bible, I Corinthians 14:8

When you have to interpret instructions from your commander, think of what he wants to accomplish most; then carry out your instructions in such a way to help him to accomplish this mission.

General Bruce C. Clarke

Everything should be made as simple as possible, but not simpler.

Albert Einstein
Quoted in *Reader's Digest,* October 1977

The teams and staffs through which the modern commander absorbs information and exercises his authority must be a beautifully interlocked, smooth-working mechanism. Ideally, the whole should be practically a single mind.

General Dwight D. Eisenhower

Training in all its phases must be intensive. . . . It must be intelligently directed so that every individual, including the last private in the ranks, can understand the reasons for the exertions he is called upon to make.

General Dwight D. Eisenhower
Eisenhower Papers, 1970

To be disciplined . . . means that one frankly adopts the thoughts and views of the superior in command, and that one uses all humanly practicable means in order to give him satisfaction.

Marshal Ferdinand Foch
Precepts, 1919

I do not propose to lay down for you a plan of campaign; but simply to lay down the work it is desirable to have done and leave you free to execute it in your own way.

General Ulysses Simpson Grant
To General William Tecumseh Sherman
on the destruction of General Johnston's army, April 1862

It has been said that one bad general is better than two good ones, and the saying is true if taken to mean no more than that an army is better directed by a single mind, the inferior, than by two superior ones at variance and cross-purposes with each other.

Abraham Lincoln
First Annual Message to Congress, 3 December 1861

Nothing is more important in war than unity of command.

Napoleon Bonaparte
Maxims, LXIV, 1831

There are certain things in war of which the commander alone comprehends the importance. Nothing but his superior firmness and ability can subdue and surmount all difficulties.

Napoleon Bonaparte
Maxims, LXVI, 1831

One [cause] affected all our efforts and contributed much to turning our defeat into disaster—the failure, after the fall of Rangoon, to give the forces in the field a clear strategic object for the campaign. . . . Burma was not the first, nor was it to be the last campaign that had been launched on no clear realization of its political or military objects. A study of such campaigns points emphatically to the almost inevitable disaster that must follow. Commanders on the field, in fairness to them and their troops, must be clearly and definitely told what is the object they are locally to attain.

Field Marshal Sir William Slim
Defeat into Victory, 1961

This acting without orders, in anticipation of orders, or without waiting for approval, yet always within the over-all intention, must become second nature in any form of warfare where formations do not fight en cadre, and must go down to the smallest units.

Field Marshal Sir William Slim
Defeat into Victory, 1961

Sensible initiative is based upon an understanding of the commander's intentions.

Soviet Army Field Service Regulations, 1936

Every individual from the highest commander to the lowest private must always remember that inaction and neglect of opportunities will warrant more severe censure than an error of judgment in the action taken. The criterion by which a commander judges the soundness of his own decision is whether it will further the intentions of the higher commander.

U.S. Army Field Manual 100-5, *Operations,* 1944

Communication

Effective leaders can communicate ideas through several organizational layers, across great distances, even through the jamming signals of special interest groups and opponents.

Warren Bennis
Training and Development Journal, August 1984

Most conversations are just alternating monologues—the question is, is there any real listening going on?

Leo Buscaglia

If you have an important point to make, don't try to be subtle or clever. Use a pile-driver. Hit the point once. Then come back and hit it a second time—a tremendous whack!

Sir Winston Churchill

Soldiers want to do what the boss wants done—and if they do not, it is because *he* has done something wrong—because he did not communicate his desires.

General Bruce C. Clarke

[A] great part of the information obtained in war is contradictory, a still greater part is false, and by far the greatest part is of doubtful character.

Karl von Clausewitz
On War, 1832

Without knowing the force of words, it is impossible to know men.
Confucius
Analects, circa 500 B.C.

Men govern with words.

Benjamin Disraeli

To think justly, we must understand what others mean; to know the value of our thoughts, we must try their effect on other minds.
William Hazlitt
The Plain Speaker, 1826

Orders and directives which can be understood are not good enough—they should not be able to be misunderstood.
Colonel Lucius Holt

The most valuable of all talents is that of never using two words when one will do.

Thomas Jefferson

He can compress the most words into the smallest idea of any man I ever met.

Abraham Lincoln

In battle, and out of it, the failure to act and to communicate is more often due to timidity in the soldier than to fear of physical danger.
Brigadier General S.L.A. Marshall
Men Against Fire, 1947

Men who can command words to serve their thoughts and feelings are well on their way to commanding men to serve their purposes.
Brigadier General S.L.A. Marshall
The Armed Forces Officer, 1950

Battles are won through the ability of men to express concrete ideas in clear and unmistakable language. All administration is carried forward along the chain of command by the power of men to make their thoughts articulate and available to others.

Brigadier General S.L.A. Marshall
The Officer as a Leader, 1966

Communication is something so simple and difficult that we can never put it in simple words.

Thomas S. Matthews

A commander must train his subordinate commanders, and his own staff, to work and act on verbal orders. Those who cannot be trusted to act on clear and concise verbal orders, but want everything in writing, are useless.

Field Marshal Bernard L. Montgomery
Memoirs of Field Marshal the Viscount Montgomery of Alamein, 1958

Issuing orders is worth about 10 percent. The remaining 90 percent consists in assuring proper and vigorous execution of the order.

General George S. Patton, Jr.

On the clarity of your ideas depends the scope of your success in any endeavor.

James Robertson

A really classical example of this art of estimating a situation psychologically was shown in the year 1917 by a brigade commander. This General said, "Each of our three regimental commanders must be handled differently. Colonel 'A' does not want an order. He wants to do everything himself, and he always does well. Colonel 'B' executes every order, but has no initiative. Colonel 'C' opposes everything he is told to do and wants to do the contrary."

A few days later the troops confronted a well-intrenched enemy whose position would have to be attacked. The General issued the following individual orders:

To Colonel "A" (who wants to do everything himself): "My dear Colonel 'A,' I think we will attack. Your regiment will have to carry the burden of the attack. I have, however, selected you for this reason.

The boundaries of your regiment are so and so. Attack at X hour. I don't have to tell you anything more."

To Colonel "C" (who opposes everything):

"We have met a very strong enemy. I am afraid we will not be able to attack with the forces at our disposal."

"Oh, General, certainly we will attack. Just give my regiment the time of attack and you will see that we are successful," replied Colonel "C."

To Colonel "B" (who must always have detailed orders) the attack order was merely sent with additional details.

Captain Adolf von Schell
Battle Leadership, 1933

Men of a few words are the best men.

William Shakespeare
Henry V, Act III, Scene i, 1600

In a battle nothing is ever as good or as bad as the first reports of excited men would have it.

Field Marshal Sir William Slim
Unofficial History, 1959

If you want to talk to men, it doesn't matter whether they are private soldiers or staff officers, if you want to talk to them as a soldier, and not as a politician, there are only two things necessary. The first is to have something to say that is worth saying, to know what you want to say; and the second, and terribly important thing, is to believe it yourself. Don't go and tell men something that you don't believe yourself, because they'll spot it and if they don't spot it at the time, they'll find out. Then you're finished.

Field Marshal Sir William Slim
Speech to U.S. Army Command and General Staff College,
8 April 1952

There are three things that ought to be considered before some things are spoken—the manner, the place, and the time.

Robert Southey

Competence

In war there is no second prize for the runner-up.

General Omar N. Bradley

The American soldier is a proud one and he demands professional competence in his leaders. In battle, he wants to know that the job is going to be done right, with no unnecessary casualties. The non-commissioned officer wearing the chevrons is supposed to be the best soldier in the platoon and he is supposed to know how to perform all the duties expected of him. The American soldier expects his sergeant to be able to teach him how to do his job. And he expects even more from his officers.

General Omar N. Bradley

It is no use saying "we are doing our best." You have got to succeed in doing what is necessary.

Sir Winston Churchill

Professional attainment, based upon prolonged study, and collective study at colleges, rank by rank, and age by age—these are the title deeds of the commanders of future armies, and the secret of future victories.

Sir Winston Churchill

50

Battles are won by slaughter and maneuver. The greater the general, the more he contributes in maneuver, the less he demands in slaughter.

Sir Winston Churchill
The World Crisis, 1923

The bedrock requirements remain for skilled and dedicated professionals to run the Army itself during a period of evolution and change. We look to these men to administer, train, and maintain in a state of razor-sharp combat readiness the farflung units of the United States Army worldwide.

General George H. Decker

There is no type of human endeavor where it is so important that the leader understands all phases of his job as that of the profession of arms.

Major General James C. Fry

'Tis skill, not strength, that governs a ship.

Thomas Fuller
Gnomologia, 1732

What is the use of running when we are not on the right road?

German proverb

The winds and waves are always on the side of the ablest navigators.

Edward Gibbon
Decline and Fall of the Roman Empire, 1776

A general thoroughly instructed in the theory of war, but not possessed of military coup d'oeil, coolness, and skill, may make an excellent strategic plan and be entirely unable to apply the rules of tactics in presence of the enemy: his projects will not be successfully carried out, and his defeat will be probable.

Baron Henri de Jomini
Précis de l'Art de la Guerre, 1838

Officers can never act with confidence until they are masters of their profession.

General Henry Knox

Our army would be invincible if it could be properly organized and officered. There never were such men in an army before. They will go anywhere and do anything if properly led. But there is the difficulty—proper commanders.

General Robert E. Lee
Letter to General John B. Hood, 21 May 1863

Weapons, equipment, tactics, and organization can achieve their full potentials only when combined with the required numbers of people operating with skill, efficiency, and devotion.

General Lyman L. Lemnitzer

Another key value in the military is professional competence—that is, proficiency in tactical and technical. Throughout history, soldiers and their leaders have always been expected to know the profession of arms and to be skillful at it.

John O. Marsh, Jr.

To be defeated is pardonable; to be surprised—never!

Napoleon Bonaparte

An irresolute general who acts without principles and without a plan, even though he lead an army numerically superior to that of the enemy, almost always finds himself inferior to the latter on the field of battle.

Napoleon Bonaparte
Maxims, LXXXIV, 1831

A competent leader can get efficient service from poor troops, while on the contrary an incapable leader can demoralize the best of troops.

General of the Armies John J. Pershing
My Experiences in the World War, 1931

The test of any man lies in action.

Pindar
Òdes, circa fifth century B.C.

It takes a long time to bring excellence to maturity.

Publilius Syrus
Moral Sayings, circa first century B.C.

We make generals today on the basis of their ability to write a damned letter. Those kinds of men can't get us ready for war.

General Lewis B. "Chesty" Puller

The requirement upon all soldiers to master their profession—always of fundamental importance—has gained new emphasis with the advent of new weapons and the resultant greater capabilities and responsibilities of the Army.

General Matthew B. Ridgway

The performance of public duty is not the whole of what makes a good life; there is also the pursuit of private excellence.

Bertrand Russell

It is not big armies that win battles; it is the good ones.

Marshal Comte de Maurice Saxe
Mes Rêveries, 1732

The true way to be popular with troops is not to be free and familiar with them, but to make them believe you know more than they do.

General William Tecumseh Sherman
Letter to the Right Reverend Henry C. Lay,
11 November 1864

Now the general is the bulwark of the state: if the bulwark is complete at all points, the state will be strong; if the bulwark is defective, the state will be weak.

Sun-Tzu
The Art of War, circa fourth century B.C.

Carefully study the well-being of your men, and do not overtax them. Concentrate your energy and hoard your strength. Keep your army continually on the move and devise unfathomable plans.

Sun-Tzu
The Art of War, circa fourth century B.C.

Professional competence is more than a display of book knowledge or of the results of military schooling. It requires the display of qualities of character which reflect inner strength and justified confidence in one's self.

General Maxwell D. Taylor

Skill in naval affairs, as in other crafts, is the result of scientific training. It is impossible to acquire this skill unless the matter be treated as of the first importance and all other pursuits are considered to be secondary to it.

Thucydides
History of the Peloponnesian War, circa 404 B.C.

Our object ought to be to have a good army rather than a large one.

General George Washington
15 September 1780

Confidence

In confidence and quietness shall be your strength.

Bible, Isaiah 30:15

If a soldier would command an army he must be prepared to withstand those who would criticize the manner in which he leads that army.

General Omar N. Bradley

An individual must have confidence in himself and have no self-doubts; he must have confidence in his weapons; and, further and most important, he must have faith and confidence in the leaders above him.

Rear Admiral John D. Bulkeley

Be always sure you're right, then go ahead.

Davy Crockett
Autobiography, 1834

As is our confidence, so is our capacity.

William Hazlitt
Characteristics, 1823

When troops once realize their inferiority, they can no longer be depended upon. If attacking, they refuse to advance. If defending, they abandon all hope of resistance. It is not the losses they have suffered but those they expect to suffer that affect them. Consequently, unless discipline and national spirit are of superior quality, and unless the soldier is animated by something higher than the habit of mechanical disobedience, panic, shirking and wholesale surrender will be the ordinary features of a campaign.

Colonel G.F.R. Henderson
Stonewall Jackson and the American Civil War, 1898

Fields are won by those who believe in winning.

Thomas W. Higginson

I do not play at war. I shall not allow myself to be ordered about by commanders-in-chief. I shall make war. I shall determine the correct moment for attack. I shall shrink from nothing.

Adolf Hitler

Who has self-confidence will lead the rest.

Horace
Epistles, circa 20–13 B.C.

The fighting man's confidence must rest on three things—his leader, his weapon, and himself. His leader can often do little to guide him once battle is on. His weapon cannot make him a smaller target to the aimed or unaimed fire of the enemy. Only the man by himself, through knowledge of what a trained fighter must do to live and fight, can handle himself as he must if battles are to be won.

Editorial in *The Infantry Journal Reader,*
"The Battle-Wise Fighting Soldier," 1942

You may be whatever you resolve to be.

General Thomas J. "Stonewall" Jackson

Nothing gives one person so much advantage over another as to remain always cool and unruffled under all circumstances.

Thomas Jefferson

Self-confidence is the first requisite to great undertakings.

Samuel Johnson
Lives of the Poets: Pope, 1868

The qualities which commonly make an army formidable are long habits of regularity, great exactness of discipline, and great confidence in the commander.

Samuel Johnson

No matter what may be the ability of the officer, if he loses the confidence of his troops, disaster must sooner or later ensue.

General Robert E. Lee
Letter to Jefferson Davis, 8 August 1863

To insure victory the troops must have confidence in themselves as well as in their commanders.

Niccolò di Bernardo Machiavelli
Discorsi, 1531

No officer can command unless he is certain of himself and confident that his orders are likely to lead to success.

Brigadier General S.L.A. Marshall
Men Against Fire, 1947

A good military leader must dominate the events which encompass him; once events get the better of him he will lose the confidence of his men, and when that happens he ceases to be of value as a leader.

Field Marshal Bernard L. Montgomery

The first thing a young officer must do when he joins the Army is to fight a battle, and that battle is for the hearts of his men. If he wins that battle and subsequent similar ones, his men will follow him anywhere; if he loses it, he will never do any real good.

Field Marshal Bernard L. Montgomery
Memoirs of Field Marshal the Viscount Montgomery of Alamein, 1958

You wrote to me that it's impossible; the word is not French.

Napoleon Bonaparte
Letter to General Lemarois, 9 July 1813

The bullet that will kill me is not yet cast.

Napoleon Bonaparte
17 February 1814

It is cruel, this accountability of good and well-intentioned men. But the choice is that or an end to responsibility and finally, as the cruel sea has taught, an end to the confidence and trust in the men who lead, for men will not long trust leaders who feel themselves beyond accountability for what they do.

And when men lose confidence and trust in those who lead, order disintegrates into chaos and purposeful ships into uncontrollable derelicts.

New York Times editorial, April 1952

The most vital quality a soldier can possess is self-confidence, utter, complete, and bumptious.

General George S. Patton, Jr.
Letter to his son, 6 June 1944

No one knows what he can do till he tries.

Publilius Syrus
Moral Sayings, circa first century B.C.

One must learn by doing the thing; though you think you know it, you have no certainty until you try.

Sophocles
Trachiniae, circa fifth century B.C.

The world stands aside to let pass the man who knows whither he is going.

Ordway Tead

Nobody holds a good opinion of a man who has a low opinion of himself.

Anthony Trollope

I'm going to fight hard. I'm going to give them hell.

Harry S. Truman
To Albert Barkley, 17 September 1948

They can do all because they think they can.

Virgil
Aeneid, 19 B.C.

Courage

First find the man in yourself if you will inspire manliness in others.
Amos Bronson Alcott
Table Talk, 1877

On the battlefield, the greatest pressure is fear of death, and the temptation is to run away. But the courageous man holds on.
Aristotle

Courage, however, is that firmness of spirit, that moral backbone, which, while fully appreciating the danger involved, nevertheless goes on with the undertaking. Bravery is physical; courage is mental and moral. You may be cold all over; your hands may tremble; your legs may quake; your knees be ready to give way—that is fear. If, nevertheless, you go forward; if in spite of this physical defection you continue to lead your men against the enemy, you have courage. The physical manifestations of fear will pass away. You may never experience them but once.
Major C. A. Bach
"Know Your Men—Know Your Business—Know Yourself,"
Address to new officers, 1917

At the bottom of a good deal of the bravery that appears in the world there lurks a miserable cowardice. Men will face powder and steel because they cannot face public opinion.
George Chapin

Courage is grace under pressure.

Sir Winston Churchill
(Also attributed to Ernest Hemingway, 30 November 1929)

To see what is right and not to do it is want of courage.

Confucius

Brave men are brave from the first blow.

Pierre Corneille
Le Cid, 1636

A hero is no braver than an ordinary man, but he is brave five minutes longer.

Ralph Waldo Emerson

A great part of courage is the courage of having done the thing before.

Ralph Waldo Emerson
The Conduct of Life, "Wealth," 1860

Life only demands from you the strength you possess. Only one feat is possible—not to have run away.

Dag Hammarskjöld
Markings, 1964

At the grave of a hero we end, not with sorrow at the inevitable loss, but with the contagion of his courage; and with a kind of desperate joy we go back to the fight.

Oliver Wendell Holmes, Jr.

Oh friends, be men, and let your hearts be strong,
And let no warrior in the heat of fight
Do what may bring him shame in others' eyes;
For more of those who shrink from shame are safe
Than fall in battle, while those who flee
Is neither glory nor reprieve from death.

Homer
The Iliad, Book XV, circa 700 B.C.

The greatest test of courage on earth is to beat defeat without losing heart.

Robert G. Ingersoll

It is a blessed thing that in every age someone has had the individuality enough and courage enough to stand by his own convictions.

Robert G. Ingersoll

One man with courage makes a majority.

Andrew Jackson

Courage is a quality so necessary for maintaining virtue that it is always respected, even when it is associated with vice.

Samuel Johnson

The most essential qualities of a general will always be: *first,* a high moral courage, capable of great resolution; *second,* a physical courage which takes no account of danger. His scientific or military acquirements are secondary to these.

Baron Henri de Jomini
Précis de l'Art de la Guerre, 1838

Bravery is being the only one who knows you're afraid.

Franklyn P. Jones

Everyone admires courage and the greenest garlands are for those who possess it.

John F. Kennedy

For without belittling the courage with which men have died, we should not forget those acts of courage with which men . . . have lived. The courage of life is often a less dramatic spectacle than the courage of a final moment; but it is no less a magnificent mixture of triumph and tragedy. A man does what he must—in spite of personal conse-quences, in spite of obstacles and dangers and pressures—and that is the basis of all human mortality.

John F. Kennedy
Profiles in Courage, 1956

In courage keep your heart. In strength lift up your hand.

Rudyard Kipling

Good order makes men bold, and confusion, cowards.

Niccolò di Bernardo Machiavelli
Arte Della Guèrra, 1520

Man on the battlefield . . . will be persuaded by the same things which induce him to face life bravely—friendship, loyalty to responsibility, and knowledge that he is a repository of the faith and confidence of others.

Brigadier General S.L.A. Marshall
Men Against Fire, 1947

On the field there is no substitute for courage, no other binding influence toward unity of action. Troops will excuse almost any stupidity; excessive timidity is simply unforgivable.

Brigadier General S.L.A. Marshall
The Armed Forces Officer, 1950

When led with courage and intelligence, an American will fight as willingly and as efficiently as any fighter in world history.

Brigadier General S.L.A. Marshall
The Armed Forces Officer, 1950

What though the field be lost?
All is not lost; th' unconquerable will,
And study of revenge, immortal hate,
And courage never to submit or yield.

John Milton
Paradise Lost, 1667

The strongest, most generous, and proudest of all virtues is true courage.

Michel Eyquem de Montaigne
Essays, 1580

I had learnt before I left school that of the many attributes necessary for success two are vital—hard work and absolute integrity. To these two I would now add a third—courage. I mean moral courage—not afraid to say or do what you believe to be right.

Field Marshal Bernard L. Montgomery

When soldiers brave death, they drive him into the enemy's ranks.

Napoleon Bonaparte

The only true wisdom in a general is determined courage.

Napoleon Bonaparte
Maxims, LXVI, 1831

It is often overlooked by junior officers that the same courage of convictions they consider so admirable in themselves is equally admirable when possessed by their senior leaders.

Major General Aubrey "Red" Newman
Follow Me, 1981

God grant me the courage to change the things I can change, the serenity to accept those I cannot change, the wisdom to know the difference—but God grant me the courage not to give up what I think is right even though I think it is hopeless.

Attributed to Admiral Chester W. Nimitz
The Armed Forces Prayer Book, 1974

Courage is an inherent quality, but it remains an unknown quantity until all of the chips are down.

Major General John W. O'Daniel

Great military leaders have always possessed undaunted courage. History abounds with stories of leaders who have dared to do those things which their opponents never would dream they would.

General Alexander M. Patch

Courage is fear holding on a minute longer.

General George S. Patton, Jr.

Untutored courage is useless in the face of educated bullets.

Major George S. Patton, Jr.
Cavalry Journal, April 1922

Courage, moral and physical, . . . fosters the resolution to combat and cherishes the ability to assume responsibility, be it for successes or failures. . . . But as with the biblical candle, these traits are of no military value if concealed. A man of diffident manner will never inspire confidence. A cold reserve cannot beget enthusiasm, and so with the others there must be an outward and visible sign of the inward and spiritual grace.

Major George S. Patton, Jr.
The Cavalry Journal, "Success in War," 1931

Courage, that is the temporary domination of will over instinct, brings about victory.

Ardant du Picq
Battle Studies, 1880

Four brave men who do not know each other will dare not attack a lion. Four less brave, but knowing each other well, sure of their reliability and consequently of mutual aid, will attack resolutely. There is the science of the organization of armies in a nutshell.

Ardant du Picq
Battle Studies, 1880

A timid person is frightened before a danger, a coward during the time, and a courageous person afterwards.

Jean Paul Richter

As a fundamental institution in the development of our national life, the United States Army has played a proud historic role. It has produced leaders unsurpassed in character, competence, and courage—moral equally with physical.

General Matthew B. Ridgway

There are two kinds of courage, physical and moral, and he who would be a true leader must have both. Both are the products of the character-forming process, of the development of self-control, self-discipline, physical endurance, of knowledge of one's job and, therefore, of confidence. These qualities minimize fear and maximize sound judgment under pressure and—with some of that indispensable stuff called luck— often bring success from seemingly hopeless situations.

General Matthew B. Ridgway
Military Review, "Leadership," October 1966

Perfect courage and utter cowardice are two extremes that rarely occur.

François, Duc de La Rochefoucauld
Maximes, 1665

Courage, in soldiers, is a dangerous profession they follow to earn their living.

François, Duc de La Rochefoucauld
Maximes, 1665

Cowards die many times before their deaths;
The valiant never taste death but once.

William Shakespeare
Julius Ceasar, Act II, Scene ii, 1600

'Tis true, that we are in great danger;
The greater therefore should our courage be.

William Shakespeare
King Henry V, Act IV, Scene i, 1600

I would define true courage to be a perfect sensibility of the measure of danger, and a mental willingness to incur it.

General William Tecumseh Sherman
Personal Memoirs, 1875

A brave captain is as a root, out of which, as branches, the courage of his soldiers doth spring.

Sir Philip Sidney

There is nothing like seeing the other fellow run to bring back your courage.

Field Marshal Sir William Slim
Unofficial History, 1959

Moral courage simply means that you do what you think is right without bothering too much about the effect on yourself.

Field Marshal Sir William Slim
Speech to U.S. Army Command and General Staff College,
8 April 1952

Courage is endurance of the soul.

Socrates

It is the brave man's part to live with glory, or with glory die.

Sophocles
Ajax, circa 447 B.C.

The principle on which to manage an army is to set up one standard of courage which all must reach.

Sun-Tzu
The Art of War, circa fourth century B.C.

Self-control is the chief element in self-respect, and self-respect is the chief element in courage.

Thucydides
History of the Peloponnesian War, circa 404 B.C.

The courage of a soldier is heightened by his knowledge of his profession.

Vegetius
Dē Re Mīlĭtāri, Book I, 378

Few men are born brave; many become so through training and force of discipline.

Vegetius
Dē Re Mīlĭtāri, Book III, 378

An Army of Asses led by a Lion is vastly superior to an Army of Lions led by an Ass.

General George Washington

Courage, physical and moral, a general undoubtedly must have.

Field Marshal Sir Archibald P. Wavell
"Lees Knowles Lectures,"
Trinity College, Cambridge,
1939

Creativity, Imagination, Innovation

Imagination is that mysterious element that some people have a great deal of and others have very little of. People can be encouraged to develop imagination, however. Their leaders can tell them to explore beyond the immediate answer that comes to them when they are faced with a problem; they can tell them to reach out, not to feel bound by convention or anything else, to do the unusual or think of doing the unusual.

General Robert H. Barrow
Quoted in Karel Montor et al.,
Naval Leadership: Voices of Experience, 1987

Imagination is more important then knowledge.

Albert Einstein
Essays on Science, 1934

There is among the mass of individuals who carry rifles in war a great amount of ingenuity and efficiency. If men can talk naturally to their officers, the product of their resourcefulness becomes available to all.

General Dwight D. Eisenhower

Thinking always of trying to do more brings a state of mind in which nothing seems impossible.

Henry Ford

Everything which the enemy least expects will succeed the best.

Frederick the Great
Instructions for His Generals, 1747

It is absolutely necessary to change your methods often and to imagine new decoys. If you always act in the same manner you soon will be interpreted, for you are surrounded with fifty thousand curious who want to know everything that you think and how you are going to lead them.

Frederick the Great
Instructions for His Generals, 1747

Originality, not conventionality, is one of the main pillars of generalship. To do something that the enemy does not expect, is not prepared for, something which will surprise him and disarm him morally. To be always thinking ahead and to be always peeping around corners. To spy out the soul of one's adversary, and to act in a manner which will astonish and bewilder him, this is generalship. . . . This is the foundation of success.

Major-General J.F.C. Fuller

The more elastic a man's mind is, that is the more it is able to receive and digest new impressions and experiences, the more commonsense will be the actions resulting.

Major-General J.F.C. Fuller
Generalship: Its Diseases and Their Cure, 1936

The impossible can only be overborne by the unprecedented.

General Sir Ian Hamilton
Gallipoli Diary, 1920

Cowardice, as distinguished from panic, is almost always simply a lack of ability to suspend the functioning of the imagination.

Ernest Hemingway
Men at War, 1942

Many ideas grow better when transplanted into another mind than in the one where they sprang up.

Oliver Wendell Holmes, Jr.

Māter inventĭum nĕcessĭtās.
[Necessity is the mother of invention.]

Italian proverb

Always mystify, mislead, and surprise the enemy if possible.

General Thomas J. "Stonewall" Jackson

A man may die, nations may rise and fall, but an idea lives on. Ideas have endurance without death.

John F. Kennedy
Address in Greenville, North Carolina,
8 February 1963

The problems of the world cannot possibly be solved by skeptics or cynics whose horizons are limited by the obvious realities. We need men who can dream of things that never were.

John F. Kennedy
Address in Dublin, Ireland, 28 June 1963

Originality is the most vital of all military virtues.

B. H. Liddell Hart
Thoughts on War, 1944

Long training tends to make a man more expert in execution, but such expertness is apt to be gained at the expense of fertility of ideas, originality, and elasticity.

B. H. Liddell Hart
Defense of the West, 1950

A mind stretched by a new idea never returns to its original dimension.

James Lincoln

The thinker dies, but his thoughts are beyond the reach of destruction. Men are mortal; but ideas are immortal.

Walter Lippmann
A Preface to Morals, 1929

A good soldier, whether he leads a platoon or an army, is expected to look backward as well as forward, but he must think only forward.

General Douglas MacArthur

Sixty percent of the art of command is the ability to anticipate; forty percent of the art of command is the ability to improvise.

Brigadier General S.L.A. Marshall
Men Against Fire, 1947

Imagination grows by exercise and contrary to common belief is more powerful in the mature than in the young.

William Somerset Maugham
The Summing Up, 1938

If a manager is really willing to listen, he or she will find that the average employee is loaded with ideas, most of which the manager can allow the person to try. So the first step toward innovation is getting into the habit of listening. The second is getting into the habit of letting your employees try to do their work in slightly different ways.

Tom Peters
Quoted in *Supervisory Management*, February 1984

Figure out how to do things so that you can get the maximum effect and least bloodshed.

Sun-Tzu
The Art of War, circa fourth century B.C.

It is particularly important to remember that under any circumstances it is necessary to be ahead of the enemy even at the very first encounter.

Marshal Georgii K. Zhukov
The Memoirs of Marshal Zhukov, 1971

Danger

The stout heart is also a warm and kind one; affection dwells with danger, all the holier and lovelier for such stern environment.

Thomas Carlyle
1832

Danger is part of the friction of war. Without an accurate conception of danger we cannot understand war.

Karl von Clausewitz
On War, 1832

A vaincre sans péril, on triomphe sans gloire.
[To conquer without danger is to triumph without glory.]

Pierre Corneille,
Le Cid, 1637

A coward turns away, but a brave man's choice is danger.

Euripides
Iphigenia in Tauris, circa 412 B.C.

Should the general consistently live outside the realm of danger, then, though he may show high moral courage in making decisions, by his never being called upon to breathe the atmosphere of danger his men are breathing, this lens will become blurred, and he will seldom experience the moral influences his men are experiencing.

Major-General J.F.C. Fuller
Generalship: Its Diseases and Their Cure, 1936

In comradeship is danger countered best.

Johann Wolfgang von Goethe
Faust: Part II, 1832

Any danger spot is tenable if men—brave men—will make it so.

John F. Kennedy
Speech, 25 July 1961

The major battle is only a skirmish multiplied by one hundred. The frictions, confusions, and disappointments are the same. But there is this absolute difference—that the supreme trial of the commander in war lies in his ability to overcome the weaknesses of human nature in the danger, and those are matters which he cannot know in full unless he has served with men where danger lies.

Brigadier General S.L.A. Marshall
Men Against Fire, 1947

There is nothing more dangerous than a sailor with a rifle, except a young, inexperienced staff officer with a pencil.

Major General Aubrey "Red" Newman
Follow Me, 1981

One can't answer for his courage when he has never been in danger.

François, Duc de La Rochefoucauld
Maximes, 1665

Man always fears the consequences of danger more than danger itself.

Marshal Comte de Maurice Saxe
Mes Rêveries, 1732

They are surely to be esteemed the bravest spirits who, having the clearest sense of both the pains and pleasures of life, do not on that account shrink from danger.

Thucydides
History of the Peloponnesian War, circa 404 B.C.

Decision Making

Any reasonable order in an emergency is better than no order. The situation is there. Meet it. It is better to do something and do the wrong thing than to hesitate, hunt around for the right thing to do and wind up by doing nothing at all. And, having decided on a line of action, stick to it. Don't vacillate. Men have no confidence in an officer who doesn't know his own mind.

Major C. A. Bach
"Know Your Men—Know Your Business—Know Yourself,"
Address to new officers, 1917

A good leader must sometimes be stubborn. Armed with the courage of his convictions, he must often fight to defend them. When he has come to a decision after thorough analysis—and when he is sure he is right—he must stick to it even to the point of stubbornness.

General Omar N. Bradley
Speech to U.S. Army Command and General Staff College,
16 May 1967

What can be more detestable than to be continually changing our minds.

Cleon of Athens

Not to decide is to decide.

Harvey Cox

He who gains time gains everything.

Benjamin Disraeli
Tancred, 1847

Without very good reasons a decision once made should not be abandoned. However, in the vicissitudes of war an inflexible maintenance of the original decision may lead to great mistakes. Timely recognition of the conditions and the time which call for a new decision is an attribute of the art of leadership.

German Army Leadership Manual (*Truppenführung*), 1933

In action it is better to order than to ask.

General Sir Ian Hamilton
Gallipoli Diary, 1920

In all operations a moment arrives when brave decisions have to be made if an enterprise is to be carried through.

Admiral Sir Roger Keyes

It is in the minds of the commanders that the issue of battle is really decided.

B. H. Liddell Hart
Thoughts on War, 1944

To take no action is to take undecided action.

Robert S. McNamara
4 July 1965

The problem is to grasp, in innumerable special cases, the actual situation which is covered by the midst of uncertainty and to guess the unknown elements, to reach a decision quickly and then to carry it out forcefully and relentlessly.

Field Marshal Count Helmuth von Moltke

The commander must decide how he will fight the battle before it begins. He must then decide how he will use the military effort at his disposal to force the battle to swing the way he wishes it to go.

Field Marshal Bernard L. Montgomery

When all is said and done the greatest quality required in a commander is "decision"; he must be able to issue clear orders and have the drive to get things done. Indecision and hesitation are fatal in any officer; in a C-in-C they are criminal.

Field Marshal Bernard L. Montgomery
Memoirs of Field Marshal the Viscount Montgomery of Alamein, 1958

He who wars walks in a mist through which the keenest eye cannot always discern the right path.

General Sir William Napier

Nothing is more difficult, and therefore more precious, than to be able to decide.

Napoleon Bonaparte

In forming the plan of a campaign, it is requisite to foresee everything the enemy may do, and be prepared with the necessary means to counteract it.

Napoleon Bonaparte
Maxims, II, 1831

The first qualification in a general is a cool head—that is, a head which receives accurate impressions, and estimates things and objects at their real value. He must not allow himself to be elated by good news, or depressed by bad.

Napoleon Bonaparte
Maxims, LXXIII, 1831

The first principle of a general-in-chief is to calculate what he must do, to see if he has all the means to surmount the obstacles with which the enemy can oppose him and, when he has made his decision, to do everything to overcome them.

Napoleon Bonaparte
Maxims, LXXIX, 1831

The higher you go in rank and responsibility, the greater the need to get all the facts as the best means of avoiding mistakes in decisions, and the greater need for carefully considered good judgment.

Major General Aubrey "Red" Newman
Follow Me, 1981

A good plan violently executed *now* is better than a perfect plan next week.

General George S. Patton, Jr.
War as I Knew It, 1947

It has long seemed to me that the hard decisions are not the ones you make in the heat of battle. Far harder to make are those involved in speaking your mind about some hare-brained scheme which proposes to commit troops to action under conditions where failure seems almost certain, and the only results will be the needless sacrifice of priceless lives. When all is said and done, the most precious asset any nation has is its youth, and for a battle commander ever to condone the unnecessary sacrifice of his men is inexcusable. In any action you must balance the inevitable cost in lives against the objectives you seek to attain. Unless the results to be expected can reasonably justify the estimated loss of life the action involves, then for my part I want none of it.

General Matthew B. Ridgway

Bold decisions give the best promise of success.

Field Marshal Erwin Rommel
"Rules of Desert Warfare," n.d.
Paper prepared as an introduction
to his account of the war in Africa

He who knows when he can fight and when he cannot will be victorious.

Sun-Tzu
The Art of War, circa fourth century B.C.

Once a decision was made, I did not worry about it afterward.

Harry S. Truman
Memoirs, 1955

In military operations, time is everything.

Arthur Wellesley, Duke of Wellington
30 June 1800

Discipline

If men are to give their best in war they must be united. Discipline seeks through drill to instill into all ranks this sense of unity, by requiring them to obey orders as one man. A Ceremonial parade, moreover, provides an occasion for men to express pride in their performance, pride in the Regiment or Corps and pride in the Profession of Arms.

General Sir Harold Alexander
November 1968

There is a difference between being a "hard-ass" and being a "dumb-ass."

Anonymous

Remember as you follow where you may be led to regard discipline and vigilance as of first importance, and to obey with alacrity the orders transmitted to you; as nothing contributes so much to the credit and safety of an army as the union of large bodies by a single discipline.

Archidamus, King of Sparta
Exhorting the Spartans and allies
at the start of the Peloponnesian War
(quoted by Thucydides)

You would deceive yourself greatly if you were to imagine that, in order to obtain the love of your regiment, you should let discipline slide or give in easily to the desires of each of your officers; this method would be neither certain nor glorious.

Marshal de Belle-Isle
Letter to his son

As the severity of military operations increases, so also must the sternness of the discipline. The zeal of the soldiers, their warlike instincts, and the interests and excitements of war may ensure obedience of orders and the cheerful endurance of perils and hardships during a short and prosperous campaign. But when fortune is dubious or adverse; when retreats as well as advances are necessary; when supplies fail, arrangements miscarry, and disasters impend, and when the struggle is protracted, men can only be persuaded to accept evil things by the lively realization of the fact that greater terrors await their refusal.

Sir Winston Churchill
The River War, 1899

The superior man is firm in the right way, and not merely firm.

Confucius
Analects, circa 500 B.C.

Discipline is as necessary to the soldier as the air he breathes. It is not only the source of his strength, it is the source of his contentment.

Jean Dutourd

The commander should practice kindness and severity, should appear friendly to the soldiers, speak to them on the march, visit them while they are cooking, ask them if they are well cared for, and alleviate their needs if they have any. Officers without experience in war should be treated kindly. Their good actions should be praised. Small requests should be granted and they should not be treated in an overbearing manner, but severity is maintained about everything regarding duty. The negligent officer is punished; the man who answers back is made to feel your severity by being reprimanded with the authoritative air that superiority gives; pillaging or argumentative soldiers, or those whose obedience is not immediate, should be punished.

Frederick the Great
Instructions for His Generals, 1747

The sterner the discipline the better the soldier. A strong discipline is the foundation of heroic exploits in the field.

Private Stephen Graham

Discipline is summed up in one word—obedience.

Lord Admiral John Jervis, Earl of St. Vincent

Without discipline, well planned and strictly supported, a military corps or a ship's crew are no better than a disorderly mob; it is well-formed discipline that gives force, preserves order, obedience, and cleanliness, and causes alertness and dispatch in execution of business.

Admiral Richard Kempenfelt
Letter to Sir Charles Middleton, 28 December 1779

Above all, discipline; eternally and inevitably, discipline. Discipline is the screw, the nail, the cement, the glue, the nut, the bolt, the rivet that holds everything tight. Discipline is the wire, the connecting rod, the chain that coordinates. Discipline is the oil that makes machines run fast, and the oil that makes parts slide smooth, as well as the oil that makes the metal bright. They know about discipline here. The principle of discipline here is divinely simple; you lay it on thick and fast, all the time.

Private Gerald Kersh

He who conquers others is strong;
He who conquers himself is mighty.

Lao-Tzu
The Way of Lao-Tzu, circa sixth century B.C.

Discipline, in the sense in which it is restrictive, [is] submergent of individuality. . . . The aim is to render the unit a unit, and the man a type, in order that their effort shall be calculable, their collective output even in grain and bulk. The deeper the discipline, the lower the individual efficiency, and the more sure the performance. It is a deliberate sacrifice of capacity in order to reduce the uncertain element, the bionomic factor, in enlisted humanity.

Thomas E. Lawrence
The Science of Guerrilla Warfare, 1929

I cannot trust a man to control others who cannot control himself.

General Robert E. Lee

A compliance with the minutiae of military courtesy is a mark of well-disciplined troops.

General John A. Lejeune

I don't mind being called tough, since I find in this racket it's the tough guys who lead the survivors.

Colonel Curtis Le May
1943

The spirit of discipline, as distinct from its outward and visible guises, is the result of association with martial traditions and their living embodiment.

B. H. Liddell Hart
Thoughts on War, 1944

Few men are brave by nature, but good order and experience make many so. Good order and discipline in any army are more to be depended upon than courage alone.

Niccolò di Bernardo Machiavelli
Arte Della Guèrra, 1520

The main end and design of all the care and pains that are bestowed in keeping up good order and discipline is to fit and prepare an army to engage an enemy in a proper manner.

Niccolò di Bernardo Machiavelli
Arte Della Guèrra, 1520

To give reputation to the army of any state, it is necessary to revive the discipline of the ancients, cherish and honor it, and give it life, so that in return it may give reputation to the state.

Niccolò di Bernardo Machiavelli
Discorsi, 1531

The first thing to be taken care of in the disciplining of men is to dress them, to teach them the air of a soldier, and to drive out the clown.

Lieutenant John MacIntire
*A Military Treatise on the Discipline of the Marine
Forces When at Sea,* 1763

The power of an army cannot be measured in mere numbers. It is based on a high state of discipline and training; on a readiness to carry out its mission wherever and whenever the Commander in Chief and Congress decide. Any compromise with those requirements and that purpose not only minimizes our efforts but largely vitiates our development of military power.

General George C. Marshall
Selected Speeches and Statements of General of the Army George C. Marshall, edited by Major H. A. Deweerd, 1945

No leader ever fails his men—nor will they fail him—who leads them in respect for the disciplined life. Between these two things—discipline in itself and a personal faith in the military value of discipline—lies all the difference between military maturity and mediocrity.

Brigadier General S.L.A. Marshall
The Armed Forces Officer, 1950

While modern warfare and weapons demand a very high order of intelligence, and offer greater advantage than ever to intelligent soldiers, such as the Americans are, they make it ever more necessary that intelligence should be guided and controlled by instruction and discipline to produce the most useful and inexpensive results.

General George B. McClellan
American Military Thought, 1878

Discipline is essential in military service but, unfortunately, it cannot be maintained unless stern measures are taken when circumstances call for them.

Major General Aubrey "Red" Newman
Follow Me, 1981

You cannot be disciplined in great things and undisciplined in small things. There is only one sort of discipline—perfect discipline. . . . Discipline is based on pride in the profession of arms, on meticulous attention to details, and on mutual respect and confidence. [It] can only be obtained when all officers are so imbued with the sense of their lawful obligation to their men and to their country that they cannot tolerate negligence.

General George S. Patton, Jr.

When a man enters the Army, he leaves home, usually for the first time, and also he leaves behind him the inhibitions resulting from his respect for the opinion of his parents and his friends; which inhibitions, unknown to himself, have largely guided his existence. When he joins a unit and lacks this corrective influence, he is apt to slip in morals, in neatness, and in energy. Administrative discipline must replace the absent inhibitions.

All human beings have an innate resistance to obedience. Discipline removes this resistance and, by constant repetition, makes obedience habitual and subconscious. . . . No sane man is unafraid in battle, but discipline produces in him a form of vicarious courage which, with his manhood, makes for victory. Self-respect grows directly from discipline. The Army saying, "Who ever saw a dirty soldier with a medal?" is largely true.

General George S. Patton, Jr.

Aeons and aeons ago a small band of natural fighters arose in their might and beat all the timid, primitive men into submission. At last, however, because there were more of them, the timid men organized into armies and beat the fighters. The fighters in turn had to figure out a way to regain prestige. Unfortunately there were not enough of them to make up a great army, so they resorted to hiring soldiers. This, however, did not work either. The mercenaries ran away. At length they hit on the solution. They simply beat the heads of the deserters together until their brains fell on the ground. Then the other mercenaries obeyed them and defeated the timid men. The fighters had learned the art of discipline.

General George S. Patton, Jr.

If you can't get them to salute when they should salute and wear the clothes you tell them to wear, how are you going to get them to die for their country?

General George S. Patton, Jr.

There is only one sort of discipline—perfect discipline. If you do not enforce and maintain discipline, you are potential murderers.

General George S. Patton, Jr.
Instructions to his corps and division commanders, 1944

Administrative discipline is the index of combat discipline. Any commander who is unwilling or unable to enforce administrative discipline will be incapable of enforcing combat discipline. An experienced officer can tell, by a very cursory administrative inspection of any unit, the caliber of its commanding officer.

General George S. Patton, Jr.
War as I Knew It, 1947

No man is fit to command another that cannot command himself.

William Penn
No Cross, No Crown, 1669

Discipline is not made to order, cannot be created offhand; it is a matter of the institution of tradition.

Ardant du Picq
Battle Studies, 1880

Pardon one offense and you encourage the commission of many.

Publilius Syrus

Only those who have disciplined themselves can exact disciplined performance from others.

General Matthew B. Ridgway
Military Review, "Leadership," October 1966

But as soon as discipline is neglected in a nation, as soon as comfort becomes an aim, it needs no inspiration to foretell that its ruin is near.

Marshal Comte de Maurice Saxe
Mes Rêveries, 1732

After the organization of troops, military discipline is the first matter that presents itself. It is the soul of armies. If it is not established with wisdom and maintained with unshakable resolution you will have no soldiers.

Marshal Comte de Maurice Saxe
Mes Rêveries, 1732

The discipline which makes the soldiers of a free country reliable in battle is not to be gained by harsh or tyrannical treatment. On the contrary, such treatment is far more likely to destroy than to make an army. It is possible to impart instruction and to give commands in such manner and such a tone of voice to inspire in the soldier no feeling but an intense desire to obey, while the opposite manner and tone of voice cannot fail to excite strong resentment and a desire to disobey. The one mode or the other of dealing with subordinates springs from a corresponding spirit in the breast of the commander. He who feels the respect which is due to others cannot fail to inspire in them regard for himself, while he who feels, and hence manifests, disrespect toward others, especially his inferiors, cannot fail to inspire hatred against himself.

Major General John M. Schofield
Address to corps of cadets, 11 August 1879

A true military discipline stems not from knowledge but from habit.

General Hans von Seeckt

The more modern war becomes the more essential appear the basic qualities that from the beginning of history have distinguished armies from mobs. The first of these is discipline.

Field Marshal Sir William Slim
Defeat into Victory, 1961

Regard your soldiers as your children, and they will follow you into the deepest valleys; look upon them as your own beloved sons, and they will stand by you even unto death.

If, however, you are indulgent, but unable to make your authority felt; kind-hearted but unable to enforce your commands; and incapable, moreover, of quelling disorder, then your soldiers must be likened to spoilt children; they are useless for any practical purpose.

Sun-Tzu
The Art of War, circa fourth century B.C.

When the general is weak and without authority; when his orders are not clear and distinct; when there are no fixed duties assigned to the officers and men, and the ranks are formed in a slovenly haphazard manner, the result is utter disorganization.

Sun-Tzu
The Art of War, circa fourth century B.C.

If soldiers are punished before they have grown attached to you, they will not prove submissive; and unless submissive, they will be practically useless. If, when the soldiers have become attached to you, punishments are not enforced, they will still be useless.

Therefore soldiers must be treated in the first instance with humanity, but kept under control by means of iron discipline. This is a certain road to victory.

If in training soldiers, commands are habitually enforced, the army will be well disciplined.

If the general shows confidence in his men but always insists on his orders being obeyed, the gain will be mutual.

Sun-Tzu
The Art of War, circa fourth century B.C.

By true discipline, I mean that willing and cheerful subordination of the individual to the success of the team which is the Army. This kind of discipline is not to be confused with the external appearance of traditional discipline: the salute, the knock on the orderly room door, the formulae of deference to superiors—in short, military courtesy as it is rigidly prescribed in our field manuals. The latter have their place, particularly in the peacetime Army; but they are not the indices of the discipline which really counts.

General Maxwell D. Taylor
The Field Artillery Journal, January/February 1947

The strength of an army lies in strict discipline and undeviating obedience to its officers.

Thucydides
History of the Peloponnesian War, circa 404 B.C.

The first point we must remember is that discipline is not created by edict. You do not achieve discipline simply by giving orders; discipline is inspired, created and maintained by leadership. Without that inspiration and without that necessary leadership, you will never get discipline.

Brigadier J. H. Thyer
Lecture to officers, warrant officers, and sergeants,
Changi POW camp, 18 June 1942

Troops who march in an irregular and disorderly manner are always in great danger of being defeated.

Vegetius
Dē Re Mīlitāri, Book I, 378

The necessity of discipline cannot be too often inculcated.

Vegetius
Dē Re Mīlĭtāri, Book I, 378

No state can be either happy or secure that is remiss and negligent in the discipline of its troops.

Vegetius
Dē Re Mīlĭtāri, Book I, 378

In war discipline is superior to strength; but if that discipline is neglected, there is no longer any difference between the soldier and the peasant.

Vegetius
Dē Re Mīlĭtāri, Book II, 378

Inquiries are now no longer made about customs that have been so long neglected, because in the midst of peace, war is looked upon as an object too distant to merit consideration. But former instances will convince us that the re-establishment of ancient discipline is by no means impossible, although now so totally lost.

Vegetius
Dē Re Mīlĭtāri, Book III, 378

The ancients, taught by experience, preferred discipline to numbers.

Vegetius
Dē Re Mīlĭtāri, Book III, 378

But it is much more to the credit of a general to form his troops to submission and obedience by habit and discipline than to be obliged to force them to their duty by the terror of punishment.

Vegetius
Dē Re Mīlĭtāri, Book III, 378

Discipline is the soul of an army. It makes small numbers formidable; procures success to the weak and esteem to all.

General George Washington
Letter to captains of Virginia regiments, 29 July 1759

To bring Men to a proper degree of Subordination is not the work of a day, a Month, or even a year.

General George Washington
Letter to the president of Congress,
24 September 1776

Discipline is teaching which makes a man do something which he would not, unless he had learnt that it was the right, the proper, and the expedient thing to do. At its best, it is instilled and maintained by pride in oneself, in one's unit, in one's profession; only at its worst by a fear of punishment.

Field Marshal Sir Archibald P. Wavell
Soldiers and Soldiering, 1953

It is discipline that makes one feel safe, while lack of discipline has destroyed many people before now.

Xenophon
Speech to Greek officers after the defeat
of Cyrus at Cunaxa, 401 B.C.

Duty

In doing what we ought, we deserve no praise, because it is our duty.

Saint Augustine

Only tyrants seem to have difficulty in comprehending the American mind, and their most famous last words have been, "The Americans won't fight."

Lieutenant General Milton G. Baker

For most men, the matter of learning is one of personal preference. But for Army officers, the obligation to learn, to grow in their profession, is clearly a public duty.

General Omar N. Bradley

Duty be habit is to pleasure tuned.

Samuel E. Bridges

We give thanks to God for the noblest of all His blessings, the sense that we had done our duty.

Sir Winston Churchill

Neither the physician not the general can ever, however praiseworthy he may be in the theory of his art, perform anything highly worthwhile without experience in the rules laid down for the conservation of all small duties.

Marcus Tullius Cicero

Faîtes votre devoir et laisser-faire aux dieux.
[Do your duty, and leave the rest to heaven.]

Pierre Corneille
Horace, Act II, Scene viii, 1639

Duty is never simple, never easy, and rarely obvious.

Jean Dutourd

So nigh is grandeur to our dust,
So near to God is man,
When Duty whispers low, *Thou must.*
The youth replies, *I can.*

Ralph Waldo Emerson
Voluntaries, III, 1867

Don't flinch from that fire, boys. There's a hotter fire than that for those who don't do their duty! Give that rascally little tug a shot, and don't let her go off with a whole coat.

Rear Admiral David G. Farragut
Action near Fort St. Philip (New Orleans), 24 April 1862

It is wonderful what strength and boldness of purpose and energy will come from feeling that we are in the way of duty.

John W. Foster

Ave Caesar, morturi te sălūtant.
[Hail Caesar, we who are about to die salute you.]

Gladiator salute

The very efficiency of the army depends upon fortitude, integrity, self-restraint, personal loyalty to other persons, and the surrender of the individual to the common good.

General Sir John Hackett

The duty of the men at Stalingrad is to be dead.

Adolf Hitler

Our business in the field of fight
Is not to question, but to prove our might.

Homer
The Iliad, Book XX, circa 700 B.C.

The first duty of a soldier or good citizen is to attend to the safety and interest of his country.

Andrew Jackson
To Henry Dearbon, 8 January 1807

The brave man, inattentive to his duty, is worth little more to his Country than the coward who deserts her in the hour of danger.

Andrew Jackson
At the Battle of New Orleans
to the troops who had abandoned their positions,
8 January 1815

Duty is ours; consequences are God's.

General Thomas J. "Stonewall" Jackson
1862

This generation learned from bitter experience that either brandishing or yielding to threats can only lead to war. But firmness and reason can lead to the kind of peaceful solution in which my country profoundly believes.

John F. Kennedy

Duty is the most beautiful word in the English language.

General Robert E. Lee

Do your duty in all things. You cannot do more. You should never wish to do less.

General Robert E. Lee

I think and work with all my power to bring the troops to the right place at the right time; then I have done my duty. As soon as I order them forward into battle, I leave my army in the hands of God.

General Robert E. Lee

Let us have faith that right makes might, and in that faith let us to the end dare to do our duty as we understand it.

Abraham Lincoln
Speech at Cooper Union, New York, 27 February 1859

I firmly believe that any man's finest hour, his greatest fulfillment to all he holds dear, is the moment when he has worked his heart out in a good cause and lies exhausted on the field of battle victorious.

Vince Lombardi

Old soldiers never die; they just fade away. And like the old soldier in that ballad, I now close my military career and just fade away, an old soldier who tried to do his duty as God gave him the sight to see that duty.

General Douglas MacArthur
Speech to Congress after he was relieved by
President Harry S. Truman, 19 April 1951

A Marine on duty has no friends.

Marine Corps motto
Marine Corps Officer's Guide, 1967

Every mission constitutes a pledge of duty. Every man is bound to consecrate his every effort to its fulfillment. He will derive his rule of action from the profound conviction of that duty.

Giuseppe Mazzini

Perish discretion when it interferes with duty.

Hannah More

Duty—the sublimest word in the English language.

Attributed to Lord Admiral Horatio Nelson

Duty is the great business of a sea officer; all private considerations must give way to it, however painful it may be.

Lord Admiral Horatio Nelson
Letter for Frances Nisbet, 1786

England expects every man to do his duty.

Lord Admiral Horatio Nelson
Aboard the HMS *Victory* before the Battle of Trafalgar,
21 October 1805

Thank God, I have done my duty.

Lord Admiral Horatio Nelson
After the Battle of Trafalgar, October 1805

A soldier can have no greater professional asset than a high sense of duty. This applies with equal force to menial administrative tasks as well as to major military responsibilities.

Major General Aubrey "Red" Newman
Follow Me, 1981

I pray daily to do my duty, retain my self confidence and accomplish my destiny.

General George S. Patton, Jr.
Diary entry, 20 June 1943

If I do my full duty, the rest will take care of itself.

General George S. Patton, Jr.
Diary entry prior to North African landing,
8 November 1943

Any commander who fails to attain his objective, and who is not dead or severely wounded, has not done his full duty.

General George S. Patton, Jr.
War as I Knew It, 1947

You've got to perform without flinching whatever duty is assigned you, regardless of the difficulty or the danger attending it. If it is garrison duty, you must attend to it. If it is meeting fever, you must be willing. If it is the closest kind of fighting, anxious for it. You must know how to ride, how to shoot, how to live in the open. Absolute obedience to every command is your first lesson. No matter what comes you mustn't squeal. Think it over—all of you. If any man wishes to withdraw he will be gladly excused, for others are ready to take his place.

Theodore Roosevelt
Address to U.S. Army recruits, 1898

A soldier's vow to his country is that he will die for the guardianship of her domestic virtue, of her righteous laws, and her anyway challenged or endangered honor. A state without virtue, without laws, without honor, he is bound not to defend.

John Ruskin
The Crown of Wild Olive, 1866

I hold my duty as I hold my soul.

William Shakespeare
Hamlet, Act II, Scene ii, 1601

Theirs not to make reply,
Theirs not to reason why,
Theirs but to do and die.

Alfred, Lord Tennyson
The Charge of the Light Brigade, 1854

Duty, Honor, Country.

U.S. Military Academy motto

They went where duty seemed to call,
They scarcely asked the reason why;
They only knew they could but die,
And death was not the worst of all!

John Greenleaf Whittier
Lexington, 1875

War is only a sort of dramatic representation, a sort of dramatic symbol of a thousand forms of duty.

Woodrow Wilson
Speech at Brooklyn, New York, 11 May 1914

But an officer on duty knows no one—to be partial is to dishonor both himself and the object of his ill-advised favor. What will be thought of him who exacts of his friends that which disgraces him? Look at him who winks at and overlooks offenses in one, which he causes to be punished in another, and contrast him with the inflexible soldier who does his duty faithfully, notwithstanding it occasionally wars with his private feelings. The conduct of one will be venerated and emulated, the other detested as a satire upon soldiership and honor.

Brevet Major William Jenkins Worth
Battalion orders, West Point, New York,
22 December 1820

Emotion

If you wish to do something foolish, follow the counsel of your anger.

Anonymous

It is easy to fly into a passion—anybody can do that—but to be angry with the right person to the right extent and at the right time and with the right object and in the right way—that is not easy, and it is not everyone who can do it.

Aristotle
Nicomachean Ethics, circa 340 B.C.

Never let yourself be driven by impatience or anger. One always regrets having followed the first dictates of his emotions.

Marshal de Belle-Isle
Letter to his son

Let not the sun go down on your wrath.

Bible, Ephesians 4:26

Let every man be swift to hear, slow to speak, slow to wrath.

Bible, James 1:19

He *that is* slow to anger *is* better than the mighty.

Bible, Proverbs 16:32

Speak when you are angry and you will make the best speech you will ever regret.

Ambrose Bierce
The Devil's Dictionary, 1906

All men who reflect on controversial matters should be free from hatred, friendship, anger, and pity.

Julius Caesar

Nothing in life is so exhilarating as to be shot at without result.

Sir Winston Churchill
The Malakand Field Force, 1898

When anger arrives, think of the consequences.

Confucius

Man is only truly great when he acts from the passions.

Benjamin Disraeli

A man in a passion rides a horse that runs away with him.

Thomas Fuller
Gnomologia, 1732

Nothing great in the world has ever been accomplished without passion.

Hegel
Philosophy of History, 1832

Īra fŭror brĕvis est.
[Anger is a short madness.]

Horace

I have one sentiment for soldiers living and dead: cheers for the living; tears for the dead.

Robert G. Ingersoll
Speech at Indianapolis, Indiana, 21 September 1876

If you aren't fired with enthusiasm, you'll be fired with enthusiasm.

Vince Lombardi

Always shun whatever may make you angry.

Publilius Syrus
Moral Sayings, circa first century B.C.

Always remember that when you are in the right you can afford to keep your temper, and when you are in the wrong you cannot afford to lose it.

John J. Reynolds

Of all base passions, fear is most accurs'd.

William Shakespeare
Henry VI, Act V, Scene ii, 1591

I have always believed that a motto for generals must be "No regrets," no crying over spilt milk.

Field Marshal Sir William Slim
Defeat into Victory, 1961

Esprit

All that can be done with the soldier is to give him *esprit de corps*—i.e., a higher opinion of his own regiment than all the other troops in the country.

Frederick the Great
Military Testament, 1768

Esprit, then, is the product of a thriving mutual confidence between the leader and the led, founded in the faith that together they possess a superior quality and capability.

Brigadier General S.L.A. Marshall
The Armed Forces Officer, 1950

Shrewd critics have assigned military success to all manner of things—tactics, shape of frontiers, speed, happily placed rivers, mountains or woods, intellectual ability, or the use of artillery. All in a measure true, but none vital. The secret lies in the inspiring spirit which lifted weary, footsore men out of themselves and made them march forgetful of agony . . . with an army it is the result of external impetus—leadership.

Major George S. Patton, Jr.
The Infantry Journal Reader, "Success in War," 1931

The ability to produce endurance is but an instance of that same martial soul which arouses in its followers that resistless emotion defined as elan, the will to victory.

Major George S. Patton, Jr.
The Infantry Journal Reader, "Success in War," 1931

Wars may be fought with weapons, but they are won by men. It is the spirit of the men who follow and the man who leads that gains victory.

Major George S. Patton, Jr.
Cavalry Journal, 1933

Moreover, it is more the nature of men to be less interested in things which relate to others than about those in which they themselves are concerned. The reputation of an organization becomes personal just as soon as it is an honor to belong to it.

Marshal Comte de Maurice Saxe
Mes Rêveries, 1732

Esprit de corps thrives not only on success, but on hardships and adversity shared with courage and fortitude.

Major General Orlando Ward

Experience

Experience is what you get when you are looking for something else.
Anonymous

Fools say that they learn from their own experience. I have always contrived to get my experience at the expense of others.
Prince Otto von Bismarck-Schönhausen

A great captain can only be formed by long experience and intense study.
Archduke Karl Ludwig Johann Charles of Austria

If men could learn from history, what lessons it might teach us. But passion and party blind our eyes, and the light which experience gives us is a lantern on the stern, which shines only on the waves behind us.
Samuel Taylor Coleridge
18 December 1831

Experience keeps a dear school, yet Fools will learn in no other.
Benjamin Franklin
Poor Richard's Almanac, 1743

War, like most things, is a science to be acquired and perfected by diligence, by perseverance, by time, and by practice.

Alexander Hamilton
The Federalist, 1787

I have but one lamp by which my feet are guided, and that is the lamp of experience. I know of no way of judging of the future but by the past.

Patrick Henry
Speech to Virginia Convention, 23 March 1775

Experience is not what happens to a man; it is what a man does with what happens to him.

Aldous Huxley
Reader's Digest, March 1956

Experience enables you to recognise a mistake when you make it again.

Franklyn P. Jones

The first quality of a general in chief is a great knowledge of the art of war. This is not intuitive, but the result of experience. A man is not born a commander. He must become one. Not to be anxious; to be always cool; to avoid confusion in his commands; never to change countenance; to give his orders in the midst of battle with as much composure as if he were perfectly at ease. These are the proofs of valor in a general.

Count de Montecuccoli
Commentarii Bellici, 1740

Our business, like any other, is to be learned by constant practice and experience; and our experience is to be had in war, not at reviews.

General Sir John Moore

Given time and adequate guidance, junior officers are forged into mature professional soldiers in the only way possible: by experience.

Major General Aubrey "Red" Newman
Follow Me, 1981

Do not despise the bottom rungs in the ascent to greatness.

Publilius Syrus
Moral Sayings, circa first century B.C.

The profit on a good action is to have done it.

Seneca
Letters to Lucilius, A.D. 63

If history repeats itself, and the unexpected always happens, how incapable must man be of learning from experience.

George Bernard Shaw

Marriage and family life are education. Sport, play, and entertainment are education. Religious training is education. Friendship is education. Military service is education. Any and every encounter with nature and society is education. Some social scientists call education in this comprehensive sense "acculturation." I prefer to call it more simply—"experience."

Vice Admiral James Bond Stockdale
Military Ethics,
"Education for Leadership and Survival," 1987

Military men who spend their lives in the uniform of their country acquire experience in preparing for war and waging it. No theoretical studies, no intellectual attainments on the part of the layman can be a substitute for the experience of having lived and delivered under the stress of war.

General Maxwell D. Taylor
Speech to graduating U.S. Military Academy cadets,
June 1963

Failure

It must be a rare occurrence if a battle is fought without many errors and failures, but for which more important results would have been obtained, and the exposure of these diminishes the credit due, impairs the public confidence, undermines the morale of the army, and works evil to the cause for which men have died.

Jefferson Davis
After the Battle of Chickamauga, 3 October 1863

Who never climbed high never fell low.

Thomas Fuller
Gnomologia, 1732

There is no failure except in no longer trying.

Elbert Hubbard

The greatest achievement is not in never falling, but in rising again after you fall.

Vince Lombardi

Show me a good loser and I will show you a loser.

Vince Lombardi

The history of failure in war can be summed up in two words: too late. Too late in comprehending the deadly purpose of a potential enemy; too late in realizing the mortal danger; too late in preparedness;

too late in uniting all possible forces for resistance; too late in standing with one's friends.

General Douglas MacArthur

Death is nothing, but to live defeated is to die every day.

Napoleon Bonaparte

When a man blames others for his failures, it's a good idea to credit others with his successes.

Howard W. Newton

Success is not a harbor but a voyage with its own perils to the spirit. The game of life is to come up a winner, to be a success, or to achieve what we set out to do. Yet there is always the danger of ailing as a human being. The lesson that most of us on this voyage never learn, but can never quite forget, is that to win is sometimes to lose.

Richard M. Nixon

The difference between failure and success is doing a thing nearly right and doing a thing exactly right.

Edward Simmons

I would prefer even to fail with honor than win by cheating.

Sophocles
Philoctetes, 409 B.C.

The problem for education is not to teach people how to deal with success but how to deal with failure.

Vice Admiral James Bond Stockdale
Military Ethics,
"Machiavelli, Management, and Moral Leadership," 1987

In the game of life it's a good idea to have a few early losses, which relieves you of the pressure of trying to maintain an undefeated season.

Bill Vaughan

Faith

The commander's will must rest on iron faith; faith in God, in his cause, or in himself.

Correlli Barnett
The Sword Bearers, 1963

For we walk by faith, not by sight.

Bible, II Corinthians 5:7

Blessed *are* they that have not seen, and *yet* have believed.

Bible, John 20:29

If thou canst believe, all things *are* possible to him that believeth.

Bible, Mark 9:23

All the strength and force of man comes from his faith in things unseen. He who believes is strong; he who doubts is weak. Strong convictions precede great actions.

James F. Clarke

If you think you can win, you can win. Faith is necessary to victory.

William Hazlitt
Literary Remains, 1836

Loss of hope, rather than loss of life, is the factor that really decides wars, battles, and even the smallest combats. The all-time experience of warfare shows that when men reach the point where they see, or feel, that further effort and sacrifice can do no more than delay the end, they commonly lose the will to spin it out, and bow to the inevitable.

B. H. Liddell Hart

Sempĕr fidēlis.
[Ever faithful.]

Marine Corps motto

Faith may be defined briefly as an illogical belief in the occurrence of the improbable.

Henry Louis Mencken
Prejudices, 1922

I'm convinced that, if each and every one of us would renew his faith in the principles of our freedom and would use the highly developed talent for merchandising our principles that we use to sell our products, our country would remain strong spiritually as well as physically.

Captain Edward V. Rickenbacker
Rickenbacker, 1967

Hope encourages men to endure and attempt everything; in depriving them of it, or in making it too distant, you deprive them of their very soul.

Marshal Comte de Maurice Saxe
Mes Rêveries, 1732

Be bloody, bold, and resolute.

William Shakespeare
Macbeth, Act IV, Scene i, 1606

Morality and faith are the pillars of our society. May we never forget that.

General George Washington

When faith is lost, when honor dies,
The man is dead!

John Greenleaf Whittier
Ichabod, 1850

Fear

Fear is stronger than arms.

Aeschylus
Seven Against Thebes, 467 B.C.

Nothing is terrible except fear itself.

Sir Francis Bacon
Dē Augmĕntis Scĭentĭarum, 1623

The ugly truth is revealed that fear is the foundation of obedience.
Sir Winston Churchill

It is not death or pain that is to be dreaded, but the fear of pain or death.

Epictetus
Discourses, circa A.D. 100

Since officers must necessarily lead them into the greatest dangers, the soldiers should fear their officers more than all the dangers to which they are exposed. . . . Good will can never induce the common soldier to stand up to such dangers; he will only do so through fear.
Frederick the Great

Far better is it to have a stout heart always and suffer one's share of evils than to be ever fearing what may happen.
Herodotus

On the battlefield the real enemy is fear and not the bayonet or bullet. All means of union of power demand union of knowledge.

Robert Jackson

Never take counsel of your fears.

General Thomas J. "Stonewall" Jackson
To Major Hotchkiss, 18 June 1862,
quoted in Douglas Southall Freeman's *Lee's Lieutenants*, 1944

We should never let our fears hold us back from pursuing our hopes.

John F. Kennedy
Address in Washington, D.C., 11 December 1959

A man killed is merely one man less, whereas a man unnerved is a highly infectious carrier of fear, capable of spreading an epidemic of panic.

B. H. Liddell Hart

In the normal man it is an absolutely normal impulse to move away from danger. Yet within an army it is recognized by all that personal flight from danger, where it involves dereliction of duty, is the final act of cowardice and of dishonor. During combat the soldier may become so gripped by fear that most of his thought is directed toward escape. But if he is serving among men whom he has known for a long period or whose judgment of him counts for any reason, he still will strive to hide his terror from them.

Brigadier General S.L.A. Marshall
Men Against Fire, 1947

The thing of which I have most fear is fear.

Michel Eyquem de Montaigne
Essays, 1580

There are only two forces that unite men—fear and interest.

Napoleon Bonaparte

All men are timid on entering any fight whether it is the first fight or the last fight. All of us are timid. Cowards are those who let their timidity get the better of their manhood.

General George S. Patton, Jr.
Letter to his son, 6 June 1944

All men are frightened. The more intelligent they are, the more they are frightened. The courageous man is the man who forces himself, in spite of his fear, to carry on. Discipline, pride, self-respect, self-confidence, and love of glory are attributes which will make a man courageous even when he is afraid.

General George S. Patton, Jr.
War as I Knew It, 1947

No sane man is unafraid in battle, but discipline produces in him a form of vicarious courage.

General George S. Patton, Jr.
War as I Knew It, 1947

An army of stags led by a lion is more to be feared than an army of lions led by a stag.

Attributed to Philip of Macedonia

Fear makes men forget, and skill which cannot fight is useless.

Phormio of Athens
To Athenian forces before the Battle of Crisaean Gulf, 429 B.C.

Tactics is an art based on the knowledge of how to make men fight with maximum energy against fear, a maximum which organization alone can give.

Ardant du Picq
Battle Studies, 1880

Ad dētĕriŏra crēdĕnda prōni mĕtŭo.
[Fear makes men ready to believe the worst.]

Quintus Curtius Rufus
Dē Rēbus Gesti Ălexandri Magni,
circa second century

111

In time of battle, when victory hangs in the balance, it is necessary to put down any sign of weakness, indecision, lack of aggressiveness, or panic, whether the man wears stars on his shoulders or chevrons on his sleeve, for one frightened soldier can infect his whole unit.

General Matthew B. Ridgway
Soldier: The Memoirs of Matthew B. Ridgway, 1956

That a few men break is understandable. But I prefer to remember the others who did not break, the men who stood and fought and died. What quality in them sustained and strengthened them I do not know. Surely it was not fearlessness, for in battle no normal man is entirely free from fear. I think perhaps Housman gave one answer in his lines:

"Here dead we lie because we did not choose to live and shame the land from which we sprung. Nor did they choose to shame their comrades, or themselves."

General Matthew B. Ridgway
Soldier: The Memoirs of Matthew B. Ridgway, 1956

We promise according to our hopes, and perform according to our fears.

François, Duc de La Rochefoucauld
Maximes, 1665

I believe that anyone can conquer fear by doing the things he fears to do, provided he keeps doing them until he gets a record of successful experiences behind him.

Eleanor Roosevelt

The only thing we have to fear is fear itself—nameless, unreasoning, unjustified terror which paralyzes needed efforts to convert retreat into advance.

Franklin D. Roosevelt
Presidential nomination acceptance speech, 1936

The fear of war is worse than war itself.

Seneca
Hercules Furens, circa A.D. 50

112

No man should possess him with any appearance of fear, lest he, by showing it, should dishearten his army.

William Shakespeare
King Henry V, Act IV, Scene i, 1600

Keep your fears to yourself but share your courage.

Robert Louis Stevenson

Soldiers when in desperate straits lose the sense of fear. . . . If there is no help for it, they will fight hard. Thus without waiting to be marshalled, the soldiers will be constantly on the *qui vive;* without waiting to be asked, they will do your will; without restrictions, they will be faithful; without giving orders, they can be trusted.

Prohibit the taking of omens, and do away with superstitious doubts. Then, until death comes, no calamity need be feared.

Sun-Tzu
The Art of War, circa fourth century B.C.

Even the bravest are frightened by sudden terrors.

Tacitus

Nothing is so much to be feared as fear.

Henry David Thoreau
7 September 1851

Courage is resistance to fear, mastery of fear—not absence of fear. Except a creature be part coward it is not a compliment to say it is brave.

Mark Twain
Pudd'nhead Wilson's Calendar, 1894

For, as the well-trained soldier is eager for action, so does the untaught fear it.

Vegetius
Dē Re Mīlitāri, Book II, 378

The only thing I am afraid of is fear.

Arthur Wellesley, Duke of Wellington
3 November 1831

Flexibility, Change

Learn then to make dispositions in such a fashion that the fate of your army does not depend on the good or bad conduct of a single minor officer.

Frederick the Great
Instructions for His Generals, 1747

All is flux, nothing stays still.

Heraclitus

Nothing endures but change.

Heraclitus

Plus ça change, plus c'est la même chose.
[The more things change, the more they remain the same.]

Alphonse Karr
Les Guepes, January 1849

The unexpectancy of combat is inevitable, and in view of this fact he who invokes the memory of the glorious maneuvers that led to Marengo, Austerlitz and Jena is open to censure. . . . Now one arrives on the ground and one fights there: that is the war of the future.

Jules Lewis Lewal

No rule of war is so absolute as to allow no exceptions.

Napoleon Bonaparte
Maxims, XLII, 1831

Beware not of changes, but of premature changes—particularly when those changes are based on personal preference, motivated by a desire to create an impression rather than to fill a need.

Major General Aubrey "Red" Newman
Follow Me, 1981

Omnĭa mūtāntur, nĭhil intĕrĭt.
[All things change; nothing perishes.]

Ovid
Mĕtămorphōsēs, circa A.D. 5

There is no approved solution to any tactical situation.

General George S. Patton, Jr.
War as I Knew It, 1947

It is true that in war determination by itself may achieve results, while flexibility, without determination in reserve, cannot, but it is only the blending of the two that brings fine success.

Field Marshal Sir William Slim
Defeat into Victory, 1961

Things do not change; we change.

Henry David Thoreau
Walden, 1854

The art of war is, in the last result, the art of keeping one's freedom of action.

Xenophon

Honor

Fame is like a river, that beareth up things light and swollen, and drowns things weighty and solid.

Sir Francis Bacon
Essays, "Of Praise," 1625

Honor is often what remains after faith, love, and hope are lost.

Jacob Burckhardt
The Civilization of the Renaissance in Italy, 1929

My honor is dearer to me than my life.

Miguel de Cervantes
Don Quixote, 1615

What is life without honor? Degradation is worse than death.

General Thomas J. "Stonewall" Jackson
1862

Nobody can acquire honor by doing what is wrong.

Thomas Jefferson
To Manchot, war chief of the Potawatomies,
21 December 1808

It matters not how a man dies, but how he lives.

Samuel Johnson
26 October 1769

I would lay down my life for America, but I cannot trifle with my honor.

Admiral John Paul Jones
Letter to A. Livingson, 4 September 1777

He has honor if he holds himself to an ideal of conduct though it is inconvenient, unprofitable, or dangerous to do so.

Walter Lippmann
A Preface to Morals, 1929

The difference between a moral man and a man of honor is that the latter regrets a discreditable act, even when it has worked and he has not been caught.

Henry Louis Mencken
Prejudices: Fourth Series, 1924

What is left when honor is lost?

Publilius Syrus
Sententiae, circa 50 B.C.

If I lose mine honor, I lose myself.

William Shakespeare
Antony and Cleopatra, Act III, Scene iv, 1607

War must be carried on systematically, and to do it you must have men of character activated by principles of honor.

General George Washington

Human Nature

The task of leadership is not to put greatness into humanity, but to elicit it, for the greatness is already there.

John Buchan

Human nature is the same everywhere; the modes only are different.

Earl of Chesterfield
Letters to His Godson, 1773

By nature, men are nearly alike; by practice, they get to be wide apart.

Confucius
Analects, circa 500 B.C.

It is a law of nature common to all mankind, which no time shall annul or destroy, that those who have strength shall bear rule over those who have less.

Dionysius the Younger

It is characteristic of the military mentality that non-human factors . . . are held essential, while the human being, his desires and thoughts—in short, the psychological factors—are considered as unimportant and secondary.

Albert Einstein
Out of My Later Life, 1950

Remember also that one of the requisite studies for an officer is *man*. Where your analytical geometry will serve you once, a knowledge of men will serve you daily. As a commander, to get the right man in the right place is one of the questions of success or defeat.

Admiral David G. Farragut
Letter to his son, 13 October 1864

A perfect general, like Plato's republic, is a figment. Either would be admirable, but it is not characteristic of human nature to produce beings exempt from human weaknesses and defects.

Frederick the Great

It was, I think, ever increasing size, with its concomitant complexity of control, which more than any factors created this change both in industrial and military organizations. The more management, or command, became methodized, the more dehumanized each grew, the worker, or the soldier, becoming a cog in a vast soulless machine, was de-spiritualized, the glamour of work, or of war, fading from before his eyes, until working, or fighting, became drudgery.

Major-General J.F.C. Fuller
Generalship: Its Diseases and Their Cure, 1936

Beneath the dingy uniformity of international fashions in dress, man remains what he has always been—a splendid fighting animal, a self-sacrificing hero, and a bloodthirsty savage.

Dean William Ralph Inge
Outspoken Essays: First Series, 1919

A commander should have a profound understanding of human nature, the knack of smoothing out troubles, the power of winning affection while communicating energy, and the capacity for ruthless determination where required by circumstances. He needs to generate an electrifying current, and to keep a cool head in applying it.

B. H. Liddell Hart
Thoughts on War, 1944

Human nature will not change. In any future great national trial, compared with the men of this, we shall have as weak and as strong, as silly and as wise, as bad and as good.

Abraham Lincoln
10 November 1864

The art of leading, in operations large or small, is the art of dealing with humanity, of working diligently on behalf of men, of being sympathetic with them, but equally, of insisting they make a square facing toward their own problems.

Brigadier General S.L.A. Marshall
Men Against Fire, 1947

Despite the near presence of the enemy, troops will always let down at every opportunity and it is the task of leadership to keep them picked up. They will always bunch unless they are insistently told by voice to stop bunching. They will always run if they see others running and do not understand why. In these natural tendencies lie the chief dangers to battlefield control and the chief causes of battlefield panic.

Brigadier General S.L.A. Marshall
Men Against Fire, 1947

The art of leading, in operations large or small, is the art of dealing with humanity.

Brigadier General S.L.A. Marshall
Men Against Fire, 1947

People will sometimes forgive you the good you have done them, but seldom the harm you have done them.

William Somerset Maugham

Unlike steel, an army is a most sensitive instrument and can easily become damaged; its basic ingredient is men and, to handle an army well, it is essential to understand human nature.

Field Marshal Bernard L. Montgomery

We need less "pipe clay" and less seclusion at the Military Academy—in a word, more democracy. During their four year term the cadets see about as little of the world as inmates of a convent. When they graduate they know little of human nature and the only men they have handled are themselves.

New York Times, 21 May 1919

As long as armies are made up of people, the human element will remain an irreplaceable consideration in command and leadership.

Major General Aubrey "Red" Newman
Follow Me, 1981

In my experience, all very successful commanders are prima donnas, and must be so treated.

General George S. Patton, Jr.

Since the necessary limitations of map problems inhibit the student from considering the effects of hunger, emotion, personality, fatigue, leadership, and many other imponderable yet vital factors, he first neglects and then forgets them.

Major George S. Patton, Jr.
The Infantry Journal Reader, "Success in War," 1931

What you must know is how man reacts. Weapons change but man who uses them changes not at all. To win battles you do not beat weapons—you beat the soul of the enemy man.

General George S. Patton, Jr.
Letter to his son, 6 June 1944

The man is the first weapon in battle: let us then study the soldier in battle, for it is he who brings reality to it. Only study of the past can give us a sense of reality, and show us how the soldier will fight in the future.

Ardant du Picq
Battle Studies, 1880

If we had no faults of our own, we would not take so much pleasure in noticing those of others.

François, Duc de La Rochefoucauld
Reflections, 1678

Few men are gifted with sound reasoning powers, thus it is the human heart that we must search. Without having studied this most profound and sublime side of war, one can scarcely hope for the favors of fortune.

Marshal Comte de Maurice Saxe

The human heart is . . . the starting point in all matters pertaining to war.

Marshal Comte de Maurice Saxe

Nobody likes the man who brings bad news.

Sophocles
Antigone, circa 442 B.C.

There is no need to suppose that human beings differ very much one from another; but it is true that the ones who come out on top are the ones who have been trained in the hardest school.

Thucydides
History of the Peloponnesian War, circa 404 B.C.

Common sense is not so common.

Voltaire
Dictionnaire Philosophique, 1764

Sarcasm is always resented and seldom forgiven.

Field Marshal Sir Archibald P. Wavell
"Lees Knowles Lectures,"
Trinity College, Cambridge, 1939

The only thing that one really knows about human nature is that it changes. Change is the one quality we can predicate on it.

Oscar Wilde
The Soul of Man Under Socialism, 1895

The facts are that times change, technology changes, weapons change, but basic human nature doesn't change. A leader must keep up to date on every aspect of his job, weigh all facts, and seek other people's advice.

General Louis H. Wilson
Quoted in Karel Montor et al.,
Naval Leadership: Voices of Experience, 1987

The line between firmness and harshness, between strong leadership and bullying, between discipline and chicken-_____ is a fine one. It is difficult to define, but those of us who are professionals and also have accepted as a career the leadership of men, must find that line. It is because judgments and people and human relationships are involved in leadership that only men can lead men, and not computers.

Major General Melvin Zais
Lucky Eagle Says, 1969

Humor

Men will let you abuse them if only you will make them laugh.

Henry Ward Beecher
Proverbs from Plymouth Pulpit, 1887

It is good to make a jest, but not to make a trade of jesting.

Thomas Fuller

Take heed of jesting; many have been ruined by it. It is hard to jest, and not sometimes leer too, which often sinks deeper than we intended or expected.

Thomas Fuller

Better lose a jest than a friend.

Thomas Fuller
Gnomologia, 1732

There is no defense against adverse fortune which is, on the whole, so effectual as a habitual sense of humor.

Thomas W. Higginson

A jest often decides matters of importance more effectively and happily than seriousness.

Horace
Satires, 23 B.C.

You are not angry with people when you laugh at them. Humour teaches tolerance.

William Somerset Maugham
The Summing Up, 1938

Humor is an effective but tricky technique in command and leadership, beneficial when used wisely and with skill, but it can backfire into a dangerous booby trap if overworked or crudely employed.

Major General Aubrey "Red" Newman
Follow Me, 1981

Mix empathy with your humor; consider how the jest you have in mind will affect others before you utter it.

Major General Aubrey "Red" Newman
Follow Me, 1981

Fortune and humour govern the world.

François, Duc de La Rochefoucauld
Maximes, 1665

A jest's prosperity lies in the ear
Of him that hears it, never in the tongue
Of him that makes it.

William Shakespeare
Love's Labour's Lost, Act V, Scene ii, 1595

People are afraid of a leader who has no sense of humor. They think that he is not capable of relaxing, and as a result of this there is a tendency for that leader to have a reputation for pomposity, which may not be the case at all. Humor has a tendency to relax people in times of stress.

General Louis H. Wilson
Quoted in Karel Montor et al.,
Naval Leadership: Voices of Experience, 1987

Initiative

You must be able to underwrite the honest mistakes of your subordinates if you wish to develop their initiative and experience.

General Bruce C. Clarke

Nature knows no pause in progress and development, and attaches her curse on all inaction.

Johann Wolfgang von Goethe

Time is neutral with a bias in favour of the side that exhibits the more intelligent initiative.

Major Reginald Hargreaves

Once begun, a task is easy; half the work is done.

Horace
Epistles, circa 20–13 B.C.

There are two kinds of fools. One says, "This is old, therefore it is good." The other says, "This is new, therefore it is better."

Dean William Ralph Inge

Initiative means freedom to act, but it does not mean freedom to act in an offhand or casual manner.

Admiral Ernest J. King

126

Initiative is the agent which translates imagination into action. It must be used intelligently lest it become irresponsibility or even insubordination, but it must be used courageously when the situation warrants. Military history provides innumerable examples of commanders, who, confronted with unforeseen circumstances, have adhered slavishly to instructions and, at best, have lost an opportunity; at worst they have brought on defeat.

General Lyman L. Lemnitzer

The test of fitness in command is the ability to think clearly in the face of unexpected contingency or opportunity. Improvisation is of the essence of initiative in all combat just as initiative is the outward showing of the power of decision.

Brigadier General S.L.A. Marshall
Men Against Fire, 1947

Never tell people *how* to do things. Tell them *what* to do and they will surprise you with their ingenuity.

General George S. Patton, Jr.
War as I Knew It, 1947

Some officers require urging, others require suggestions, very few have to be restrained.

General George S. Patton, Jr.
War as I Knew It, 1947

Even if you're on the right track, you'll get run over if you just sit there.

Will Rogers

The reasonable man adapts himself to the world; the unreasonable one persists in trying to adapt the world to himself. Therefore all progress depends on the unreasonable man.

George Bernard Shaw

It takes more than tanks and guns and planes to win. It takes more than masses of men. It takes more than heroism, more than self-sacrifice, more than leadership. Modern war requires trained minds. . . . The days of unthinking masses of manpower are over. Individual intelligence, individual understanding and individual initiative in all ranks will be powerful weapons in our ultimate success.

General Brehon Somervell
Public Addresses, 1941–1942

Only by full use of your imagination and your initiative will you ever know your own capabilities as a leader. You will never know your capacity until you stretch yourself, or are stretched beyond what you think you can do or should do.

Lieutenant General Arthur G. Trudeau

Integrity

Let us be true: this is the highest maxim of art and life, the secret of eloquence and of virtue, and of all moral authority.

Henri-Frédéric Amiel
Journal, 17 December 1854

Let integrity and uprightness preserve me.

Bible, Psalms 25:21

Today's officer must have the mental flexibility, the imagination, to utilize to the fullest extent the developments of modern technology. Nevertheless, he must not lose his soldier's soul in the laboratory. Above all he must have the integrity and character of a Washington, the moral convictions of a Lincoln, and the tenacity and fighting ability of an Eisenhower, a MacArthur and a Patton. These are high standards, but they are the standards of our present dedicated leadership, and will always be the hallmarks of the great officer.

Wilbur M. Brucker

An honest man's word is as good as his bond.

Miguel de Cervantes
Don Quixote, 1615

A few honest men are better than numbers.

Oliver Cromwell
Letter to Sir W. Spring, September 1643

A single lie destroys a whole reputation for integrity.

Baltasar Gracián Y Morales
The Art of Wordly Wisdom, 1647

He is as good as his word—and his word is no good.

Seumas MacManus

Fidelity . . . because it comes of personal decision, is the jewel within reach of every officer who has the will to possess it. It is the epitome of character, and fortunately no other quality in the individual is more readily recognized and honored by one's military associates.

Brigadier General S.L.A. Marshall
The Armed Forces Officer, 1950

The characteristic which higher command always looks for in any officer is honesty. Honesty in thought, word, and deed.

General Alexander M. Patch

The "integrity of the military profession" . . . means that we must have an officer corps of such character and competence as will provide the highest professional and spiritual leadership to our citizen armies. It means a non-commissioned officer corps indoctrinated and inspired by the officer corps, whose precepts are its guides, and whose standards it emulates. This professional, long-term cadre must be adequate both in size and in quality . . . a great reservoir of character, of devotion to duty, of loyalty, of professional competence.

General Matthew B. Ridgway
Soldier: The Memoirs of Matthew B. Ridgway, 1956

Integrity is the most important responsibility of command. Commanders are dependent on the integrity of those reporting to them in every decision they make. Integrity can be ordered but it can only be achieved by encouragement and example.

General John D. Ryan

O, what a tangled web we weave,
When first we practise to deceive!

Sir Walter Scott
Marmion, 1808

No legacy is so rich as honesty.

William Shakespeare
All's Well That Ends Well, Act III, Scene v, 1602

The man in a chain of command turns over some of his rights of judgment; he must act on the judgments of his superiors, even though his own judgment differs. What he cannot turn over to anybody else is his conscience and his integrity.

Roger L. Shinn
Military Ethics, 1987

False words are not only evil in themselves, but they infect the soul with evil.

Socrates

If I had to find a single word by which to characterize the officers of the United States Army, that word would be: Integrity—absolute, uncompromising integrity.

Robert T. Stevens

Labor to keep alive in your breast that little spark of celestial fire called conscience.

General George Washington

I hold the maxim no less applicable to public than to private affairs, that honesty is the best policy.

General George Washington
Farewell Address, 1796

Judgment

Facts do not cease to exist simply because they are ignored.

Anonymous

Fixing the problem is more important than affixing the blame.

Anonymous

Never promise something you can't deliver.

Anonymous

People who jump to conclusions generally leap over the facts.

Anonymous

War, as the saying goes, is full of false alarms.

Aristotle
Nicomachean Ethics, circa 340 B.C.

Judgment, a critical element in leadership decision making, has two components. One is knowledge. A leader cannot make a judgment if he is unfamiliar with the subject about which the judgment must be made. . . . The other component is common sense, which is an attribute that individuals attain through experience.

General Robert H. Barrow
Quoted in Karel Montor et al.,
Naval Leadership: Voices of Experience, 1987

I learned that good judgment comes from experience and that experience grows out of mistakes.

General Omar N. Bradley

Judgment comes from experience and experience comes from bad judgment.

General Simon Bolivar Buckner

True genius resides in the capacity for evaluation of uncertain, hazardous, and conflicting information.

Sir Winston Churchill

During an operation decisions have usually to be made at once; there may be no time to review the situation or even to think it through. . . . If the mind is to emerge unscathed from this relentless struggle with the unforeseen, two qualities are indispensable: first, an intellect that, even in the darkest hour, retains some glimmerings of the inner light which leads to truth; and second, the courage to follow this faint light wherever it may lead.

Karl von Clausewitz

Learning is not wisdom; information does not guarantee good judgment.

John Dewey

There is nothing so useless as doing efficiently that which should not be done at all.

Peter F. Drucker

According to success do we gain a reputation for judgment.

Euripides
Hippolytus, 428 B.C.

Familiarity confounds all traits of distinction: interest and prejudice take away the power of judging.

William Hazlitt
Table Talk, 1821

The greatest commander is he whose intuitions most nearly happen.

Thomas E. Lawrence

Beyond the requirement of a modern Army for technical skill in its people, there is the necessity for judgment and imagination—for leadership.

General Lyman L. Lemnitzer

Adaptation to changing conditions is the condition of survival. This depends on the simple yet fundamental question of attitude. To cope with the problems of the modern world we need, above all, to see them clearly and analyze them scientifically. This requires freedom from prejudice combined with the power of discernment and with a sense of proportion. . . . Discernment may be primarily a gift, and a sense of proportion, too. But their development can be assisted by freedom from prejudice, which largely rests with the individual to achieve—and within his power to achieve it. Or at least to approach it. The way of approach is simple, if not easy—requiring, above all, constant self-criticism and care for precise statement.

B. H. Liddell Hart
Why Don't We Learn from History? 1971

If you take a chance, it usually succeeds, presupposing good judgment.

Lieutenant General Sir Giffard Martel

We easily enough confess in others an advantage of courage, strength, experience, activity, and beauty; but an advantage in judgment we yield to none.

Michel Eyquem de Montaigne
Essays, "Of Presumption," 1580

I have benefitted enormously from criticism and at no point did I suffer from any perceptible lack thereof.

Napoleon Bonaparte

While younger officers should guard against attacks of retarded judgment, older officers should view such occasional lapses in perspective, remembering their own salad days, when they too were green in judgment.

Major General Aubrey "Red" Newman
Follow Me, 1981

134

Fancy language is not a substitute for good judgment.
Major General Aubrey "Red" Newman
Follow Me, 1981

A hasty judgment is a first step to recantation.
Publilius Syrus
Moral Sayings, circa first century B.C.

Everyone complains of his memory, but no one complains of his judgment.
François, Duc de La Rochefoucauld
Maximes, 1665

Reason wishes that the judgment it gives be just; anger wishes that the judgment it has given seem to be just.
Seneca
On Anger, circa first century A.D.

What you have to do is to weigh all the various factors, recognizing that in war half your information may be wrong, that a lot of it is missing completely, and that there are all sorts of elements over which you have no control, such as the weather and to a certain extent the action of the enemy. You have got to weigh all these things and come to a decision as to what you want to do.
Field Marshal Sir William Slim
Speech to U.S. Army Command and General Staff College,
8 April 1952

Reason and judgment are the qualities of a leader.
Tacitus
Annals, circa A.D. 90

A general is not easily overcome who can form a true judgment of his own and the enemy's forces.
Vegetius
Dē Re Mīlītāri, Book III, 378

That quality which I wish to see the officers possess, who are at the head of the troops, is a cool, discriminating judgment when in action, which will enable them to decide with promptitude how far they can go and ought to go, with propriety; and to convey their orders, and act with such vigor and decision, that the soldier will look up to them with confidence in the moment of action, and obey them with alacrity.

Arthur Wellesley, Duke of Wellington
General Order, 15 May 1811

Just, Justice

We become just by performing just actions, temperate by performing temperate actions, brave by performing brave actions.

Aristotle
Nicomachean Ethics, circa 340 B.C.

All virtue is summed up in dealing justly.   Aristotle
Nicomachean Ethics, circa 340 B.C.

With what measure ye mete, it shall be measured to you.
Bible, Mark 4:24

He that ruleth over men *must be* just.   *Bible,* II Samuel 23:3

Justice is the crowning glory of the virtues.

Marcus Tullius Cicero
De Officiis, 44 B.C.

Justice is truth in action.

Ralph Waldo Emerson
11 February 1851

Keep alive the light of justice, and much that men say in blame will pass you by.

Euripides
The Suppliants, circa 421 B.C.

Without justice, courage is weak.   Benjamin Franklin
                                        Poor Richard's Almanac, 1732

Rigid justice is the greatest injustice.   Thomas Fuller
                                              Gnomologia, 1732

As an officer rises higher in his profession the demands made upon
him in the administration of justice increase.

                                    General Sir John W. Hackett

To do injustice is more disgraceful than to suffer it.

                                                        Plato
                            Gorgias, circa fourth century B.C.

I proclaim that might is right, justice the interest of the stronger.

                                                        Plato
                              The Republic, circa 370 B.C.

Many generals believe that they have done everything as soon as they
have issued orders, and they order a great deal because they find many
abuses. This is a false principle; proceeding in this fashion, they will
never reestablish discipline in an army in which it has been lost or
weakened. Few orders are best, but they should be followed up with
care; negligence should be punished without partiality and without
distinction of rank or birth; otherwise, you will make yourself hated.
One can be exact and just, and be loved at the same time as feared.
Severity must be accompanied by kindness, but this should not have
the appearance of pretense, but of goodness.

                              Marshal Comte de Maurice Saxe
                                            Mes Rêveries, 1732

        Be just and fear not.

                                        William Shakespeare
                        King Henry VIII, Act III, Scene ii, 1613

Knowledge, Wisdom, Intelligence

Wisdom comes only through suffering.

> Aeschylus
> *Agamemnon*, 458 B.C.

Gnothi seauton.
[Know thyself.]

> Anonymous (Inscription at temple of Delphic Oracle)

I never learned anything while I was talking.

> Anonymous

It is better to learn late—than never.

> Anonymous

With regard to excellence, it is not enough to know, but we must try to have and use it.

> Aristotle
> *Nicomachean Ethics*, circa 340 B.C.

To lead, you must know—you may bluff all your men some of the time, but you can't do it all the time. Men will not have confidence in an officer unless he knows his business, and he must know it from the ground up.

Major C. A. Bach
"Know Your Men—Know Your Business—Know Yourself,"
Address to new officers, 1917

Nam et ipsa scientia potestas est.
[Knowledge is power.]

Sir Francis Bacon
Meditationes Sacrae, 1597

He that hath knowledge spareth words; *and* a man of understanding is of an excellent spirit.

Bible, Proverbs 17:27

He who wants to move in an element such as in war should not bring along book knowledge, only a trained mind. If he has fixed ideas not conceived on the spur of the moment from his own flesh and blood his edifice will be torn down by the chain of events before it is completed.

Karl von Clausewitz
On War, 1832

When you know a thing, to hold that you know it; and when you do not know a thing, to allow that you do not know it—this is knowledge.

Confucius
Analects, circa 500 B.C.

Learning without thought is labour lost; thought without learning is perilous.

Confucius
Analects, circa 500 B.C.

Cogito, ergo sum.
[I think, therefore I am.]

René Descartes
Le Discours de la Méthode, 1637

It is not enough to have a good mind. The main thing is to use it well.

Renè Descartes
Le Discours de la Méthode, 1637

The more extensive a man's knowledge of what has been done, the greater will be his power of knowing what to do.

Benjamin Disraeli

Nothing astonishes men so much as common sense and plain dealing.

Ralph Waldo Emerson
Essays: First Series, "Art," 1841

Common sense is as rare as genius.

Ralph Waldo Emerson
Essays: Second Series, "Experience," 1844

We pay a high price for being intelligent. Wisdom hurts.

Euripides
Electra, 413 B.C.

No study is possible on the battlefield, one does simply what one can in order to apply what one knows. Therefore, in order to do even a little, one has already to know a great deal and know it well.

Marshal Ferdinand Foch

Unskillful generals race to the first trap set before them. This is why a great advantage is drawn from knowledge of your adversary, and when you know his intelligence and character you can use it to play on his weaknesses.

Frederick the Great
Instructions for His Generals, 1747

War is not an affair of chance. A great deal of knowledge, study, and meditation is necessary to conduct it well.

Frederick the Great
Instructions for His Generals, 1747

One good head is better than a hundred strong hands.

Thomas Fuller
Gnomologia, 1732

Act quickly, think slowly.

Greek proverb

Each war has to be learned while it is being fought; and it is upon the side which absorbs its lessons the more readily that victory bestows her laurels.

Major Reginald Hargreaves

Native intelligence—the ability to look at a situation, evaluate it, and then make a sensible judgment—is one of the necessary attributes of a good leader.

Admiral James L. Holloway III
Quoted in Karel Montor et al.,
Naval Leadership: Voices of Experience, 1987

Wisdom consists not so much in knowing what to do in the ultimate as in knowing what to do next.

Herbert Hoover
Reader's Digest, July 1958

The great end of life is not knowledge but action.

Thomas Henry Huxley
Technical Education, 1877

If a little knowledge is dangerous, where is the man who has so much as to be out of danger?

Thomas Henry Huxley
Elemental Instruction in Physiology, 1877

He who knows others is wise;
He who knows himself is enlightened.

Lao-Tzu
The Way of Lao-Tzu, circa sixth century B.C.

Generalship, at least in my case, came not by instinct, unsought, but by understanding, hard study and brain concentration. Had it come easy to me, I should not have done it as well.

Thomas E. Lawrence

Knowledge advances by steps, and not by leaps.

Lord Thomas Babington Macaulay
Essays and Biographical History, 1828

A general should possess a perfect knowledge of the location where he is carrying on a war.

Niccolò di Bernardo Machiavelli

A prince should therefore have no other aim or thought, nor take up any other thing for his study, but war and its organization and discipline, for that is the only art that is necessary to one who commands.

Niccolò di Bernardo Machiavelli
The Prince, 1513

[Training] means long hours of arduous work. For the officers and noncommissioned officers it means not only hard physical work but also intensive daily study of the manuals covering the latest technique in warfare. It is only through discomfort and fatigue that progress can be made toward the triumph of mind and muscles over the softness of the life to which we have become accustomed.

General George C. Marshall
Selected Speeches and Statements of General of the Army
George C. Marshall, edited by Major H. A. DeWeerd, 1945

Wisdom begins at the point of understanding that there is nothing shameful about ignorance; it is shameful only when a man would rather remain in that state than cultivate other men's knowledge.

Brigadier General S.L.A. Marshall
The Armed Forces Officer, 1950

Where there is much desire to learn, there of necessity will be much argument, much writing, many opinions; for opinion in good men is but knowledge in the making.

John Milton

One of the first requirements for effective leadership is knowledge. A leader quickly becomes aware that his people are watching him to see how he performs under certain circumstances and how he reacts to unexpected things, so the leader simply must conduct himself to the best of his ability and in a way that indicates that he understands what he is doing.

Admiral Thomas H. Moorer
Quoted in Karel Montor et al.,
Naval Leadership: Voices of Experience, 1987

An ignorant officer is a murderer. All brave men confide in the knowledge he is supposed to possess; and when the death-trial comes their generous blood flows in vain. Merciful God! How can an ignorant man charge himself with so much bloodshed? I have studied war long, earnestly and deeply, but yet I tremble at my own derelictions.

Admiral Sir Charles Napier

If I always appear prepared, it is because before entering on an undertaking, I have meditated for long and have foreseen what may occur. It is not genius which reveals to me suddenly and secretly what I should do in circumstances unexpected by others; it is thought and meditation.

Napoleon Bonaparte

Techniques which must be mastered to become an expert vary mightily, depending on the field of your expertise, the level of command and the personalities involved. But the basic requirement is simple: study and train and practice until you have more knowledge and know-how than others with whom you work.

Major General Aubrey "Red" Newman
Follow Me, 1981

Wisdom sets bounds even to knowledge.

Friedrich Wilhelm Nietzsche
Twilight of the Idols, 1888

The instruments of battle are valuable only if one knows how to use them.

Ardant du Picq
Battle Studies, 1880

No one is wise at all times.

Pliny the Elder
Natural History, A.D. 77

A general in the field should endeavor to discover in the chief that is against him, whether there be any weakness in his mind and character, through which he may be attacked with some advantage.

Polybius
Histories, circa 125 B.C.

Knowledge is the surest guarantee of self-confidence, self-control, and self-discipline. . . . From his knowledge, the leader will acquire three fundamental qualities necessary to lead men: flexibility of mind, common sense, and confidence. . . . Common sense is the assimilation of knowledge which expresses itself by the ability to compare, to discriminate, and to judge accurately. Nobody is born with it; it is acquired through experience, studies and readings.

Captain M. Rioux

Nine-tenths of wisdom is being wise in time.

Theodore Roosevelt
Address in Lincoln, Nebraska, 14 June 1917

Young officers of all Services must learn terrain or learn [the language of the conqueror].

Major General Alden K. Sibley

Education is what remains after what has been learnt has been forgotten.

Burrhus F. Skinner
"New Scientist," 21 May 1964

The only good is knowledge and the only evil is ignorance.

Socrates

How dreadful knowledge of the truth can be when there's no help in truth.

Sophocles

Wisdom outweighs any wealth.

Sophocles
Antigone, circa 442 B.C.

If you know the enemy and know yourself, you need not fear the result of a hundred battles. If you know yourself but not the enemy, for every victory gained you will also suffer a defeat. If you know neither the enemy nor yourself, you will succumb in every battle.

Sun-Tzu
The Art of War, circa fourth century B.C.

Knowledge comes, but wisdom lingers.

Alfred, Lord Tennyson
Locksley Hall, 1842

It is a characteristic of wisdom not to do desperate things.

Henry David Thoreau
Walden, 1854

It's what you know after you know it all that counts.

Harry S. Truman

Memory is not wisdom; idiots can by rote repeat whole volumes. Yet what is wisdom without memory?

Martin Tupper

The courage of a soldier is heightened by his knowledge of his profession.

Vegetius
Dē Re Mīlĭtāri, Book I, 378

It is essential to know the character of the enemy and of their principal officers—whether they be rash or cautious, enterprising or timid, whether they fight on principle or from chance and whether the nations they have been engaged with were brave or cowardly.

Vegetius
Dē Re Mīlĭtāri, Book III, 378

Judge a man by his questions rather than by his answers.

Voltaire

Leadership

There are three types of leaders: Those who make things happen; those that watch things happen; and those who wonder what happened!
Anonymous

Leaders know themselves; they know their strengths and nurture them.
Warren Bennis
Training and Development Journal, August 1984

Leaders are people who do the right thing; managers are people who do things right.
Warren Bennis
Training and Development Journal, August 1984

I am a man under authority, having soldiers under me: and I say to this *man,* Go, and he goeth: and to another, Come, and he cometh.
Bible, Matthew 8:9

We should not forget that there are far more staff officer assignments than there are command billets, and a good staff officer can and should display the same leadership as a commander. While it takes a good staff officer to initiate a plan, it requires a leader to insure that the plan is properly executed. That is why you and I have been taught that the work of collecting information, studying it, drawing a plan, and making a decision is 10 percent of the job; seeing that plan through is the other 90 percent. A well-trained officer is one who can serve effectively either as a staff officer or as a commander.

General Omar N. Bradley

Education makes a people easy to lead, but difficult to drive; easy to govern, but impossible to enslave.

General Omar N. Bradley

There's just three things I ever say. If anything goes bad, then I did it. If anything goes semi-good, then we did it. If anything goes really good, then you did it. That's all it takes.

Coach Paul "Bear" Bryant

Leadership is understanding people and involving them to help you do a job. That takes all of the good characteristics, like integrity, dedication of purpose, selflessness, knowledge, skill, implacability, as well as a determination not to accept failure.

Admiral Arleigh A. Burke
Quoted in Karel Montor et al.,
Naval Leadership: Voices of Experience, 1987

Leadership is one of the most observed and least understood phenomena on earth.

James MacGregor Burns
Leadership, 1978

And when we think we lead, we are most led.

Lord George Noel Gordon Byron
The Two Foscari, Act II, Scene i, 1821

Leadership is so much a part of the conduct of training that at times it is difficult to tell where one stops and the other starts.

Lieutenant General Arthur S. Collins, Jr.
Common Sense Training, 1978

Men are neither lions nor sheep. It is the man who leads them who turns them into either lions or sheep.

Jean Dutourd
Taxis of the Marne, 1957

Leadership is the knack of getting somebody to do something you want done because he wants to do it.

General Dwight D. Eisenhower

Ten good soldiers
    wisely led
will beat a hundred
    without a head.

Euripides

A good leader takes a little more than his share of blame; a little less than his share of credit.

Arnold H. Glasgow

The art of leadership . . . consists in consolidating the attention of the people against a single adversary and taking care that nothing will split up that attention.

Adolf Hitler
Mein Kampf, 1925

No man is a leader until his appointment is ratified in the minds and hearts of his men.

The Infantry Journal, August 1948

There go my people. I must find out where they are going so I can lead them.

Alexandre Ledru-Rollin

A strong leader knows that if he develops his associates he will be even stronger.

James F. Lincoln

The final test of a leader is that he leaves behind him in other men the conviction and the will to carry on.

The genius of a good leader is to leave behind him a situation which common sense, without the grace of genius, can deal with successfully.

Walter Lippmann
14 April 1945

The strength of the group is in the strength of the leader.

Vince Lombardi

The very essence of leadership is its purpose. And the purpose of leadership is to accomplish a task. That is what leadership does—and what it *does* is more important than what it is or how it works. The purpose of leadership is to accomplish a task.

Colonel Dandridge M. "Mike" Malone

Leadership is action, not position.

Donald H. McGannon

The beginning of leadership is a battle for the hearts and minds of men.

Field Marshal Bernard L. Montgomery

A leader is a dealer in hope.

Napoleon Bonaparte

Show me the leader and I will know his men. Show me the men and I will know the leader.

Arthur W. Newcomb

A good leader can't get too far ahead of his followers.

Franklin D. Roosevelt
1940

Every great man is always being helped by everybody; for his gift is to get good out of all things and all persons.

John Ruskin

Leadership must be based on goodwill. Goodwill does not mean posturing and, least of all, pandering to the mob. It means obvious and wholehearted commitment to helping followers. We are tired of leaders we fear, tired of leaders we love, and most tired of leaders who let us take liberties with them. What we need for leaders are men of the heart who are so helpful that they, in effect, do away with the need of their jobs. But leaders like that are never out of a job, never out of followers. Strange as it sounds, great leaders gain authority by giving it away.

Vice Admiral James Bond Stockdale
Military Ethics,
"Machiavelli, Management, and Moral Leadership," 1987

The great leaders feel themselves commanded by a power and strength which they in turn command.

Ordway Tead

A central quality of leadership, as far as I can see, is a difficult combination of receptivity and outgoingness—the ability at one and the same time to take in and to give out. It means that leadership roles are open to sensitive people, some of whom might conclude—after watching the latest war movie—that they have no chance of ever making the grade. It means, too, that the most effective leaders, and the ones who endure over the long run, may not necessarily be the tough macho types who look impressive on first acquaintance but soon come to sound like broken records. There is a time for toughness, but there are also times when toughness should definitely be turned off.

Stephen Joel Trachtenberg

Men make history and not the other way round. In periods where there is no leadership, society stands still. Progress occurs when courageous, skillful leaders seize the opportunity to change things for the better.

Harry S. Truman

A leader is a man who has the ability to get people to do what they don't want to do, and like it.

Harry S. Truman
Memoirs, 1954

Education is the mother of leadership.

Wendell Willkie

Leadership, if the word has any meaning at all, is a characteristic which inheres in individuals who have energy, faith, and ability in unusual degree.

Henry M. Wriston

Loyalty

No man can serve two masters: for either he will hate the one, and love the other; or else he will hold to one, and despise the other.

Bible, Matthew 6:24

Never in the field of human conflict was so much owed by so many to so few.

Sir Winston Churchill
Tribute to Royal Air Force, 20 August 1940

Loyalty is the one thing a leader cannot do without.

A. P. Gouthey

Loyalty is the marrow of honor.

Field Marshal Paul von Hindenburg
Out of My Life, 1920

Loyalty is the big thing, the greatest battle asset of all. But no man ever wins the loyalty of troops by preaching loyalty. It is given him by them as he proves his possession of the other virtues. The doctrine of a blind loyalty to leadership is selfish and futile military dogma except in so far as it is ennobled by a higher loyalty in all ranks to truth and decency.

Brigadier General S.L.A. Marshall
Men Against Fire, 1947

Under combat conditions, [the American soldier] will reserve his greatest loyalty for the officer who is most resourceful in the tactical employment of his forces and most careful to avoid unnecessary losses.

Brigadier General S.L.A. Marshall
The Armed Forces Officer, 1950

Discipline must be imposed, but loyalty must be earned—yet the highest form of discipline exists only when there is mutual loyalty, up and down.

Major General Aubrey "Red" Newman
Follow Me, 1981

There is a great deal of talk about loyalty from the bottom to the top. Loyalty from the top down is even more necessary and much less prevalent.

General George S. Patton, Jr.
War as I Knew It, 1947

Master, go on, and I will follow thee
To the last gasp, with truth and loyalty.

William Shakespeare
As You Like It, Act II, Scene iii, 1600

Few men of all history have had the wholehearted support of their men to the extent that Robert E. Lee held the devotion of the Army of Northern Virginia. . . . A large measure of his success was due to the fact that the [soldiers] knew that General Lee did his best to provide for their welfare. He was loyal to them and they were loyal to him. Soldiers . . . were comrades associated in the common enterprise of defeating the enemy and serving a cause to which they were all devoted. . . . General Lee lived just as simply as they did.

General Maxwell D. Taylor
The Field Artillery Journal, January/February 1947

Luck, Fate

A crystal ball is not a precise instrument.   Anonymous

Destiny is not a matter of chance, it is a matter of choice; it is not a thing to be waited for, it is a thing to be achieved.
William Jennings Bryan

Countless and inestimable are the chances of war.
Sir Winston Churchill

The nation had the lion's heart. I had the luck to give the roar.
Sir Winston Churchill

There is no human affair which stands so constantly and so generally in close connection with chance as War.
Karl von Clausewitz
On War, 1832

The history of free men is never really written by chance but by choice—their choice.
General Dwight D. Eisenhower
Address in Pittsburgh, Pennsylvania, 9 October 1956

There is in the worst of fortune the best of chances for a happy change.   Euripides
Iphigenia in Tauris, 414 B.C.

A general who has a too presumptuous confidence in his skill runs the risk of being grossly duped. War is not an affair of chance. A great deal of knowledge, study, and meditation is necessary to conduct it well, and when blows are planned whoever contrives them with the greatest of appreciation of their consequences will have a great advantage.

Frederick the Great
Instructions for His Generals, 1747

A wise man turns chance into good fortune.

Thomas Fuller
Gnomologia, 1732

There is nothing certain about war except that one side won't win.

General Sir Ian Hamilton
Gallipoli Diary, 1920

We are not permitted to choose the frame of our destiny. But what we put into it is ours.

Dag Hammarskjöld
Markings, 1964

I am the master of my fate;
I am the captain of my soul.

William E. Henley
Invictus, 1888

Adversity reveals the genius of a general; good fortune conceals it.

Horace
Satires, circa 34 B.C.

God has fixed the time for my death. I do not concern myself about that, but to be always ready, no matter when it may overtake me. That is the way all men should live, and then all would be equally brave.

General Thomas J. "Stonewall" Jackson

War is the realm of the unexpected.

B. H. Liddell Hart

To a good general luck is important. Livy
History of Rome, circa A.D. 10

There *is* such a thing as luck, and as soldiers you have to believe in it.

Brigadier General S.L.A. Marshall

Luck in the long run is given only to the efficient.

Field Marshal Count Helmuth von Moltke

Fortune or fate decides one half our life; the other half depends on ourselves.

Field Marshal Bernard L. Montgomery

The affairs of war, like the destiny of battles, as well as of empires, hang upon a spider's thread.

Napoleon Bonaparte
Political Aphorisms, 1848

War is composed of nothing but accidents, and, although holding to general principles, a general should never lose sight of everything to enable him to profit from these accidents; that is the mark of genius.
   In war there is but one favorable moment; the great art is to seize it.

Napoleon Bonaparte
Maxims, XCV, 1831

With a great general there is never a continuity of great actions which can be attributed to chance and good luck; they always are the result of calculation and genius.

Napoleon Bonaparte
Maxims, LXXXII, 1831

Something must be left to chance; nothing is sure in a sea fight beyond all others.

Lord Admiral Horatio Nelson
9 October 1805

In war we must always leave room for strokes of fortune, and accidents that cannot be foreseen.

Polybius
Histories, circa 125 B.C.

Opportunity seems to strike at the door of only those men who have prepared themselves for greater things.

Captain M. Rioux

Opportunity plays a great role in the career of any man. Churchill needed a war to show his statesmanship, de Gaulle was given power because of the threat of a civil war.

Captain M. Rioux

Fortune turns everything to the advantage of those she favours.

François, Duc de La Rochefoucauld
Maximes, 1665

However great the advantages given us by nature, it is not she alone, but fortune with her, which makes heroes.

François, Duc de La Rochefoucauld
Maximes, 1665

Men are not prisoners of fate, but only prisoners of their own minds.

Franklin D. Roosevelt
Pan American Day Address, 15 April 1939

And without knowledge of the human heart, one is dependent on the favor of fortune, which sometimes is very inconsistent.

Marshal Comte de Maurice Saxe
Mes Rêveries, 1732

We should make war without leaving anything to chance, and in this especially consists the talent of a general.

Marshal Comte de Maurice Saxe
Mes Rêveries, 1732

"They couldn't hit an elephant at this dist . . ."
Last words of General John Sedgwick
Battle of Spotsylvania, 1864

The fortunes of war are always doubtful.
Seneca
Phoenissae, circa A.D. 60

Luck never made a man wise.
Seneca
Letters to Lucilius, A.D. 63

Whatever God has brought about is to be borne with courage.
Sophocles
Oedipus at Colonus, circa fifth century B.C.

Fortune is not on the side of the faint-hearted.
Sophocles
Phaedra, 430 B.C.

Audentĭa fortūna iŭvat.
[Fortune favors the brave.]
Terence
Phormia, 161 B.C. (also by Virgil, *Aeneid*)

"I did not mean to be killed today."
Dying words of Vicomte de Turenne
French commander, Battle of Salzbach, 1675

Opportunity in war is often more to be depended on than courage.
Vegetius
Dē Re Mīlĭtāri, Book III, 378

Management

Success cannot be administered.

Admiral Arleigh A. Burke
1962

Soldiers will go all out for an officer who does not waste their time through poor management when he has a tough job to do.

General Bruce C. Clarke

There has been a constant struggle on the part of the military element to keep the end—fighting, or readiness to fight—superior to mere administrative considerations. . . . The military man, having to do the fighting, considers that the chief necessity; the administrator equally naturally tends to think the smooth running of the machine the most admirable quality.

Rear Admiral Alfred T. Mahan
Naval Administration and Warfare, 1903

That which soldiers are willing to sacrifice their lives for—loyalty, team spirit, morale, trust and confidence—cannot be infused by managing.

General Edward C. Meyer
Military Review, July 1980

Leadership and management are neither synonymous nor interchangeable. Clearly good civilian managers must lead, and good military leaders must manage. Both qualities are essential to success.

General Edward C. Meyer
Military Review, July 1980

An army cannot be administered. It must be led.

Franz-Joseph Strauss
Speech to German Bundestag, 1957

This modern tendency to scorn and ignore tradition and to sacrifice it to administrative convenience is one that wise men will resist in all branches of life, but more especially in our military life.

Field Marshal Sir Archibald P. Wavell

Obviously, a good leader is a good manager, but a good manager in the narrow sense of the word is not necessarily a good leader. Managers imply to me those who are more of an administrative sort, whereas leadership implies all the broad aspects, which is getting others to do what you want them to do even though they might not undertake the task of their own volition.

General Louis H. Wilson
Quoted in Karel Montor et al.,
Naval Leadership: Voices of Experience, 1987

Mentor

Leadership is a quality that one nurtures with experience and the proper guidance. Senior officers must act as mentors to their youthful counterparts, trusting them with real responsibilities, and allowing them to make their own decisions.

David M. Abshire
Washington Quarterly Review, 30 March 1983

Leadership can be taught by good coaching.

General Bruce C. Clarke

The relation between officers and men should in no sense be that of superior and inferior nor that of master and servant, but rather that of teacher and scholar. In fact, it should partake of the nature of the relation between father and son, to the extent that officers, especially commanding officers, are responsible for the physical, mental, and moral welfare, as well as the discipline and military training, of the young men under their command.

General John A. Lejeune
Marine Corps Manual, 1920

Men think as their leaders think.

General Charles P. Summerall

Military Ethics

The consequences of a degenerating ethical climate are bad enough in our current time of peace; they would be disastrous in war. War places men under unparalleled pressure, no matter where in the forces they serve. At all levels tough decisions must be made—decisions that can cost lives. There is no room for anything but an eye toward the common good here. Mutual trust is indispensable if the forces are to operate the way they must. The whole structure of discipline and esprit de corps will disintegrate if officers cannot see past their own wants and aspirations.

Major R. I. Aitken

Following the path of least resistance is what makes rivers and men crooked.

Anonymous

Neither by nature nor contrary to nature do the moral excellences arise in us, rather we are adapted by nature to receive them, and made perfect by habit.

Aristotle
Nicomachean Ethics, circa 340 B.C.

An officer should never apologize to his men; also an officer should never be guilty of an act for which his sense of justice tells him he should apologize.

Major C. A. Bach
"Know Your Men—Know Your Business—Know Yourself,"
Address to new officers, 1917

Men may be inexact or even untruthful in ordinary matters and suffer as a consequence only the disesteem of their associates or even the inconvenience of unfavorable litigation. But the inexact or untruthful soldier trifles with the lives of his fellow men and the honor of his government.

Newton D. Baker

The principal armed service of its country—in its professional attitudes, its equipment, its officer corps—is an extension, a reflection, of that country's whole society.

Correlli Barnett
The Swordbearers, 1963

Expedients are for the hour, but principles are for the ages.

Henry Ward Beecher
Proverbs from Plymouth Pulpit, 1887

Consider yourself the judge, the headmaster, the magistrate, and the father of your regiment. As judge and magistrate, you will watch over the maintenance of moral standards. Concern yourself particularly with this objective, always forgotten or too neglected by military commanders. Where there are high morals, laws are observed, and what is worth even more, they are respected. Look to purifying morals but do not think that they can be established through orders. They must be taught by example and inspiration.

Marshal de Belle-Isle
Letter to his son

We should be willing to assume that most men have sufficient desire to live a moral life, that they will profit from instruction that helps them to become more alert to ethical issues, and to apply their moral values more carefully and rigorously to the ethical dilemmas they encounter in their professional lives.

Derek C. Bok
Change, "Can Ethics Be Taught?" 1976

The world has achieved brilliance without conscience. Ours is a world of nuclear giants and ethical infants.

General Omar N. Bradley
Armistice Day speech, 1948

A fish begins to rot at the head.

Chinese proverb

The soldier trade, if it is to mean anything at all, has to be anchored to an unshakeable code of honor. Otherwise, those of us who follow the drums become nothing more than a bunch of hired assassins walking around in gaudy clothes . . . a disgrace to God and mankind.

Karl von Clausewitz
On War, 1832

The wise man is informed in what is right. The inferior man is informed in what will pay.

Confucius

Integrity in all of its diverse meanings, interpretations, and nuances is the most important ingredient in the moral and personal psyche of an officer or NCO.

Lieutenant General Edward M. Flanagan, Jr.

One of the more disturbing aspects of this problem of moral conduct is the revelation that among so many influential people morality has become identified with legality. We are certainly in a tragic plight if the accepted standard by which we measure the integrity of a man in public life is that he keeps within the law.

Senator William Fulbright
Speech before the Senate, 28 January 1967

The task of building an ethical environment where leaders and all personnel are instructed, encouraged, and rewarded for ethical behavior is a matter of first importance. All decisions, practices, goals, and values of the entire institutional structure which make ethical behavior difficult should be examined, beginning with the following:

First, blatant or subtle forms of ethical relativism which blur the issue of what is right or wrong or which bury it as a subject of little or no importance.

Second, the exaggerated loyalty syndrome, where people are afraid to tell the truth and are discouraged from it.

Third, the obsession with image, where people are not even interested in the truth.

And last, the drive for success, in which ethical sensitivity is bought off or sold because of the personal need to achieve.

Chaplain (Major General) Kermit D. Johnson
Parameters,
"Ethical Issues of Military Leadership," 1974

I want to make it clear beyond any question that absolute integrity of an officer's word, deed, and signature is a matter that permits no compromise. Inevitably, in the turmoil of the times, every officer will be confronted by situations which test his character. On these occasions he must stand on his principles, for these are the crucial episodes that determine the worth of a man.

On a practical level, there are two vital steps to ethical behavior: knowing what is right and doing it.

Michael Josephson

For ethically committed persons, laws simply establish baseline standards of impropriety. Ultimately, these persons seek to do what is right in terms of universal moral principles such as honesty, integrity, loyalty, fairness, caring and respect for others, accountability and protection of the public trust. Laws cannot coerce these values.

Michael Josephson

Ethical and legal aren't the same. One can be dishonest, unprincipled, untrustworthy, unfair, and uncaring, without breaking the law.

Michael Josephson

A man has honor if he holds himself to a course of conduct because of a conviction that it is in the general interest, even though he is well aware that it may lead to inconvenience, personal loss, humiliation, or grave personal risk.

Brigadier General S.L.A. Marshall
The Armed Forces Officer, 1950

Moderation in temper is always a virtue, but moderation in principle is always a vice.

Thomas Paine
Rights of Man, 1792

The principles of leadership in the military are the same as they are in business, in the church, and elsewhere: a. Learn your job. (This involves study and hard work.) b. Work hard at your job. c. Train your people. d. Inspect frequently to see that the job is being done properly.

Admiral Hyman G. Rickover
Rickover, 1982

The ordinary soldier has a surprisingly good nose for what is true and what is false.

Field Marshal Erwin Rommel

In these perilous times which face mankind the world over, I would like to stress the moral and ethical side of leadership responsibility. For it is in the area of moral courage, truth and honor that the fibers of character are strengthened sufficiently to sustain men under the great stresses and responsibilities facing our military leaders today.

General David M. Shoup

Peace is best secured by those who use their strength justly, but whose attitude shows that they have no intention of submitting to wrong.

Thucydides

If there is no vital center to man that is dynamic and unique that acts in terms of higher standards then all expressions are equally valid.

Alvin Toffler
Future Shock, 1970

Men who take up arms against another in public war do not cease on this account to be moral beings responsible to one another.

U.S. Army General Order 100
1863

Lastly, our ancestors established their system of government on morality and religious sentiment. Moral habits, they believed, cannot safely be trusted on any other foundation than religious principle, nor any government be secure which is not supported by moral habits.

Daniel Webster

While basic laws underlie command authority, the real foundation of successful leadership is the moral authority derived from professional competence and integrity. Competence and integrity are not separable. The officer who sacrifices his integrity sacrifices all; he will lose the respect and trust of those he seeks to lead, and he will degrade the reputation of his profession. The good repute of the officer corps is a responsibility shared by every officer. Each one of us stands in the light of his brother, and each shares in the honor and burden of leadership. Dedicated and selfless service to our country is our prime motivation. This makes our profession a way of life rather than a job.

General William C. Westmoreland

As in the past, our service must rest upon a solid ethical base, because those who discharge such moral responsibilities must uphold and abide by the highest standards of behavior.

General John A. Wickham

Military History

Look at Jackson's Brigade! It stands there like a stone wall.
                              Brigadier General Bernard E. Bee
                              Battle of First Bull Run, 21 July 1861

History is the source on which you must constantly draw. Do not read history to learn history, but to learn war, morals, and politics.
                              Marshal de Belle-Isle
                              Letter to his son

Providence is always on the side of the big battalions and against the small ones.
                              Roger Comte de Bussy-Rabutin
                              Letter to Comte de Limoges, 18 October 1677

From Stettin on the Baltic to Trieste on the Adriatic an iron curtain has descended across Europe.
                              Sir Winston Churchill
                              Address at Westminster College, 5 March 1946

The Army is not what it used to be—in fact, it never has been.
                              General Bruce C. Clarke

Only the study of military history is capable of giving those who have no experience of their own a clear picture of what I have just called the friction of the whole machine.

Karl von Clausewitz
Principles of War, 1812

Gentlemen, we are being killed on the beaches. Let's go inland and be killed.

General Norman Cota
Omaha Beach, June 1944

Let it be admitted that the modern technological revolution has confronted us with military problems of unprecedented complexity, problems made all the more difficult because of the social and political turbulence of the age in which we live. But precisely because of these revolutionary developments, let me suggest that you had better study military history, indeed all history, as no generation of military men have studied it before.

Frank Craven

Here once the embattled farmers stood,
And fired the shot heard round the world.

Ralph Waldo Emerson
Sung at dedication of Concord Battle Monument,
4 July 1837

Mon centre cède, ma droite recule; situation excellente. J'attaque!
[My center is giving way, my right is in retreat; situation excellent. I am attacking.]

Marshal Ferdinand Foch
Dispatch to Marshal Joffre at the Battle of the Marne,
September 1914

Great results in war are due to the commander. History is therefore right in making generals responsible for victories—in which they are glorified; and for defeats—in which case they are disgraced.

Marshal Ferdinand Foch
Precepts, 1919

Praise the Lord and pass the ammunition.

Chaplain Howell M. Forgy
Chaplain for cruiser USS *New Orleans*, 7 December 1941

By push of bayonets, no firing till you see the whites of their eyes.

Frederick the Great
Battle of Prague, 6 May 1757

God is always with the strongest battalions.

Frederick the Great
Letter to the Duchess von Gotha, 8 May 1760

Don't ignore the yesterdays of war in your study of today and tomorrow.

Douglas Southall Freeman
Lecture at U.S. Marine Corps School,
Quantico, Virginia, 1950

The differences brought about between one war and another by social or technological changes are immense, and an unintelligent study of military history which does not take adequate account of these changes may quite easily be more dangerous than no study at all. Like the statesman, the soldier has to steer between the dangers of repeating the errors of the past because he is ignorant that they have been made, and of remaining bound by theories deduced from past history although changes in conditions have rendered these theories obsolete.

Michael Howard
Journal of the Royal United Service Institution,
"The Use and Abuse of Military History," 1962

That men do not learn very much from the lessons of history is the most important of all the lessons that history has to teach.

Aldous Huxley
Collected Essays, 1959

No, no, let us pass over the river and rest under the shade of the trees.

Dying words of General Thomas J. "Stonewall" Jackson
10 May 1863

For a people who are free, and who mean to remain so, a well-organized and armed militia is their best security.

Thomas Jefferson
Message to Congress, November 1808

I don't know who won the Battle of the Marne, but if it had been lost, I know who would have lost it.

Marshal Joseph Joffre
Speech to Briey parliamentary commission, 1919

Military history, accompanied by sound criticism, is indeed the true school of war.

Baron Henri de Jomini
Précis de l'Art de la Guerre, 1838

I don't know much about this thing called logistics. All I know is that I want some.

Admiral Ernest J. King

[History] provides us with the opportunity to profit by the stumbles and tumbles of our forerunners.

B. H. Liddell Hart

It should be the duty of every soldier to reflect on the experiences of the past, in the endeavor to discover improvements, in his particular sphere of action, which are practicable in the immediate future.

B. H. Liddell Hart
Thoughts on War, 1944

It is only possible to probe into the mind of a commander through historical examples.

B. H. Liddell Hart
Strategy, 1967

Upon the fields of friendly strife are sown the seeds that, upon other fields, on other days, will bear the fruits of victory.

General Douglas MacArthur

The military student does not seek to learn from history the minutia of method and technique. In every age these are decisively influenced by the characteristics of weapons currently available and by means at hand for maneuvering, supplying and controlling combat forces. But research does bring to light those fundamental principles, and their combinations and applications, which, in the past, have been productive of success. These principles know no limitation of time. Consequently, the Army extends its analytical interest to the dust-buried accounts of wars long past as well as to those still reeking with the scent of battle. It is the object of the search that dictates the field for its pursuit.

General Douglas MacArthur
Annual Report of the Chief of Staff, U.S. Army,
for the Fiscal Year Ending June 30, 1935

We need to learn from the past.

General Edward C. Meyer
Address to Leadership Conference at the 1982
U.S. Army Command and General Staff College,
16 December 1982

An army marches on its stomach.

Attributed to Napoleon Bonaparte

Read over and over again the campaigns of Alexander, Hannibal, Caesar, Gustavus, Turenne, Eugene and Frederick. Make them your models. This is the only way to become a great general and to master the secrets of the art of war. With your own genius enlightened by this study, you will reject all maxims opposed to those of these great commanders.

Napoleon Bonaparte
Maxims, LXXVIII, 1831

Russia has two generals whom she can trust—Generals Janvier and Fevrier [Generals January and February].

Nicholas I of Russia
10 March 1853

In order for a man to become a great soldier . . . it is necessary for him to be so thoroughly conversant with all sorts of military possibilities that whenever an occasion arises he has at hand without effort on his

173

part a parallel. To attain this end . . . it is necessary . . . to read military history in its earliest and hence crudest form and to follow it down in natural sequence permitting his mind to grow with his subject until he can grasp without effort the most obtuse question of the science of war because he is already permeated with all its elements.

General George S. Patton, Jr.

The history of war is the history of warriors; few in number, mighty in influence. Alexander, not Macedonia, conquered the world. Scipio, not Rome, destroyed Carthage. Marlborough, not the Allies, defeated France. Cromwell, not the Roundheads, dethroned Charles.

Major George S. Patton, Jr.
The Infantry Journal Reader, "Success in War," 1931

To be a successful soldier, you must know history.

General George S. Patton, Jr.
Letter to his son, 6 June 1944

Ils ne passeront pas.
[They shall not pass.]

Marshal Henri-Philippe Pétain
To General de Castelnau at Verdun, 26 February 1916

Don't cheer, boys; the poor devils are dying.

Captain John W. Philip
As USS *Texas* passed Spanish cruiser *Vizcaya,*
Battle of Santiago, 1898

Only study of the past can give us a sense of reality, and show us how the soldier will fight in the future.

Ardant du Picq
Battle Studies, 1880

Don't fire until you see the whites of their eyes.

Israel Putnam
Battle of Bunker Hill, 17 June 1775
(Also attributed to William Prescott)

174

We have had the lesson before us over and over again—nations that were not ready and were unable to get ready found themselves overrun by the enemy.

Franklin D. Roosevelt
Message to Congress, May 1940

If history is not necessary to your career, there is no point in reading it unless you enjoy it and find it interesting. I do not mean that the only point of history is to give pleasure—far from it. It has many other uses. . . . But it will not have these uses except for those that enjoy it.

Bertrand Russell

Those who cannot remember the past are condemned to repeat it.

George Santayana
The Life of Reason, 1905

History shows that there are no invincible armies and never have been.

Josif V. Stalin
Speech to Soviet people, 3 July 1941

The single most important foundation for any leader is a solid academic background in history. That discipline gives perspective to the problems of the present and drives home the point that there is really very little new under the sun.

Vice Admiral James Bond Stockdale
The Washington Quarterly,
"Educating Leaders," 30 March 1983

Knowledge of detail is of infinitely more value to the officer than the more obtuse subjects and it is harder to obtain. It is therefore recommended that the study of military history should be supplemented by the detailed study of at least one campaign.

Major Eben Swift
1906

The gods are on the side of the stronger.

Tacitus
Histories, circa A.D. 109

Today's military leaders cannot have scientific knowledge alone. They must be students of warfare with an imagination capable of projecting forward the principles of the past to the specific requirements of the future.

General Maxwell D. Taylor

God is always on the side of the big battalions.

Vicomte de Turenne

At West Point, much of the history we teach was made by the people we taught.

U.S. Military Academy poster

Dieu n'est pas pour les gros bataillons, mais pour ceux qui tirent le mieux.
[God is on the side not of the heavy battalions, but of the best shots.]

Voltaire

God is always on the side of the heaviest battalions.

Voltaire
Letter to M. le Riche, 1770

The real way to get value out of the study of military history is to take particular situations, and as far as possible get inside the skin of the man who made a decision, realize the conditions in which the decision was made, and then see in what way you could have improved on it.

Field Marshal Sir Archibald P. Wavell
Lecture to officers at Aldershot, 1930

Though the military art is essentially a practical one, the opportunities of practicing it are rare. Even the largest-scale peace maneuvers are only a feeble shadow of the real thing. So that a soldier desirous of acquiring skill in handling troops is forced to theoretical study of great captains.

Field Marshal Sir Archibald P. Wavell
Lecture to officers at Aldershot, 1930

Nothing except a battle lost can be half so melancholy as a battle won.
Arthur Wellesley, Duke of Wellington
Dispatch from Waterloo, 1815

The battle of Waterloo was won on the playing fields of Eton.
Attributed to Arthur Wellesley, Duke of Wellington

If we ignore the historical importance of our profession, the society from which it comes, and why it is worth preserving, we run the risk of the guardians not valuing what they guard.
General John A. Wickham

Military Leadership

Military leadership is the art of influencing and directing people to an assigned goal in such a way as to command their obedience, confidence, respect, and loyal cooperation.

Department of the Army Training Circular 6, *Leadership*
19 July 1948

Leadership is the art of influencing human behavior.

Department of the Army Pamphlet 22-1, *Leadership*
December 1948

Leadership is the art of influencing and directing others to an assigned goal in such a way as to obtain their obedience, confidence, respect, and loyal cooperation. Military leadership is this same art demonstrated and applied within the profession of arms.

Leadership for Commanders of Divisions and Higher Units,
U.S. Army Command and General Staff College,
1 January 1949

Leadership is the art of influencing human behavior—the ability to handle men. The techniques will vary depending on the size of the command, the types of men, the personality of the commander, and the particular situation.

U.S. Army Field Manual 22-10, *Leadership*
6 March 1951

The military leader must build a command relationship between himself and his men that will result in immediate and effective action on their part to carry out his will in any situation.

U.S. Army Field Manual 22-100,
Command and Leadership for the Small Unit Leader,
26 February 1953

Military leadership—the art of influencing and directing men in such a way as to obtain their willing obedience, confidence, respect and loyal cooperation in order to accomplish the mission.

U.S. Army Field Manual 22-100, *Military Leadership*
2 December 1958, June 1961, and 1 November 1965

Leadership is defined as the process of influencing the actions of individuals and organizations in order to obtain desired results.

Department of the Army Pamphlet 600-15,
Leadership at Senior Levels of Command, October 1968

Military leadership is the process of influencing men in such a manner as to accomplish the mission.

U.S. Army Field Manual 22-100, *Military Leadership*
29 June 1973

The most essential element of combat power is competent and confident leadership. Leadership provides purpose, direction, and motivation in combat. It is the leader who will determine the degree to which maneuver, firepower, and protection are maximized; who will ensure these elements are effectively balanced; and who will decide how to bring them to bear against the enemy.

U.S. Army Field Manual 100-5, *Operations*
20 August 1982 and 5 May 1986

Military leadership—the process by which a soldier influences others to accomplish the mission. He carries out this process by applying his leadership attributes (beliefs, values, ethics, character, knowledge, and skills).

U.S. Army Field Manual 22-100, *Military Leadership*
31 October 1983

Leadership and command at senior levels is the art of direct and indirect influence and the skill of creating the conditions for sustained organizational success to achieve the desired result.

U.S. Army Field Manual 22-103,
Leadership and Command at Senior Levels, 21 June 1987

Our job is to develop bold audacious leaders, competent enough to know the difference between risk and gamble, and willing to take risk to get inside the decision cycle of the enemy in order to wrest the initiative from him. We must develop commanders who trust their subordinates, who delegate responsibility and authority to them, and who encourage them to exercise initiative within the framework of their intent.

Lieutenant General Gerald T. Bartlett

Leadership in a democratic Army means firmness, not harshness; understanding, not weakness; justice, not license; humanness, not intolerance; generosity, not selfishness; pride, not egotism.

General Omar N. Bradley

General Patton demonstrated his point with a china plate and a wet noodle. Holding the plate almost perpendicular, he attempted to push the wet noodle up the slippery, slick surface. His effort was not successful.

General Omar N. Bradley

At the top there are great simplifications. An accepted leader has only to be sure of what it is best to do, or at least have his mind made up about it. The loyalties which center upon number one are enormous. If he trips, he must be sustained. If he makes mistakes, they must be covered. If he sleeps, he must not be wantonly disturbed. If he is no good, he must be pole-axed.

Sir Winston Churchill
Their Finest Hour, 1949

The Commander of an Army neither requires to be a learned explorer of history nor a publicist, but he must be well versed in the higher affairs of state; he must know and be able to judge correctly of traditional tendencies, interests at stake, the immediate questions at issue, and the characters of leading persons; he need not be a close observer of men, a sharp dissector of human character, but he must know the character, the feelings, the habits, the peculiar faults and inclinations, of those whom he is to command. . . . These are matters only to be gained by the exercise of an accurate judgment in the observation of things and men.

Karl von Clausewitz
On War, 1832

For, in truth, there is no position in which man can be placed which asks so much of his intellect in so short a space as that of the general, the failure or success, the decimation or security of whose army hangs on his instant thought and unequivocal instruction under the furious and kaleidoscopic ordeal of the field. To these qualities of heart and head add one factor more—opportunity—and you have the great soldier.

Colonel Theodore A. Dodge
Great Captains, 1889

Men willingly take orders to die only from those they regard as superior beings.

Theodore R. Fehrenbach

Leadership is a timeless subject; it has been described, discussed, dissected and analyzed by management experts (who sometimes confuse management and leadership) for centuries.

Lieutenant General Edward M. Flanagan, Jr.

If you command wisely, you'll be obeyed cheerfully.

Thomas Fuller
Gnomologia, 1732

The prize of the general is not a bigger tent, but command.

Oliver Wendell Holmes, Jr.
Law and the Court, 1913

If officers desire to have control over their commands, they must remain habitually with them, industriously attend to their instruction and comfort, and in battle lead them well.

General Thomas J. "Stonewall" Jackson
Instructions to his commanding officers, November 1861

[A leader] should be the soul of tact, patience, justice, firmness, and charity. No meritorious act of a subordinate should escape his attention or be left to pass without its reward, even if the reward is only a word of approval. Conversely, he should not be blind to a single fault in any subordinate, though, at the same time, he should be quick and unfailing to distinguish error from malice, thoughtlessness from incompetency, and well-meant shortcomings from heedless or stupid blunders.

Admiral John Paul Jones

An ingredient as essential as leadership to a free society . . . is what I would like to refer to as "followership." To me, "followers" are the backbone of any great nation or organization, for without loyal, dedicated "followers," there can be no effective leaders. And without effective leaders, no viable organization could survive.

General P. X. Kelly
Quoted in Karel Montor et al.,
Naval Leadership: Voices of Experience, 1987

A leader is best when he is neither seen nor heard. Not so good when he is adored and glorified. Worst when he is hated and despised.
"Fail to honor people, they will fail to honor you." But of a Great Leader, when his work is done, his aim fullfilled, the people will all say, "We did this ourselves."

Lao-Tzu
Way of Lao-Tzu, circa sixth century B.C.

Being an Army leader means that in the final analysis, that leader must be ready someday, somewhere, to lead soldiers to accomplish an ultimate task that no one wants to do, under conditions that no one else wants to tolerate. Those intolerable conditions exist with an Army at war in combat—killing and dying.

Colonel Dandridge M. "Mike" Malone

Success comes when leaders lead instead of pushing.

Brigadier General S.L.A. Marshall
Sinai Victory, 1958

Get your major purpose clear, take off your plate all which hinders that purpose and hold hard to all that helps it, and then go ahead with a clear conscience, courage, sincerity, and selflessness.

Field Marshal Bernard L. Montgomery

No man can justly be called a great captain who does not know how to organize and form the character of an army, as well as to lead it when formed.

General Sir William Napier

Nothing is more important in war than unity of command.

Napoleon Bonaparte
Maxims, LXIV, 1831

Command and leadership are two quite different functions, yet they are inextricably interrelated—each supplementing and strengthening the other. I think of them as Siamese twins, each essential to the life of the other, joined at the head and heart—with the head symbolizing command and the heart symbolizing leadership.

Major General Aubrey "Red" Newman
Follow Me, 1981

Leadership gimmicks, gambits, and grandstand plays, if used with judgment and selectivity, can be helpful in special circumstances. But nothing can replace the most effective principle of company-level leadership; the day-to-day personal interest of the commander.

Major General Aubrey "Red" Newman
Follow Me, 1981

To do great things is difficult; but to command great things is more difficult.

Friedrich Wilhelm Nietzsche
Thus Spoke Zarathustra, 1883–1892

Superiority of material strength is given to a commander gratis. Superior knowledge and superior tactical skill he must himself acquire. Superior morale, superior cooperation, he must himself create.

Admiral Joseph Mason Reeves

What you cannot enforce,
Do not command.

Sophocles
Oedipus at Colonus, circa fifth century B.C.

Every great leader I have known has been a great teacher, able to give those around him a sense of perspective and to set the moral, social, and motivational climate among his followers.

Vice Admiral James Bond Stockdale
The Washington Quarterly,
"Educating Leaders," 30 March 1983

When troops flee, are insubordinate, distressed, collapse in disorder, or are routed, it is the fault of the general. None of the disorders can be attributed to natural causes.

Sun-Tzu
The Art of War, circa fourth century B.C.

Sorting out muddles is really the chief job of a commander.

Field Marshal Sir Archibald P. Wavell
Royal United Service Institution Journal,
February 1933

A general good at commanding troops is like one sitting in a leaking boat or lying under a burning roof. For there is no time for the wise to offer counsel nor the brave to be angry. All must come to grips with the enemy.

Wu Ch'i

In modern warfare the correct commanding of troops is of great importance. This embraces a wide range of military-political, moral, material and psychological factors, and constitutes an important integral part of military science and art.

Marshal Georgii K. Zhukov
The Memoirs of Marshal Zhukov, 1971

Mistakes

If you ever make any mistakes, be quick to admit and especially to correct them. While this manner of conducting oneself is totally natural and is not deserving of praise, it will however draw praise for you, will win you hearts and will allow you to pardon mistakes in others.

Marshal de Belle-Isle
Letter to his son

Leaders value learning and mastery, and so do people who work for leaders. Leaders make it clear that there is no failure, only mistakes that give us feedback and tell us what to do next.

Warren Bennis
Training and Development Journal, August 1984

Wise men learn by other men's mistakes, fools by their own.

Henry George Bohn

I can pardon everyone's mistakes but my own.

Marcus Porcius Cato

Any man can make mistakes, but only an idiot persists in his error.

Marcus Tullius Cicero
Philippics, 44 B.C.

You must be able to underwrite the honest mistakes of your subordinates if you wish to develop their initiative and experience.

General Bruce C. Clarke

Nothing is easy in war. Mistakes are always paid for in casualties and troops are quick to sense any blunder made by their commanders.

General Dwight D. Eisenhower
Crusade in Europe, 1948

Man must strive, and striving he must err.

Johann Wolfgang von Goethe
Faust: Part I, 1808

The man who makes no mistakes does not usually make anything.

Bishop W. C. Magee

The greatest general is he who makes the fewest mistakes.

Napoleon Bonaparte

To inquire if and when we made mistakes is not to apologize. War is replete with mistakes because it is full of improvisations. In war we are always doing something for the first time. It would be a miracle if what we improvised under the stress of war would be perfect.

Vice Admiral Hyman G. Rickover
Testimony before the House Military
Appropriations Subcommittee, April 1964

Happily for the result of the battle—and for me—I was, like other generals before me, to be saved from the consequences of my mistakes by the resourcefulness of my subordinate commanders and the stubborn valor of my troops.

Field Marshal Sir William Slim
Defeat into Victory, 1961

When a general makes no mistakes in war, it is because he has not been at it long.

Vicomte de Turenne
After the Battle of Marienthal, 1645

Love truth, but pardon error.

Voltaire
Sept Discours en vers sur l'Homme, 1738

Experience is the name everyone gives to their mistakes.

Oscar Wilde
Lady Windemere's Fan, 1892

Moral Courage, Will

A man does not flee because he is fighting in an unrighteous cause, he does not attack because his cause is just; he flees because he is the weaker, he conquers because he is the stronger, or because his leader has made him feel the stronger.

Anonymous (from World War I)

[Will] is a moral quality which grows to maturity in peace and is not suddenly developed on the outbreak of war . . . for war . . . has no power to transform, it merely exaggerates the good and evil that are in us, till it is plain for all to read; it cannot change, it exposes. Man's fate in battle is worked out before war begins.

Aristotle

War is a contest of wills.

Sir Winston Churchill
Middle East Planning Conference, 27 April 1941

If the military leader is filled with high ambition and if he pursues his aims with audacity and strength of will, he will reach them in spite of all obstacles.

Karl von Clausewitz

The best arms are dead and useless material as long as the spirit is missing which is ready, willing, and determined to use them.

Adolf Hitler
Mein Kampf, 1925

People do not lack strength. They lack will.

Victor Hugo

In war the chief incalculable is the human will.

B. H. Liddell Hart
Strategy, 1967

It is fatal to enter any war without the will to win it.

General Douglas MacArthur
Speech to Republican National Convention,
7 July 1952

Courage is a moral quality; it is not a chance gift of nature . . . it is a cold choice between two alternatives, the fixed resolve not to quit; an act of renunciation which must be made not once but many times by the power of will. Courage is will power.

Lord Charles Moran
The Anatomy of Courage, 1967

In war, the moral is to the material as three to one.

Napoleon Bonaparte

A man does not have himself killed for a few half-pense a day or for a petty distinction. You must speak to the soul in order to electrify the man.

Napoleon Bonaparte

Quant au courage moral, il quait trouvé fort rare, disait-il, celui de deux heures après minuit; c'est-a-dire le courage de l'improviste.
[As to moral courage, I have very rarely met with two-o'clock-in-the-morning courage; I mean instantaneous courage.]

Napoleon Bonaparte
4–5 December 1815

Physical courage is an animal instinct; moral bravery is a much higher and truer courage.

Wendell Phillips

New weapons are worthless in the hands of soldiers who have neither the will nor the intelligence to use them.

Ardant du Picq

In battle, two moral forces, even more than two material forces, are in conflict. The stronger conquers.

Ardant du Picq
Battle Studies, 1880

Man is and always will be the supreme element in combat, and upon the skill, the courage and endurance, and the fighting heart of the individual soldier the issue will ultimately depend.

General Matthew B. Ridgway

It is not the critic that counts, not the man who points out how the strong man stumbled, or where the doer of deeds could have done them better. The credit belongs to the man in the arena, whose face is marred by dust and sweat and blood; who strived valiantly; who errs and comes short again and again; who knows great enthusiasms, the great devotions and spends himself in a worthy cause; who at the best knows at the end the triumph of high achievement; and who at the worst if he fails at least fails while daring greatly, so that his place shall never be with those cold timid souls who know neither victory nor defeat.

Theodore Roosevelt

To fight and conquer in all your battles is not supreme excellence; supreme excellence consists in breaking the enemy's resistance.

Sun-Tzu
The Art of War, circa fourth century B.C.

We must have "character," which simply means that he knows what he wants and has the courage and determination to get it. He should have a genuine interest in, and a real knowledge of, humanity, the raw materials of his trade, and, most vital of all, he must have what we call the fighting spirit, the will to win.

Field Marshal Sir Archibald P. Wavell
"Lees Knowles Lectures,"
Trinity College, Cambridge, 1939

Morale

Morale is when your hands and feet keep working when your head says it can't be done.

Anonymous

The by-products of good leadership are good morale and motivation.

General Bruce C. Clarke

The morale of soldiers comes from three things: a feeling that they have an important job to do, a feeling that they are trained to do it well, and a feeling that their good work is appreciated and recognized.

General Bruce C. Clarke
Soldiers, March 1985

Soldiers like to see the men who are directing operations; they properly resent any indication of neglect or indifference to them on the part of their commanders and invariably interpret a visit, even a brief one, as evidence of the commander's concern for them. Diffidence or modesty must never blind the commander to his duty of showing himself to his men, of speaking to them, of mingling with them to the extent of physical limitation. It pays big dividends in terms of morale, and morale, given rough equality in other things, is supreme on the battlefield.

General Dwight D. Eisenhower

Morale is the greatest single factor in successful war. . . . In any long and bitter campaign morale will suffer unless all ranks thoroughly believe that their commanders are concerned first and always with the welfare of the troops who do the fighting.

General Dwight D. Eisenhower
Crusade in Europe, 1948

Morale, of course, is the most highly important of any military attribute, but we must produce the type of morale that results from self-respect, thorough discipline, intensive training and adequate leadership—we should not make the mistake of believing that morale can be produced by pampering or by the lowering of standards to permit greater ease of living.

General Dwight D. Eisenhower
Eisenhower Papers, 1970

Battles are beyond all else struggles of morale. Defeat is inevitable as soon as the hope of conquering ceases to exist. Success comes not to him who has suffered the least but to him whose will is firmest and morale strongest.

French Army Field Regulations, 1913

The morale of an army and its chief officers has an influence upon the fate of a war; and this seems to be due to a certain physical effect produced by the moral cause. For example, the impetuous attack upon a hostile line of twenty thousand brave men whose feelings are thoroughly enlisted in their cause will produce a much more powerful effect than the attack of forty thousand demoralized or apathetic men upon the same point.

Baron Henri de Jomini
Précis de l'Art de Guerre, 1838

It is the morale of armies, as well as of nations, more than anything else, which makes victories and their results decisive.

Baron Henri de Jomini
Précis de l'Art de Guerre, 1838

No system of tactics can lead to victory when the morale of an army is bad.

Baron Henri de Jomini
Précis de l'Art de Guerre, 1838

Machines are as nothing without men. Men are as nothing without morale.

Admiral Ernest J. King
Graduation address to the U.S. Naval Academy,
19 June 1942

The unfailing formula for production of morale is patriotism, self-respect, discipline, and self-confidence within a military unit, joined with fair treatment and merited appreciation from without. It cannot be produced by pampering or coddling an army, and is not necessarily destroyed by hardship, danger, or even calamity. Though it can survive and develop in adversity that comes as an inescapable incident of service, it will quickly wither and die if soldiers come to believe themselves the victims of indifference or injustice on the part of their government, or of ignorance, personal ambition, or ineptitude on the part of their military leaders.

General Douglas MacArthur
Annual Report of the Chief of Staff, U.S. Army,
for the Fiscal Year Ending 30 June 1933

It is not enough to fight. It is the spirit which we bring to the fight that decides the issue. It is morale that wins the victory.

General George C. Marshall
Selected Speeches and Statements of General of the Army
George C. Marshall, edited by Major H. A. DeWeerd, 1945

Morale is the state of mind. It is steadfastness and courage and hope. It is confidence and zeal and loyalty. It is elan, esprit de corps and determination. It is staying power, the spirit which endures to the end—the will to win. With it all things are possible, without it everything else, planning, preparation, production count for naught.

General George C. Marshall
Selected Speeches and Statements of General of the Army
George C. Marshall, edited by Major H. A. DeWeerd, 1945

The efficiency of an army depends on many different things, but one is outstanding—and that is morale. You can have all the materiel in the world, but without morale it is largely ineffective. You must have morale, first and foremost, and morale is determined by a great many things. Primarily it depends, of course, on leadership, the possession of equipment and, in the long run, on the people back home.

General George C. Marshall
Military Review, October 1948

The morale of the force flows from the self-discipline of the commander, and in turn, the discipline of the force is reestablished by the upsurge of its moral power.

Brigadier General S.L.A. Marshall
The Armed Forces Officer, 1950

The morale of the soldier is the greatest single factor in war and the best way to achieve a high morale in wartime is by success in battle.

Field Marshal Bernard L. Montgomery
Memoirs of Field Marshal Viscount Montgomery of Alamein, 1958

In war, everything depends on morale; and morale and public opinion comprise the better part of reality.

Napoleon Bonaparte

Note the army organizations and tactical formations on paper are always determined from the mechanical point of view, neglecting the essential coefficient, that of morale. They are almost always wrong.

Ardant du Picq
Battle Studies, 1880

In the last analysis, success in battle is a matter of morale. In all matters which pertain to an army, organization, discipline and tactics, the human heart in the supreme moment of battle is the basic factor.

Ardant du Picq
Battle Studies, 1880

Morale, only morale, individual morale as a foundation under training and discipline, will bring victory.

Field Marshal Sir William Slim
To the officers of the 10th Indian Infantry Division,
June 1941

So when I took command, I sat quietly down to work out this business of morale. I came to certain conclusions, based not on any theory that I had studied, but on some experience and a good deal of hard thinking. It was on these conclusions that I set out consciously to raise the fighting spirit of my army.

Field Marshal Sir William Slim
Defeat into Victory, 1961

Morale is a state of mind. It is that intangible force which will move a whole group of men to give their last ounce to achieve something, without counting the cost to themselves; that makes them feel they are part of something greater than themselves.

Field Marshal Sir William Slim
Serve to Lead, 1959

You are well aware that it is not numbers or strength that bring victories in war. No, it is when one side goes against the enemy with the gods' gift of a stronger morale that their adversaries, as a rule, cannot withstand them.

Xenophon
Speech to Greek officers after the defeat
of Cyrus at Cunaxa, 401 B.C.

Morale can be thought of as a significant subset of individual capacity. . . . The capability of an individual and the capability of a ship can be enhanced by some 20 to 30 percent if morale is high. Morale, then, which certainly is a significant contributor to mission performance, is a large part of capability.

Admiral Elmo R. Zumwalt, Jr.
Quoted in Karel Montor et al.,
Naval Leadership: Voices of Experience, 1987

Motivation

Never lead on any of your subordinates with hopes that you have no possibility of fulfilling. When the persons who hold them see them dashed, they will accuse you of having neglected their interests.

Marshal de Belle-Isle
Letter to his son

Education makes a people easy to lead, but difficult to drive; easy to govern, but impossible to enslave.

General Omar N. Bradley

Ten pats on the back for each kick in the shins is a very good ratio for a commander.

General Bruce C. Clarke

Awards that motivate only the top men are of little value in raising the ability of a unit. It takes awards to motivate the lower third to do that. A unit is measured by the ability of the lower third personnel in it to carry their part of the load.

General Bruce C. Clarke

The first step in motivating soldiers is to tell them the reason why.

General Bruce C. Clarke

The key word in training soldiers is motivation.

General Bruce C. Clarke

O Lord God, when Thou givest to thy servants to endeavour any great matter, grant us also to know that it is not the beginning, but the continuing of the same until it is thoroughly finished, which yieldeth the true glory.

Sir Francis Drake (prayer)

Genius is one percent inspiration and ninety-nine percent perspiration.

Thomas Alva Edison
Life, 1932

Nothing great was ever achieved without enthusiasm.

Ralph Waldo Emerson
Essays: First Series, "Circles," 1841

A battle is lost less through the loss of men than by discouragement.

Frederick the Great
Instructions for His Generals, 1747

Correction does much, but encouragement does more. Encouragement after censure is as the sun after a shower.

Johann Wolfgang von Goethe

The harder you work, the harder it is to surrender.

Vince Lombardi

A soldier will fight long and hard for a bit of colored ribbon.

Napoleon Bonaparte
To British captain of HMS *Bellerophon*, 15 July 1815

It is not by harangues at the moment of engaging that soldiers are rendered brave. Veterans hardly listen to them and recruits forget them at the first discharge of a cannon.

Napoleon Bonaparte
Maxims, LXI, 1831

You can order people to come to work, but you can't order them to be excellent in what they do. Excellence on the production line or office floor is a matter of a 100 percent voluntary commitment. Getting that commitment is what identifies the superior manager.

Tom Peters

On occasion a hobnailed boot can advance a faltering skirmish line far better than a stirring appeal to a man's higher nature.

R. M. Sandusky

There are no gains without pains.

Adlai Stevenson
Presidential nomination acceptance speech, 1952

It is said of Caesar that he never lacked a pleasant word for his soldiers. He remembered the face of anyone who had done a gallant deed and, when not in the presence of the enemy, joined his men in soldier games. Such little human acts as these inspired his legionnaires with the devotion which went so far to account for his success as a great captain.

General Maxwell D. Taylor
Speech to Citadel cadets, 21 January 1956

Zeal is always at its height at the commencement of an undertaking.

Thucydides

Study the human side of history. . . . To learn that Napoleon in 1796 with 20,000 beat combined forces of 30,000 by something called economy of force or operating on interior lines is a mere waste of time. If you can understand how a young unknown man inspired a half-starved, ragged, rather Bolshie, crowd; how he filled their bellies; how he outmarched, outwitted, outbluffed and defeated men who had studied war all their lives and waged it according to the text-books of their time, you will have learnt something worth knowing.

Field Marshal Sir Archibald P. Wavell

Men who think that their officer recognizes them are keener to be seen doing something honorable and more desirous of avoiding disgrace.

Xenophon

NCO Corps

If a selection of good sergeants and corporals be made by the officer at the head of the regiment, and if that officer will only allow those individuals to do their duty, there is not the least doubt that they will do it.

Anonymous diary entry of a British sergeant,
War of 1812

There never has been a good army without a good noncommissioned officer corps.

General Bruce C. Clarke

The command sergeant major is the principal enlisted staff assistant to his commander. As such, he makes suggestions and recommendations to his commander as called for and as is appropriate. But he is more; he sets the standards in leadership, performance of duty, conduct, discipline, morale, and community relations for the non-commissioned. officers of his unit.

General Bruce C. Clarke

Any officer can get by on his sergeants. To be a sergeant you have to know your stuff. I'd rather be an outstanding sergeant than just another officer.

Gunnery Sergeant Daniel Daly

If a soldier during an action looks about as if to fly, or so much as sets foot outside the line, the non-commissioned officer standing behind him will run him through with his bayonet and kill him on the spot.

Frederick the Great

The backbone of the Army is the noncommissioned man!

Rudyard Kipling
The 'Eathen, 1896

The primary responsibility for the quality of training falls squarely on the shoulders of our sergeants. They are the primary link in the leadership chain.

General Edward C. Meyer

The essential central characteristic for sergeants is the same as that for generals: *character.*

Major General Aubrey "Red" Newman
Follow Me, 1981

Sergeants operate where the action is, in direct control of men who get the job done. That is why they need that rawhide toughness they are famous for, and why they have the human understanding that so few of the American public give them credit for.

Major General Aubrey "Red" Newman
Follow Me, 1981

We have good corporals and sergeants, and some good lieutenants and captains, and those are far more important than good generals.

General William Tecumseh Sherman

The choice of non-commissioned officers is an object of the greatest importance: The order and discipline of a regiment depends so much upon their behavior, that too much care cannot be taken in preferring none to that trust but those who by their merit and good conduct are entitled to it. Honesty, sobriety, and a remarkable attention to every point of duty, with a neatness in their dress, are indispensable requisites

200

. . . nor can a sergeant or corporal be said to be qualified who does not write and read in a tolerable manner.

Baron Frederic von Steuben
*Regulations for the Order and Discipline
of the Troops of the United States,* 1779

Nothing does so much honor to the abilities or application of the tribune as the appearance and discipline of the soldiers, when their apparel is neat and clean, their arms bright and in good order and when they perform their exercises and evolutions with dexterity.

Vegetius
Dē Re Mīlĭtāri, Book II, 378

Obedience

He who has never learned to obey cannot be a good commander.
Aristotle
Politics, circa fourth century B.C.

The man who commands efficiently must have obeyed others in the past, and the man who obeys dutifully is worthy of being some day a commander.
Marcus Tullius Cicero
Legibus, circa 52 B.C.

There is nothing in war which is of greater importance than obedience.
Karl von Clausewitz
On War, 1832

Obedience is a hard profession.

Pierre Corneille
Nicomède, 1671

Not for fame or reward, not for place or for rank, not lured by ambition or goaded by necessity, but in simple obedience to duty as they understood it, these men suffered all, sacrificed all, dared all, and died.
Inscription at Arlington National Cemetery

Men must be habituated to obey or they cannot be controlled in battle, and the neglect of the least important order impairs the proper influence of the officer.

General Robert E. Lee
Instruction to the army of northern Virginia, 1865

The [soldiers] must learn to keep their ranks, to obey words of command and signals by drum and trumpet, and to observe good order, whether they halt, advance, retreat, are upon a march, or engaged with an enemy.

Niccolò di Bernardo Machiavelli
Arte Della Guèrra, 1520

He who wishes to be obeyed must know how to command.

Niccolò di Bernardo Machiavelli
Discorsi, 1531

The duty of obedience is not merely military but moral. It is not an arbitrary rule, but one essential and fundamental; the expression of a principle without which military organization would go to pieces, and military success be impossible.

Rear Admiral Alfred T. Mahan
Retrospect and Prospect, 1902

To know how to command obedience is a very different thing from making men obey. Obedience is not the product of fear, but of understanding, and understanding is based on knowledge.

Brigadier General S.L.A. Marshall
The Armed Forces Officer, 1950

Soldiers must obey in all things. They may and do laugh at foolish orders, but they nevertheless obey, not because they are blindly obedient, but because they know that to disobey is to break the backbone of their profession.

Admiral Sir Charles Napier

Let your character be above reproach, for that is the way to earn men's obedience.

Field Marshal Johann von Schulenburg
Letter to Marshal Comte de Saxe, 1709

We cannot all be masters, nor all masters
Cannot be truly followed.

William Shakespeare
Othello, Act I, Scene i, 1605

Learn to obey before you command.

Solon of Athens

Willing obedience always beats forced obedience.

Baron Frederic von Steuben

Without arrogance or the smallest deviation from the truth, it may be said that no history now extant can furnish an instance of an Army's suffering such uncommon hardships as ours have done, and bearing them with the same patience and fortitude. To see men without clothes to clothe their nakedness, without blankets to lie on, without shoes, by which their marches might be traced by the blood from their feet, and almost as often without provisions as with; marching through frost and snow, and at Christmas taking up their winter quarters within a day's march of the enemy, without a house or hut to cover them till they could be built, and submitting to it without a murmur, is a mark of patience and obedience which in my opinion can scarce be paralleled.

General George Washington

The leader must himself believe that willing obedience always beats forced obedience, and that he can get this only by really knowing what should be done. Thus he can secure obedience from his men because he can convince them that he knows best, precisely as a good doctor makes his patients obey him. Also he must be ready to suffer more hardships than he asks of his soldiers, more fatigue, greater extremes of heat and cold.

Xenophon
Cyropaedia, circa 360 B.C.

Officer Corps

He is to take notice of what discords, quarrels, and debates arise among the souldiers of his band; he is to pacify them if it may be; otherwise to commit them; he is to judge and determine such disputes with gravity and good speeches, and where the fault is, to make him acknowledge it and crave pardon of the party he hath abused. . . . He is to be careful that every souldier hath a sufficient lodging in garrison, and in the field a hut; he is also to take due care of the sick and maymed, that they perish not for want of means or looking into; he is to take care that the sutlers do not opresse and rack the poor souldiers in their victuals and drinks.

Seventeenth-century instructions for British officers

War is an art, to attain perfection in which much time and experience, particularly for the officers, are necessary.

John C. Calhoun

There are no poor companies in the Army—only poor company commanders.

General Bruce C. Clarke

The officer should wear his uniform as the judge his ermine, without a stain.

Rear Admiral John A. Dahlgren
12 July 1870

Perhaps one of the greatest mysteries of the military profession is the fact that so often the officer who is willing to sacrifice his life in combat is hesitant to risk his career to correct an abuse in the system, to suffer the embarrassment by speaking out for justice, or to stand firm on moral standards when the accepted practice follows a discordant tune. Being a brave combat leader does not guarantee that an officer will have the courage to overcome pressures to behave unethically in a bureaucracy. It all comes down to his personal standards of integrity and a sense of conviction for his service calling.

Major Francis Galligan

A Captain of the Navy ought to be a man of Strong and well-connected Sense with a tolerable education, a Gentleman as well as a Seaman both in Theory and Practice.

Admiral John Paul Jones
19 May 1776

An ignorant officer is a murderer. All brave men confide in the knowledge he is supposed to possess; and when the death-trial comes their generous blood flows in vain. Merciful God! How can an ignorant man charge himself with so much bloodshed? I have studied war long, earnestly and deeply, but yet I tremble at my own derelictions.

Admiral Sir Charles Napier

As you from this day start the world as a man, I trust that your future conduct in life will prove you both an officer and a gentleman. Recollect that you must be a seaman to be a good officer; and also that you cannot be a good officer without being a gentleman.

Attributed to Lord Admiral Horatio Nelson
Advice to new midshipman

Officers are responsible not only for the conduct of their men in battle, but also for their health and contentment when not fighting. An officer must be the last man to take shelter from fire, and the first to move forward. He must be the last man to look after his own comfort at the close of a march. The officer must constantly interest himself in the welfare of his men and their rations. He should know his men so well that any sign of sickness or nervous strain will be apparent to him. He must look after his men's feet and see that they have properly fitting shoes in good condition; that their socks fit, for loose or tight socks make sore feet. He must anticipate change of weather and see that proper clothing and footgear are asked for and obtained.

General George S. Patton, Jr.

We, as officers of the army, are not only members of the oldest of honorable professions, but are also the modern representatives of the demi-gods and heroes of antiquity. Back of us stretches a line of men whose acts of valor, of self-sacrifice and of service have been the theme of song and story since long before recorded history began. . . . In the days of chivalry . . . knights-officers were noted as well for courtesy and gentleness of behavior as for death-defying courage. . . . From their acts of courtesy and benevolence was derived the word, now pronounced as one, Gentle Man. . . . Let us be gentle. This is, courteous and considerate of the rights of others. Let us be Men. That is, fearless and untiring in doing our duty. . . . Our calling is most ancient and like all other old things it has amassed through the ages certain customs and traditions which decorate and ennoble it, which render beautiful the otherwise prosaic occupation of professional men-at-arms: killers.

General George S. Patton, Jr.

You are always on parade.

General George S. Patton, Jr.
Letter to his son, 6 June 1944

First, foremost, and always, we must have an Officer Corps, comprising a professional, long-term cadre adequate both in size and quality. This is the heart and soul of any military organization.

General Matthew B. Ridgway

As Army officers, we should prepare our men psychologically as well as physically, and inspire them with the necessity to prepare themselves for the arduous task of fighting and winning upon any battlefield.

General Matthew B. Ridgway

The Officer Corps is the heart and soul of any military organization. It must be the reservoir of character and integrity, the fountainhead of professional competence, and the dynamo of leadership.

General Matthew B. Ridgway

The business of a naval officer is one which above all others needs daring and decision.

Admiral William S. Sims

Battle is the ultimate to which the whole life's labor of an officer should be directed. He may live to the age of retirement without seeing a battle; still, he must always be getting ready for it as if he knew the hour and the day it is to break upon him. And then, whether it come late or early, he must be willing to fight—he must fight.

Major General Charles F. Smith
To Colonel Lew Wallace, September 1861

This is the officer's part, to make men continue to do things, they know not wherefore; and, when, if choice was offered, they would lie down where they were and be killed.

Robert Louis Stevenson
Kidnapped, 1886

When the common soldiers are too strong and their officers too weak, the result is *insubordination*. When the officers are too strong and the common soldiers too weak, the result is *collapse*.

Sun-Tzu
The Art of War, circa fourth century B.C.

War must be carried on systematically, and to do it, you must have good Officers, there are, in my Judgment, no other possible means to obtain them but by establishing your Army upon a permanent basis; and giving your Officers good pay; this will induce Gentlemen, and Men of Character to engage; and till the bulk of your officers are composed of such persons as are actuated by principles of Honor, and a spirit of enterprise, you have little to expect from them. . . . An Army formed of good Officers moves like clockwork.

General George Washington
Letter to Congress, 24 September 1776

There is one quality above all which seems to me essential for a good commander, the ability to express himself clearly, confidently, and concisely, in speech and on paper. . . . It is a rare quality amongst Army Officers, to which not nearly enough attention is paid in their education. It is one which can be acquired, but seldom is, because it is seldom taught.

Field Marshal Sir Archibald P. Wavell
Soldiers and Soldiering, 1953

No man can be a good officer who does not undergo more than those he commands.

Xenophon
Cyropaedia, circa 360 B.C.

You are generals, you are officers and captains. In peace time you got more pay and more respect than they did. Now, in war time, you ought to hold yourselves to be braver than the general mass of men.

Xenophon
To the Greek officers after the defeat
of Cyrus at Cunaxa, 401 B.C.

Patriotism

I am well aware of the toil, and blood, and treasure, that it will cost to maintain this declaration, and support and defend these states; yet, through all the gloom I can see the rays of light and glory. I can see the end is worth more than all the means.

John Quincy Adams

Posterity—you will never know how much it has cost my generation to preserve your freedom. I hope you will make good use of it.

John Quincy Adams

These POWs now appear to us to embody precisely those moral qualities of honor, patriotism, discipline and purpose which many of us feel have largely disappeared from American life.

Shana Alexander
Newsweek, "Prisoners of Peace," 5 March 1973

Patriotism is not so much protecting the land of our fathers as preserving the land of our children.

Anonymous

I pledge allegiance to the flag of the United States of America and to the republic for which it stands, one nation under God, indivisible, with liberty and justice for all.

Francis Bellamy and James B. Upham
1892

He who loves not his country, can love nothing.

Lord George Noel Gordon Byron
The Two Foscari, 1821

Protection and patriotism are reciprocal.

John C. Calhoun
Speech to Congress, 12 December 1811

Es dulce el amor de la patria.
[Sweet is the love of one's country.]

Miguel de Cervantes
Don Quixote, 1615

Eternal vigilance is the price of liberty.

John Philpot Curran, 10 July 1790
(Inscription on statue in front of Department of Justice Building)

And they who for their country die
Shall fill an honored grave,
For glory lights the soldier's tomb,
And beauty weeps the brave.

Joseph Rodman Drake
To the Defenders of New Orleans, 1814

Forever float that standard sheet!
Where breathes the foe but falls before us,
With Freedom's soil beneath our feet,
And Freedom's banner streaming o'er us?

Joseph Rodman Drake
New York Evening Post, "The American Flag," 29 May 1819

In the final choice, a soldier's pack is not so heavy a burden as a prisoner's chains.

General Dwight D. Eisenhower
Inaugural address, 20 January 1953

If our country is worth dying for in time of war let us resolve that it is truly worth living for in time of peace.

Hamilton Fish

He is a poor patriot whose patriotism does not enable him to understand how all men everywhere feel about their altars and their hearthstones, their flags and their fatherland.

Harry Emerson Fosdick

We must all hang together, or assuredly we shall hang separately.

Benjamin Franklin
At the signing of the Declaration of Independence, 4 July 1776

I only regret that I have but one life to lose for my country.

Nathan Hale
Prior to being hanged by the British as a spy,
22 September 1776

In the great fulfillment we must have a citizenship less concerned about what the government can do for it and more anxious about what it can do for the nation.

Warren G. Harding

Is life so dear or peace so sweet as to be purchased at the price of chains and slavery? Forbid it, Almighty God! I know not what course others may take, but as for me, give me liberty or give me death!

Patrick Henry
Speech to the Virginia Convention, 23 March 1775

It is not unseemly for a man to die fighting in defense of his country.

Homer
The Iliad, Book XV, circa 700 B.C.

The single best augury is to fight for one's country.

Homer
The Iliad, Book XII, circa 700 B.C.

Dulce et děcōrum est pro patřia mŏřĭ.
[It is a sweet and glorious thing to die for one's country.]

Horace
Odes, 23 B.C.

My God! how little do my countrymen know what precious blessings they are in possession of, and which no other people on earth enjoy!

Thomas Jefferson
Letter to James Monroe, 17 June 1785

I am a free man, an American, a United States Senator, and a Democrat, in that order.

I am also a liberal, a conservative, a Texan, a taxpayer, a rancher, a businessman, a consumer, a parent, a voter, and not as young as I used to be nor as old as I expect to be—and I am all these things in no fixed order.

I am unaware of any descriptive word in the second paragraph which qualifies, modifies, amends, or is related by hyphenation to the terms listed in the first paragraph. In consequence, I am not able—not even the least interested in trying—to define my political philosophy by the choice of a one-word or two-word label. This may be against the tide, but, if so, the choice is deliberate.

Lyndon B. Johnson
My Political Philosophy, 1958

We say pay any price, bear any burden, meet any hardship, support any friend, oppose any foe to assure the survival and the success of liberty.

John F. Kennedy

And so, my fellow Americans: ask not what your country can do for you—ask what you can do for your country.

John F. Kennedy
Inaugural Address, 20 January 1961

These are the three virtues: duty, loyalty, patriotism.

G. Gordon Liddy

By focusing on our roots as an Army, we have rekindled our patriotism. We have also brightened the Army's awareness of the lessons of history as contributors to readiness. Soldiers everywhere are absorbing these lessons through case studies, terrain walks, and staff rides.

John O. Marsh, Jr.

An officer's ultimate commanding loyalty at all times is to his country, and not to his service or to his superiors.

General George C. Marshall

Blessed is the country whose defenders are patriots. . . . We cannot exalt patriotism too high; we cannot too much encourage love of country; for, my fellow-citizens, as long as patriotism exists in the hearts of the American people, so long will our matchless institutions be secure and permanent.

William McKinley
Address in Syracuse, New York, 24 August 1897

We cannot defend freedom abroad by deserting it at home.

Edward R. Murrow

God gave men dominion over the beasts and not over his fellow men unless they submit of their own free will.

Napoleon Bonaparte

A good general, a good corps of officers, good organization, good training, rigid discipline, make good troops, independently of the cause for which they fight. Nevertheless, fanaticism, love of country, national glory, may also inspire young troops to advantage.

Napoleon Bonaparte
Maxims, LVI, 1831

One should encourage soldiers by all possible means to remain with the colors; this will be easily attained by showing great consideration to old soldiers. Pay should also be increased for length of service; because it is a great injustice not to pay the veteran more than the recruit.

Napoleon Bonaparte
Maxims, LX, 1831

I believe that every man in uniform is a citizen first and a serviceman second, and we must resist any attempt to isolate or separate the defenders from the defended.

Richard M. Nixon

These are times that try men's souls. The summer soldier and the sunshine patriot will, in this crisis, shrink from the service of their country; but he that stands it now, deserves the love and thanks of man and woman. Tyranny, like hell, is not easily conquered; yet we have this consolation with us, that the harder the conflict, the more glorious the triumph. What we obtain too cheap, we esteem too lightly; 'tis dearness only that gives everything its value. Heaven knows how to put a price upon its goods, and it would be strange indeed if so celestial an article as freedom should not be highly rated.

Thomas Paine
The American Crisis, 23 December 1776

Those who expect you to reap the blessings of freedom, must, like men, undergo the fatigue of supporting it.

Thomas Paine
The American Crisis, 12 September 1777

This empire has been acquired by men who knew their duty and had the courage to do it, who in the hour of conflict had the fear of dishonor always present to them, and who, if ever they failed in an enterprise, would not allow their virtues to be lost to their country, but freely gave their lives to her as the fairest offering which they could present at her feast.

Pericles
Funeral oration for the Athenian dead, 431 B.C.

Man was not born for himself alone, but for his country.

Plato
Epistle to Archytas, 385 B.C.

As for the enemies of freedom, to those who are potential adversaries, they will be reminded that peace is the highest aspiration of the American people. We will negotiate for it, sacrifice for it; we will not surrender for it—now or ever.

Ronald Reagan
20 January 1981

Patriotism should be an integral part of our feeling at all times, for it is merely another name for those qualities of soul which make a man in peace or in war, by day or by night, think of his duty to his fellows, and of his duty to the nation through which their and his loftiest aspirations must find their fitting expression.

Theodore Roosevelt
1916

Our country right or wrong. When right, to be kept right; when wrong, to be put right.

Carl Schurz
Address at Anti-Imperialistic Conference,
Chicago, 17 October 1899

Breathes there a man with soul so dead
Who never to himself hath said,
This is my own, my native land!
Whose heart hath ne'er within him burn'd.
As home his footsteps he hath turn'd
From wandering on a foreign strand?

Sir Walter Scott
The Lay of the Last Minstrel, 1805

A country and government such as ours are worth fighting for, and dying for, if need be.

General William Tecumseh Sherman
Personal Memoirs, 1875

Let's face it. Let's talk sense to the American people. Let's tell them the truth, that there are no gains without pains, that we are now on the eve of great decisions, not easy decisions, like resistance when you're attacked, but a long, patient, costly struggle which alone can assure triumph over the great enemies of man—war, poverty, and tyranny—and the assaults upon human dignity which are the most grievous consequences of each.

Adlai E. Stevenson
Acceptance speech, Democratic National Convention,
July 1952

Citizenship finds an equilibrium between two essential ingredients—that of rights, and that of duties. When the idea of citizenship is losing its grip, one or the other of these elements becomes eroded. Either freedom is on the losing end, or the sense of duty, of obligation, goes down the drain. We are living at a time when the idea of citizenship has been seriously weakened. We have a strong sense of the rights of a citizen. But we've lost much of the sense of the corresponding duties and obligations of citizenship.

Vice Admiral James Bond Stockdale
Military Ethics,
"Education for Leadership and Survival," 1987

Fix your eyes on the greatness of Athens as you have it before you day by day. Fall in love with her, and when you feel her great, remember that this greatness was won by men with courage, with knowledge of their duty, and with a sense of honor in action.

Thucydides
History of the Peloponnesian War, circa 404 B.C.

Total war means total national effort. An army can be only as strong as the determination and the patriotism of the nation behind it.

General Jonathan M. Wainwright
Hero of Bataan, 1981

Let our object be, our country, our whole country, and nothing but our country.

Daniel Webster
Address at Bunker Hill Monument, 17 June 1825

A nation which does not remember what it was yesterday does not know what it is today, nor what it is trying to do. We are trying to do a futile thing if we do not know where we came from or what we have been about.

Woodrow Wilson

The things that the flag stands for were created by the experiences of a great people. Everything that it stands for was written by their lives. The flag is the embodiment, not of sentiment, but of history.

Woodrow Wilson
14 June 1915

Peace

We make war that we may live in peace.

Aristotle
Nicomachean Ethics, circa 340 B.C.

It takes twenty years or more of peace to make a man; it takes only twenty seconds of war to destroy him.

King Baudouin I of Belgium
Speech to U.S. Congress, 12 May 1959

The first blessing is peace, as is agreed upon by all men who have even a small share of reason. . . . The best general, therefore, is that one who is able to bring about peace from war.

Belisarius

Peace through strength works.

George Bush
Presidential debates, 13 October 1988

In war, resolution; in defeat, defiance; in victory, magnanimity; in peace, goodwill.

Sir Winston Churchill
The Gathering Storm, 1948

The god of Victory is said to be one-handed, but Peace gives victory to both sides.

Ralph Waldo Emerson
Journals, 1867

Mankind has grown strong in eternal struggles and it will only perish through eternal peace.

Adolf Hitler
Mein Kampf, 1925

Arms alone are not enough to keep the peace. It must be kept by men.

John F. Kennedy
State of the Union Message, 11 January 1962

War is only a cowardly escape from the problems of peace.

Thomas Mann

It isn't enough to talk about peace. One must believe in it. And it isn't enough to believe in it. One must work at it.

Eleanor Roosevelt
11 November 1951

Peace, like charity, begins at home.

Franklin D. Roosevelt
14 August 1936

Peace, like war, can succeed only where there is a will to enforce it, and where there is available power to enforce it.

Franklin D. Roosevelt
Address in New York City, 21 October 1944

Peace is not only better than war, but infinitely more arduous.

George Bernard Shaw

Making peace is harder than making war.

Adlai Stevenson

Sī vīs pācem, pare bellum.
[If you wish for peace, prepare for war.]

Vegetius
Dē Re Mīlītāri, Book III, 378

To be prepared for war is one of the most effectual means of preserving peace.

General George Washington
Address to Congress, 8 January 1790

Peace hath higher tests of manhood
Than battle ever knew.

John Greenleaf Whittier
The Hero, 1853

Perseverance, Determination

Never give in! Never give in! Never, never, never, never—in nothing great or small, large or petty, never give in, except to convictions of honor and good sense.

Sir Winston Churchill

We shall not flag or fail. We shall go on to the end, we shall fight in France, we shall fight in the seas and oceans, we shall fight with growing confidence and growing strength in the air, we shall defend our island, whatever the cost may be, we shall fight on the beaches, we shall fight on the landing grounds, we shall fight in the fields and in the streets, we shall fight in the hills; we shall never surrender.

Sir Winston Churchill
Speech to the House of Commons after Dunkirk,
4 June 1940

There must be a beginning of any great matter, but the continuing unto the end until it be thoroughly finished yields the true glory.

Sir Francis Drake
Dispatch to Sir Francis Walsingham, 17 May 1587

What counts is not the size of the dog in the fight, but the size of the fight in the dog.

General Dwight D. Eisenhower

No great thing is created suddenly.

Epictetus
Discourses, circa A.D. 100

To persevere, trusting in what hopes he has, is courage in a man. The coward despairs.

Euripides
Heracles, circa 422 B.C.

Victory will come to the side that outlasts the other.

Marshal Ferdinand Foch
At the Battle of the Marne, 7 September 1914

In the pursuit of excellence, there is no finish line.

Lieutenant General Robert H. Forman

Who hangs on, wins.

German proverb

I propose to fight it out on this line, if it takes all summer.

General Ulysses S. Grant
Dispatch to Washington, from Spottsylvania Courthouse,
11 May 1864

We fight, get beat, rise, and fight again.

Major General Nathanael Greene
Letter regarding the Carolina Campaign, 22 June 1781

Every position must be held to the last man: there must be no retirement. With our backs to the wall, and believing in the justice of our cause, each one of us must fight on to the end.

Field Marshal Earl Douglas Haig

I am only one, but I am one. I cannot do everything, but I can do something. What I can do, I should do and, with the help of God, I will do!

Everett Hale

A man can be destroyed but not defeated.

Ernest Hemingway
The Old Man and the Sea, 1952

'Tis a lesson you should heed:
Try, try, try again.
If at first you don't succeed,
Try, try, try again.

William Edward Hickson
Try and Try Again, circa 1850

I have not yet begun to fight.

Admiral John Paul Jones
On the USS *Bonhomme Richard*
against the HMS *Serapis,* 23 September 1779

God helps those who persevere.

Koran

Don't give up the ship.

Admiral James Lawrence
On the USS *Chesapeake,* 1 June 1813

Man in war is not beaten, and cannot be beaten, until he owns himself
beaten.

B. H. Liddell Hart
Thoughts on War, 1944

I shall return.

General Douglas MacArthur
Departing Corregidor, Philippines,
11 March 1942

I have returned.

General Douglas MacArthur
Landing at Leyte, Philippines, 20 October 1944

Tenacity of purpose and untiring energy in execution can repair a first mistake and baffle deeply laid plans.

Rear Admiral Alfred Thayer Mahan

Nuts!

Brigadier General Anthony McAuliffe
Response to German demand for surrender at Bastogne,
Battle of the Bulge, 22 December 1944

In case of doubt, push on just a little further and then keep on pushing.

General George S. Patton, Jr.

We have met the enemy, and they are ours.

Oliver Perry
Battle of Lake Erie, 10 September 1813

Perseverance, dear my lord, keeps honor bright.

William Shakespeare
Troilus and Cressida, Act III, Scene iii, 1603

Wherever public spirit prevails, liberty is secure.

Noah Webster

Do all the good you can,
In all the ways you can,
In all the places you can,
At all the times you can,
To all the people you can,
As long as ever you can.

John Wesley
Rules of Conduct, circa 1770

Physical Presence

Perhaps he had never spoken to them personally, but when the going was rough, when fear slowed them down, he had been up there with them, sharing their dangers and leading them forward. At times he asked of them the impossible, but they did it, because he did it with them.

Description of LTC Batchelder
Commander, 1st Battalion, 67th Armored Regiment,
in the *History of 67th Armored Regiment*

The successful commander in battle is at the critical place at the critical time.

General Bruce C. Clarke

The troops should be exercised frequently, cavalry as well as infantry, and the general should often be present to praise some, to criticize others, and to see with his own eyes that the orders . . . are observed exactly.

Frederick the Great
Instructions for His Generals, 1747

A divisional commander [was] in the picket line with his men and everyone confident and smiling. He was doing nothing outside showing himself, yet his presence acted like a charm—it maintained confidence. He was a man who knew the value of moral cement.

Major-General J.F.C. Fuller
Generalship: Its Diseases and Their Cure, 1936

It was an example of inflexibility in the pursuit of previously conceived ideas that is, unfortunately, too frequent in modern warfare. Final decisions are made not at the front by those who are there, but many miles away by those who can but guess at the possibilities and potentialities.

General Douglas MacArthur
Reminiscences, 1964

The front is to be seen and its conditions are to be understood only through the eyes and words of the men who fight there.

Brigadier General S.L.A. Marshall

In the rear areas the commander, high or low, wins the hearts of men primarily through a zealous interest in their general welfare. This is the true basis of his prestige and the qualifying test placed upon his soldierly abilities by those who serve under him. But at the front he commands their respect as it becomes proved to them that he understands their tactical problem and will do all possible to help them solve it.

Brigadier General S.L.A. Marshall
Men Against Fire, 1947

Squad, platoon and company commanders go first into the fire. Should the attack temporarily stall because of strong resistance, or become unhinged from severed communications, battalion and brigade commanders go posthaste to the center of the action and restore movement.

Brigadier General S.L.A. Marshall
Sinai Victory, 1966

I also think that the commander, no matter what his rank, should go to the "hot spot," to the place where judgment counts, where a true feel of the actual situation can be gained that just simply is not transmitted by telephone or radio—in fact is transmitted in no other way than through the six senses of the man who is there. How far forward this is will depend on his rank and upon the situation at the time. There is no set rule, unless the rule is that when in doubt err toward the front and not toward the rear.

Major General Aubrey "Red" Newman
Follow Me, 1981

If you want an army to fight and risk death, you've got to get up there and lead it. An army is like spaghetti. You can't push a piece of spaghetti, you've got to pull it.

General George S. Patton, Jr.

Promulgation of an order represents not over ten percent of your responsibility. The remaining ninety percent consists in assuring through personal supervision on the ground, by yourself and your staff, proper and vigorous execution.

General George S. Patton, Jr.

When the battle becomes hot, they must see their commander, know him to be near. It does not matter even if he is without initiative, incapable of giving an order. His presence creates a belief that direction exists, that orders exist, and that is enough.

Ardant du Picq
Battle Studies, 1880

I held to the old-fashioned idea that it helped the spirits of the men to see the Old Man up there, in the snow and sleet and the mud, sharing the same cold, miserable existence they had to endure.

General Matthew B. Ridgway

The job of a commander was to be up where the crisis of action was taking place. In time of battle, I wanted division commanders to be up with their forward battalions, and I wanted corps commanders up with the regiment that was in the hottest action. If they had paper work to do, they could do it at night. By day their place was up there where the shooting was going on.

General Matthew B. Ridgway
Soldier: The Memoirs of Matthew B. Ridgway, 1956

It is the basic responsibility of a field commander to anticipate where the crisis of battle will occur, and to be there when it develops. Only in this way can he see with his own eyes what is happening.

General Matthew B. Ridgway
Soldier: The Memoirs of Matthew B. Ridgway, 1956

The commander must be the prime mover of the battle and the troops must always have to reckon with his appearance in personal control.

Field Marshal Erwin Rommel

In moments of panic, fatigue, or disorganization, or when something out of the ordinary has to be demanded . . . the personal example of the commander works wonders, especially if he has the wit to create some sort of legend 'round himself.

Field Marshal Erwin Rommel

Be there, be with your soldiers. You're not the leader if you're not there at the critical point. That isn't necessarily always the fun place. Sometimes it may even be your desk, because there are promotion or court martial papers, say. The officer who'd rather go out, just to be seen by his men, violates the principle. But the thing is, you've got to find the critical point. And *be* there.

Lieutenant General Willard W. Scott, Jr.

Some men think that modern armies may be so regulated that a general can sit in an office and play his several columns as on the keys of a piano; this is a fearful mistake. The directing mind must be at the very head of the army—must be seen there, the effect of his mind and personal energy must be felt by every officer and man present with it, to secure the best results. Every attempt to make war easy and safe will result in humiliation and disaster.

General William Tecumseh Sherman

To do these things he must know perfectly the strength and quality of each part of his own Army, as well as that of his opponent, and he must be where he can personally see and observe with his own mind. No man can properly command an Army from the rear, he must be "at its front"; and when a detachment is made, the commander thereof should be informed of the object to be accomplished, and left as free as possible to execute it in his own way; and when an Army is divided up into several parts, the superior should always attend to that one which he regards as most important.

General William Tecumseh Sherman
Memoirs of General William T. Sherman, 1875

One of the most valuable qualities of a commander is a flair for putting himself in the right place at the vital time.

Field Marshal Sir William Slim
Unofficial History, 1959

One contributing factor to American reverses was the command method of most of the American commanders, who conducted their battles from a command post which they seldom left. . . . Few commanders in the higher echelons ever spent much time in personal reconnaissance, visiting troops, or inspecting dispositions. . . . Once orders are issued, a commander's primary responsibility is to insure that they are carried out, which makes personal visits of inspection imperative.

General Lucian K. Truscott, Jr.
Command Missions, 1954

What troops and subordinate commanders appreciate is that a general should be constantly in personal contact with them, and should not see everything simply through the eyes of his staff. The less time a general spends in his office and the more with his troops the better.

Field Marshal Sir Archibald P. Wavell
"Lees Knowles Lectures,"
Trinity College, Cambridge, 1939

The real reason why I succeeded in my own campaigns is because I was always on the spot.

Arthur Wellesley, Duke of Wellington

Physical Stamina

War is highly competitive; we are trying to train people to endure the hardships and strain of war and we would be doing ourselves and our country a disservice to adopt measures which would soften the fibre of men in uniform.

Admiral Robert B. Carney

Physical fitness in today's Army is even more important than it has been in the past, and this is especially true in USAREUR [United States Army, Europe] where, to meet any Communist bloc aggression, the fighting man on the ground is the "ultimate weapon"—the fundamental factor of decision.

General Bruce C. Clarke

The infantry soldier must be given long marches with full pack, up hill and down so that he can withstand the fatigue of carrying a burden, so that he can withstand exposure in cold and wet weather without getting sick, so that he can be several days without food.

Major General Ernest N. Harmon

Nations have passed away and left no traces,
And history gives the naked causes of it—
One single, simple reason in all cases;
They fell because their peoples were not fit.

Rudyard Kipling
"Land and Sea Tales for Scouts and Guides," 1923

Fatigue makes cowards of us all.

Vince Lombardi

One does acquire experience and judgment with the years, but also, unfortunately, we lose the resiliency of tendons and muscles, and leadership in the field depends to an important extent on one's legs, and stomach, and nervous system, and on one's ability to withstand hardships, and lack of sleep, and still be disposed energetically and aggressively to command men, to dominate men on the battlefield. We may have the wisdom of the years, but we lack, I know I do in many respects, the physical ruggedness of more youthful days.

General George C. Marshall
Selected Speeches and Statements of General of the Army
George C. Marshall, edited by Major H. A. DeWeerd, 1945

You have to lead men in war by requiring more from the individual than he thinks he can do. You have to lead men in war by bringing them along to endure and to display qualities of fortitude that are beyond the average man's thought of what he should be expected to do. You have to inspire them when they are hungry and exhausted and desperately uncomfortable and in great danger; and only a man of positive characteristics of leadership, with the physical stamina that goes with it, can function under those conditions.

General George C. Marshall
Ordeal and Hope, 1963

Fatigue will beat men down as quickly as any other condition, for fatigue brings fear with it. There is no quicker way to lose a battle than to lose it on the road for lack of adequate preliminary hardening in troops.

Brigadier General S.L.A. Marshall
Men Against Fire, 1947

Work hard to keep fit. That little extra stamina may some day pull you out of some deep holes.

General Matthew B. Ridgway
Military Review, "Leadership," October 1966

I wish to preach, not the doctrine of ignoble ease, but the doctrine of the strenuous life.

Theodore Roosevelt

Continual exercise makes good soldiers because it qualifies them for military duties; by being habituated to pain, they insensibly learn to despise danger. The transition from fatigue to rest enervates them.

Marshal Comte de Maurice Saxe
Mes Rêveries, 1732

What can a soldier do who charges when out of breath?

Vegetius
Dē Re Mīlitāri, 378

Praise

Help people to reach their full potential—catch them doing something right.

Anonymous

We protest against unjust criticism, but we accept unearned praise.

Anonymous

In the arena of human life the honours and rewards fall to those who show their good qualities in action.

Aristotle
Nicomachean Ethics, circa 340 B.C.

You must get around and show interest in what your subordinates are doing even if you don't know much about the technique of their work. And when you are making these visits, try to pass out praise when due, as well as corrections or criticisms.

General Omar N. Bradley
Speech to U.S. Army Command and General Staff College,
16 May 1967

We are all motivated by a keen desire for praise, and the better a man is, the more he is inspired by glory.

Marcus Tullius Cicero
Pro Archĭa, 62 B.C.

Humility must always be the portion of any man who receives acclaim earned in the blood of his followers and the sacrifices of his friends.

General Dwight D. Eisenhower
Address in London, 12 June 1945

Hereafter, if you should observe an occasion to give your officers and friends a little more praise than is their due, and confess more fault than you can justly be charged with, you will only become the sooner for it, a great captain. Criticizing and censuring almost everyone you have to do with will diminish friends, increase enemies, and thereby hurt your affairs.

Benjamin Franklin
Letter to John Paul Jones, 1780

Praise makes good men better and bad men worse.

Thomas Fuller
Gnomologia, 1732

A nation reveals itself not only by the men it produces but also by the men it honors, the men it remembers.

John F. Kennedy
Address at Amherst College, 26 October 1963

People ask you for criticism, but they only want praise.

William Somerset Maugham
Of Human Bondage, 1915

The art of war is the most difficult of all arts; therefore military glory is universally considered the highest, and the services of warriors are rewarded by a sensible government in a splendid manner and above all other services.

Napoleon Bonaparte

Show me a republic, ancient or modern, in which there have been no decorations. Some people call them baubles. Well, it is by such baubles that one leads men.

Napoleon Bonaparte
Remark made on establishing the French
Legion of Honor, 19 May 1802

In command and leadership many qualities, attributes and techniques are required—including drive, force, judgment, perception and others. But nothing can replace the inspiration and lift that comes from commending a job well done.

Major General Aubrey "Red" Newman
Follow Me, 1981

All a soldier desires to drive him forward is recognition and appreciation of his work.

General George S. Patton, Jr.

Millions for defense but not one cent for tribute.

Charles C. Pinckney, 1796
(Also attributed to Robert G. Harper,
toast at a dinner for John Marshall, 18 June 1798)

Glory ought to be the consequence, not the motive of our actions.

Pliny the Younger
Letters, circa A.D. 100

The desire to imitate brave actions will be aroused by praise. And these trifles will diffuse a spirit of emulation among the troops which affects both officers and soldiers and in time will make them invincible.

Marshal Comte de Maurice Saxe
Mes Rêveries, 1732

You can tell the character of every man when you see how he receives praise.

Seneca
Epistles, circa first century A.D.

Mankind are tolerant of the praises of others so long as each hearer thinks he can do as well or nearly well himself.

Thucydides
History of the Peloponnesian War, circa 404 B.C.

Pride

There are two sorts of pride: one in which we approve ourselves, the other in which we cannot accept ourselves.

Henri-Frédéric Amiel
Journal, 27 October 1853

It's temper that gets most of us in trouble and pride that keeps us there.

Anonymous

Pride *goeth* before destruction, and an haughty spirit before a fall.

Bible, Proverbs 16:18

The army can pride itself on its ability to produce superior units with the ordinary run of manpower.

General Bruce C. Clarke

Though pride is not a virtue, it is the parent of many virtues.

John Churton Collins

The important thing in any organization is the creation of a soul which is based on pride.

General George S. Patton, Jr.

There is but a step between a proud man's glory and his disgrace.

Publilius Syrus
Moral Sayings, circa first century B.C.

It is as proper to have pride in oneself as it is ridiculous to show it to others.

François, Duc de La Rochefoucauld
Maximes, 1665

The soldiers of each century should make it an article of faith never to abandon their standard. It should be sacred to them; it should be respected; and every type of ceremony should be used to make them respected and precious. This is an essential point, for after troops are attached to them you can count on all sorts of successes; resolution and courage will be the natural consequences of it; and if, in desperate affairs, some determined man seizes a standard, he will render the whole century as brave as himself because it will follow him.

Marshal Comte de Maurice Saxe
Mes Rêveries, 1732

We found it a great mistake to belittle the importance of smartness in turn-out, alertness of carriage, cleanliness of person, saluting, or precision of movement, and to dismiss them as naive, unintelligent, parade-ground stuff. I do not believe that troops can have unshakable battle discipline without showing those outward and formal signs which mark the pride men take in themselves and their units and the mutual confidence and respect that exists between them and their officers.

Field Marshal Sir William Slim
Defeat into Victory, 1961

Their military pride promises much, for the first step to make a good soldier is to entertain a consciousness of personal superiority.

Report of General Anthony Wayne's Pennsylvania Line,
1781

Problem Solving

Doing easily what others find difficult is talent; doing what is impossible *for talent* is genius.

Henri-Frédéric Amiel
Journal, 17 December 1856

Any fault recognized is half corrected.

Anonymous

When things go wrong in your command, start searching for the reason in increasingly larger concentric circles around your own desk.

General Bruce C. Clarke

You have to go after the facts; they won't come to your office.

General Bruce C. Clarke

If a division commander did not have problems to solve, his rank would be much lower than that of Major General.

General Bruce C. Clarke

An organization does well only those things the boss checks.

General Bruce C. Clarke

Learn to be a good and competent inspector. Those things not inspected are neglected.

General Bruce C. Clarke

At the lower levels of command, the wise commander finds out for himself by talking to the troops, by frequently looking into all parts of his organization—the mess (I refuse to call it a dining facility), motor pool, barracks, staff sections, supply points—on an unannounced, unscheduled and varied routine.

Lieutenant General Edward M. Flanagan, Jr.

I must have assistants who will solve their own problems and tell me later what they have done.

General George C. Marshall
To General Dwight D. Eisenhower

Reflection

When eating an elephant, take one bite at a time.

General Creighton W. Abrams

Slow and steady wins the race.

Aesop
The Hare and the Tortoise, sixth century B.C.

The longest distance between two points is a short-cut.

Anonymous

Sit on the bank of a river and wait; your enemy's corpse will soon float by.

Anonymous

A job done right is too seldom complimented but it is never criticized.

General Bruce C. Clarke

Learning without thought is labor lost; thought without learning is perilous.

Confucius
Analects, circa 500 B.C.

What is the good of experience if you do not reflect?

Frederick the Great

Generalship, at least in my case, came not by instinct, unsought, but by understanding, hard study and brain concentration. Had it come easily to me, I should not have done it as well.

Thomas E. Lawrence
Letter to B. H. Liddell Hart, 1932

A good soldier, whether he leads a platoon or an army, is expected to look backward as well as forward, but he must think only forward.

General Douglas MacArthur

Nowhere can man find a quieter or more untroubled retreat than in his own soul.

Marcus Aurelius Antoninus

Be nice to people on your way up because you'll need them on your way down.

Wilson Mizner

Respect

World War II had taught me one important lesson in leadership: the most valuable soldier was one who was well informed, encouraged to use his head, and treated with respect.

> General Omar N. Bradley
> *A General's Life,* 1983

Prestige of an officer and a noncommissioned officer must be earned—it does not come with your commission or warrant.

> General Bruce C. Clarke

Respect yourself and others will respect you.

> Confucius
> *Analects,* circa 500 B.C.

If I can get them with the preservation of my own honor and fidelity and self-respect, show me the way and I will get them; but if you require me to lose my own proper good, that you may gain what is no good, consider how unreasonable and foolish you are.

> Epictetus
> *Enchiridion,* circa A.D. 100

If you treat a man as he is, he will remain as he is; if you treat him as if he were what he could be, he will become what he could be.

> Johann Wolfgang von Goethe

If you once forfeit the confidence of your fellow citizens, you can never regain their respect and esteem. It is true that you may fool all the people some of the time; you can even fool some of the people all the time; but you can't fool all the people all the time.

Abraham Lincoln
Quoted in Alexander K. McClure's
Lincoln's Yarns and Stories, 1904

All the regulations and gold braid in the Pacific Fleet cannot enforce a sailor's devotion. This, each officer in command must earn on his own.

Lieutenant Commander Arnold S. Lott
Brave Ship, Brave Men, 1965

No leader will ever fail his troops (nor will they fail him) who leads them in respect for the disciplined life.

Brigadier General S.L.A. Marshall
Men Against Fire, 1947

The fundamental cause of any breakdown of morale and discipline within the Armed Forces usually comes of this—that a commander or his subordinates transgress by treating men as if they were children or serfs instead of showing respect for their adulthood.

Brigadier General S.L.A. Marshall
The Armed Forces Officer, 1950

While men may be rallied for a short space by someone setting an example of great courage, they can be kept in line under conditions of increasing stress and mounting hardship only when loyalty is based upon a respect which the commander has won by consistently thoughtful regard for the welfare and rights of his people, and a correct measuring of his responsibility to them.

Brigadier General S.L.A. Marshall
The Armed Forces Officer, 1950

You've got to set a good example, too. You can't just talk a good line. You can fool your seniors and peers sometimes, but you can't fool the subordinates. There are a thousand little things that only the men are going to see. After six months, they know you—they'll either respect you and do anything for you, or they'll just tolerate you.

Lieutenant General James H. Merryman

Professional courtesy and good manners should be carefully integrated parts of your command and leadership principles, both up and down.

Major General Aubrey "Red" Newman
Follow Me, 1981

Most men, of whatever race, creed, or color, want to do the proper thing and they respect the man above them whose motive is the same.

General of the Armies John J. Pershing

The one mode or the other of dealing with subordinates springs from a corresponding spirit in the breast of the commander. He who feels the respect which is due to others cannot fail to inspire in them regard for himself, while he who feels, and hence manifests, disrespect towards others, especially his inferiors, cannot fail to inspire hatred against himself.

Major General John M. Schofield

There is a soul to an army as well as to the individual man, and no general can accomplish the full work of his army unless he commands the soul of his men as well as their bodies and legs.

General William Tecumseh Sherman
Personal Memoirs, 1875

Because [a good] general regards his men as infants they will march with him into the deepest valleys. He treats them as his own beloved sons and they will die with him.

Sun-Tzu
The Art of War, circa fourth century B.C.

Every great soldier has succeeded in convincing his men that he knows and respects them as individuals. To accomplish this end he goes among his men freely, mingling with them and giving the soldiers a chance to look him over and size him up. An officer who barricades himself behind his rank is properly suspected of having weaknesses to conceal—probably more than he actually has.

General Maxwell D. Taylor
Speech to Citadel cadets, 21 January 1956

In rear areas the commander, high or low, wins the hearts of men primarily through a zealous interest in their general welfare. This is the true basis of his prestige and the qualifying test placed upon his soldierly abilities by those who serve under him. But at the front he commands their respect as it becomes proved to them that he understands their tactical problem and will do all possible to help them solve it.

General Lucian K. Truscott, Jr.

- You cannot expect a soldier to be proud if you humiliate him.
- You cannot expect him to be brave if you abuse and cower him.
- You cannot expect him to be strong if you break him.
- You cannot ask for respect and obedience and willingness to assault hot LZs, hump back-breaking ridges, destroy dug-in emplacements if your soldier has not been treated with the respect and dignity which fosters unit esprit and personal pride.

Major General Melvin Zais, 1969

Responsibility

When things look good I pat the sergeants and soldiers on the back, but when somebody's arm needs twisting, I look around for the senior officer present. To get things bucked up, I work on the top.

Anonymous general

Soldiers are much like children. You must see that they have shelter, food, and clothing, the best that your utmost efforts can provide. You must be far more solicitous of their comfort than of your own. You must see that they have food to eat before you think of your own; that they have each as good a bed as can be provided before you consider where you will sleep. You must look after their health. You must conserve their strength by not demanding needless exertion or useless labor.

Major C. A. Bach
"Know Your Men—Know Your Business—Know Yourself,"
Address to new officers, 1917

For everyone to whom much is given, from him much will be required; to whom much has been committed, of him they will ask the more.

Bible, Luke 12:48

Fairness, diligence, sound preparation, professional skill and loyalty are the marks of American military leadership. Upon every young officer rests the responsibility for giving the American soldier the inspired leadership that he deserves.

General Omar N. Bradley

Each commander must always assume total responsibility for every individual in his command. If the battalion or regimental commanders fail him in the attack, then he must relieve them or be relieved himself.

General Omar N. Bradley
A Soldier's Story, 1951

Modern leadership demands officers who can accept challenge with initiative, originality, fidelity, understanding, and, above all, the willingness to assume the responsibilities of command.

General Bruce C. Clarke

The lower down the chain of command men's problems are adequately handled, the better units and Army we will have.

General Bruce C. Clarke

The now-extinct Gilly Loo bird flew backwards because he was more interested in where he had been than in where he was going. The next war will not be won by Gilly Loo birds in places of responsibility.

General Bruce C. Clarke

All commanders have the basic responsibility to insure that those they are privileged to lead received realistic training to qualify them technically, and to assure that they are well grounded in the fundamentals of leadership, discipline, and soldiering. We must help them to become true professionals! Commanders will enhance the personal pride and professionalism of their subordinates by placing greater responsibilities, authorities, trust, and confidence in them. They will make some mistakes initially and some of our statistics will suffer. We may reduce a few statistics which are being highlighted for the moment by bypassing the chain of command, but we pay a big price in a unit's effectiveness for its future missions.

General Bruce C. Clarke

The first moral obligation of any officer is to ensure that his conduct and that of his superiors is basically consonant with the values of the society and the constitution that he has sworn to uphold together with the moral constraints of the military system.

Richard A. Gabriel

Responsibility is the test of a man's courage.
                    Lord Admiral John Jervis, Earl of St. Vincent

It is a paramount and over-riding responsibility of every officer to take care of his men before caring for himself.
                    Brigadier General S.L.A. Marshall
                    The Armed Forces Officer, 1950

But every good soldier in authority should be just as concerned with his responsibility to help those under him make the right turns.
                    Major General Aubrey "Red" Newman
                    Follow Me, 1981

Man must cease attributing his problems to his environment, and learn again to exercise his will—his personal responsibility in the realm of faith and morals.

                    Albert Schweitzer

If responsibility—and particularly accountability—is most obviously upwards, moral responsibility also reaches downwards. The commander has a responsibility to those whom he commands. To forget this is to vitiate personal integrity and the ethical validity of the system.
                    Roger L. Shinn
                    Military Ethics, 1987

I tell you, as officers, that you will not eat, sleep, smoke, sit down, or lie down until your soldiers have had a chance to do these things. If you do this, they will follow you to the ends of the earth. If you do not, I will *break you in front of your regiments.*
                    Field Marshal Sir William Slim

The buck stops here.

                    Harry S. Truman
                    Sign on his desk

In a time of complexity and relative austerity, commanders must make definite, clear choices regarding priorities, and then they must support the priorities with more than words.

Major General Walter F. Ulmer, Jr.
Military Review,
"Notes on Leadership for the 1980s," July 1980

Few things help an individual more than to place responsibility upon him, and to let him know that you trust him.

Booker T. Washington

I feel the responsibility of the occasion. Responsibility is proportionate to opportunity.

Woodrow Wilson

Risk

If you never stick your neck out, you'll never get your head above the crowd.

Anonymous

We had taken a calculated risk. . . . Time has not altered that opinion. I would rather be bold than wary even though wariness may sometimes be right.

General Omar N. Bradley
A Soldier's Story, 1951

A vaincre sans peril, on triumphe sans gloire.
[When there is no peril in the fight, there is no glory in the triumph.]

Pierre Corneille
Le Cid, 1636

One does not send soldiers into battles telling them there is no risk. That is a fraud.

Jean Dutourd
Taxis of the Marne, 1957

Qui ne risque rien, n'a rien.
[He who risks nothing gets nothing.]

French proverb

Every mistake in war is excusable except inactivity and refusal to take risks.

Holloway H. Frost

Better hazard once than always be in fear.

Thomas Fuller
Gnomologia, 1732

Great deeds are usually wrought at great risks.

Herodotus
Histories, Book VII, circa 444 B.C.

He who will not risk cannot win.

Admiral John Paul Jones

It is true I must run great risk; no gallant action was ever accomplished without danger.

Admiral John Paul Jones
Letter to American commissioners in Paris, 1778

The habit of gambling contrary to reasonable calculations is a military vice which, as the pages of history reveal, has ruined more armies than any other cause.

B. H. Liddell Hart
Thoughts on War, 1944

He that leaves nothing to chance will do few things ill, but he will do very few things.

Marquess of Halifax

We need leaders who are grounded in the principles of command, yet who are responsive to new ideas; who have not only the flexibility to cope with and direct change, but the audacity to take the measured risk in order to gain victory on the battlefield.

John O. Marsh, Jr.

Troops expect to see their officers working and moving with them; morale is impaired when they see that their leaders are shirking danger. But they do not care to see them play the part of a mechanical rabbit darting to the front so as to tease the hounds. In extreme emergencies, when the stakes are high and the failure of others to act has made the need imperative, such acts are warranted. But their value lies largely in their novelty. A commander cannot rally his men by a spectacular intervention in the hour when they have lost their grip if they have grown accustomed to seeing him run unnecessary risks in the average circumstances of battle.

Brigadier General S.L.A. Marshall
Men Against Fire, 1947

True decision, by its nature, in combat and elsewhere consists in determining a line of action when choices are equally difficult. All war is a gamble. Its chief prizes fall only to the player who, weighing the odds carefully when he moves from situation to situation, will not hesitate to plunge when he feels by instinct that his hour has arrived.

Brigadier General S.L.A. Marshall
The Armed Forces Officer, 1950

War is risk. Either its ends permit of honest differences of opinion about what should best be done, or operations long since would have become an exact science and general staff work would be as routine as logarithms.

Brigadier General S.L.A. Marshall
Quoted in New York Times, 24 October 1954

First reckon, then risk.

Field Marshal Count Helmuth von Moltke

If the art of war consisted merely in not taking risks glory would be at the mercy of very mediocre talent.

Napoleon Bonaparte

Take calculated risks. That is quite different from being rash.

General George S. Patton, Jr.
Letter to his son, 6 June 1944

Far better it is to dare mighty things, to win glorious triumphs, even though checkered by failure, than to take rank with those poor spirits who neither enjoy much nor suffer much, because they live in the gray twilight that knows not victory nor defeat.

Theodore Roosevelt
Speech at Hamilton Club, Chicago, 10 April 1899

Any fool can keep a rule. God gave him a brain to know when to break the rule.

Lieutenant General Willard W. Scott, Jr.

Role Modeling,
Leadership by Example

A teacher affects eternity; he can never tell where his influence stops.

Henry B. Adams
The Education of Henry Adams, 1907

But be thou an example of the believers, in word, in conversation, in charity, in spirit, in faith, in purity.

Bible, I Timothy 4:12

As I would deserve and keep the kindness of this army, I must let them see that when I expose them, I would not exempt myself.

John Churchill, Duke of Marlborough

[The superior man] acts before he speaks, and afterwards speaks according to his actions.

Confucius
Analects, circa 500 B.C.

Example is the best General Order.

Major General George Crook

Goddamn it, you'll never get the Purple Heart hiding in a foxhole! Follow me!

Lieutenant Colonel Henry P. Crowe
Battle of Guadalcanal, 13 January 1943

As I do, so shall ye do.

Gideon
Judges 7:17, circa 1249 B.C.

Lives of great men all remind us
We can make our lives sublime,
And, departing, leave behind us
Footprints on the sands of time.

Henry Wadsworth Longfellow
A Psalm of Life, 1839

Saying is one thing and doing is another.

Michel Eyquem de Montaigne
Essays, 1580

Be an example to your men, both in your duty and in private life. Never spare yourself, and let the troops see that you don't, in your endurance of fatigue and privation. Always be tactful and well mannered and teach your subordinates to be the same. Avoid excessive sharpness or harshness of voice, which usually indicates the man who has shortcomings of his own to hide.

Field Marshal Erwin Rommel
Speech to graduating cadets, 1938

For it is often easier to fight for principles than to live up to them.

Adlai Stevenson
Speech at New York City, 27 August 1952

The need of human understanding can be summed up by saying that it is the exercise of common sense in human relations. There are times to be stern; there are times to be lenient. There are times to be exacting; there are times to be tolerant. This feeling for the right course to be taken with men is instinctive in some officers and lacking in others, but it can be cultivated and developed by all. In this connection I advise that junior officers should observe the behavior of respected senior officers, especially those who are obviously successful with soldiers. Thus, by emulation many will in due time become models themselves.

General Maxwell D. Taylor
The Field Artillery Journal, January/February 1947

The higher in rank you go . . . the more people look to you to set examples.

General John A. Wickham, Jr.

Nothing is impossible for the man who does not have to do it himself.

Earl Wilson

The only way an officer can demonstrate his leadership qualities is through personal example. . . . I for one have never believed that you should ask any person to do anything that you wouldn't do yourself.

General Louis H. Wilson
Quoted in Karel Montor et al.,
Naval Leadership: Voices of Experience, 1987

The type of leader who is the martinet can have a very efficient ship, but it may lack that special esprit that makes the ship come through against all odds. Time and time again as I came along, there were examples of squadrons in which the ship led by the martinet did not make out quite as well in individual battle efficiency competition as did the ship that was led by someone who led by example.

Admiral Elmo R. Zumwalt, Jr.
Quoted in Karel Montor et al.,
Naval Leadership: Voices of Experience, 1987

Safety

A feeling of safety kills ambition.

Henry Ford

Military service is a very dangerous profession, and safety cannot be guaranteed. . . . First, the unit must know the rules for safety—how to do things properly; second, the unit must train and practice those rules; and third, there must be a discipline in the command of that unit so that individuals will carry out the safety provisions that they understand and have trained in. The third factor is sometimes overlooked, but it is the most important of the three.

Admiral James L. Holloway III
Quoted in Karel Montor et al.,
Naval Leadership: Voices of Experience, 1987

They should be made to understand that discipline contributes no less to their safety than to their efficiency. . . . Let officers and men be made to feel that they will most effectively secure their safety by remaining steadily at their posts, preserving order, and fighting with coolness and vigor.

General Robert E. Lee
Directive to his troops, 1865

In difficult situations when hope seems feeble, the boldest plans are safest.

Livy
Ab Urbe Condita, circa 29 B.C.

In audacity and obstinacy will be found safety.

Napoleon Bonaparte
Maxims, XV, 1831

The principle is this: no safety check can ever be routine, no matter how often performed, when the lives of men are involved. It is an insidious temptation to slight checks on regulations when things have been going safely for days—but this is the danger, because it dulls alertness.

Major General Aubrey "Red" Newman
Follow Me, 1981

Out of this nettle, danger, we pluck this flower, safety.

William Shakespeare
Henry IV, Act I, Scene ii, 1598

The desire for safety stands against every great desire and noble enterprise.

Tacitus
Annals, circa A.D. 90

For they had learned that true safety was to be found in long previous training, and not in eloquent exhortations uttered when they were going into action.

Thucydides
History of the Peloponnesian War, circa 404 B.C.

Don't play for safety. It's the most dangerous thing in the world.

Hugh Walpole

Discipline apart, the soldier's chief cares are, first, his personal comfort, i.e., regular rations, proper clothing, good billets, and proper hospital arrangements (square meals and a square deal in fact); and secondly, his personal safety, i.e., that he shall be put into a fight with as good a chance as possible for victory and survival.

Field Marshal Sir Archibald P. Wavell

Second-, Third-Order Effects

Well, Mr. Secretary, it's kind of like an aircraft carrier. You fellas up here on the bridge are giving commands of left rudder, right rudder, full ahead. The wind's blowing in your face and you're feeling full of yourself, but all that's really happening is that us poor folks in the hold are getting seasick.

General Creighton W. Abrams

How great a matter a little fire kindleth!

Bible, James 3:5

In war trivial causes produce momentous events.

Julius Caesar
De Bello Gallico, 51 B.C.

When administration and orders are inconsistent, the men's spirits are low, and the officers exceedingly angry.

Chang Yu

When the general lays on unnecessary projects, everyone is fatigued.

Ch'ên Hao

Shallow men believe in luck. . . . Strong men believe in cause and effect.

Ralph Waldo Emerson
The Conduct of Life, "Worship," 1860

A bad beginning makes a bad ending.

Euripides

Laziness of mind leads to indiscipline, just as does insubordination.

Marshal Ferdinand Foch
Precepts, 1919

"Good morning; good morning!" the General said
When we met him last week on our way to the line.
Now the soldiers he smiled at are most of 'em dead,
And we're cursing his staff for incompetent swine.
"He's a cheery old card," grunted Harry to Jack
As they slugged up to Aras with rifle and pack.

But he did for them both with his plan of attack!

Siegfried Sassoon
"The General," 1917

Service

For many are called, but few *are* chosen.

Bible, Matthew 22:14

In preparing for a lifetime of service, our professionally trained military graduates must train not only for leadership in battle, but also to provide leadership for the Nation in adapting the resources of science and education to our national needs.

General Omar N. Bradley

Rank is only given you in the Army to enable you to better serve those below you and those above you. Rank is not given for you to exercise your idiosyncrasies.

General Bruce C. Clarke
Thoughts on Leadership, n.d.

The army is the people in uniform.

Benjamin Constant

The nation which forgets its defenders will itself be forgotten.

Calvin Coolidge
27 July 1920

You can only govern men by serving them. The rule is without exception.

Victor Cousin

The reward of a thing well done is to have done it.
Ralph Waldo Emerson
Essays: Second Series, "Realist," 1844

Die Tat ist alles, nichts der Ruhm.
[The deed is all, and not the glory.]
Johann Wolfgang von Goethe
Hochebirg, 1832

You have not done enough, you have never done enough, so long as it is still possible that you have something to contribute.
Dag Hammarskjöld

The noblest service comes from nameless hands,
And the best servant does his work unseen.
Oliver Wendell Holmes, Sr.
The Poet at the Breakfast Table, 1872

He serves me most, who serves his country best.
Homer
The Iliäd, Book X, circa 700 B.C.

All I am and all I have is at the service of my country.
General Thomas J. "Stonewall" Jackson
1861

What you have chosen to do for your country by devoting your life to the service of your country is the greatest contribution that any man could make.
John F. Kennedy
Address to graduating class, U.S. Naval Academy,
6 June 1961

An important part of our chances for success in any undertaking in the future depends upon the soundness of the actions which we take in the present.
General Lyman L. Lemnitzer

In a free country like our own . . . every male brought into existence should be taught from infancy that the military service of the Republic carries with it honor and distinction, and his very life should be permeated with the ideal that even death itself may become a boon when a man dies that a nation may live and fulfill its destiny.

General Douglas MacArthur

Private feelings must always be sacrificed for the public service.

Frederick Marryat
Peter Simple, 1834

Great faith, rightness of mind, influence over other people, and finally, personal success and satisfaction come of service to the ideals of the profession.

Brigadier General S.L.A. Marshall
The Armed Forces Officer, 1950

It is very difficult for a nation to create an army when it has not already a body of officers and non-commissioned officers to serve as a nucleus, and a system of military organization.

Napoleon Bonaparte
Maxims, LVII, 1831

One should encourage soldiers by all possible means to remain with the colors; this will be easily attained by showing great consideration to old soldiers. Pay should also be increased for length of service; because it is a great injustice not to pay the veteran more than the recruit.

Napoleon Bonaparte
Maxims, LX, 1831

Second to honesty and courage of purpose, I would place an unselfish attitude as the greatest attribute of a leader. . . . Place the care and protection of the men first; share their hardships without complaint and when the real test comes you will find that they possess a genuine respect and admiration for you. To do otherwise means failure at the crucial moment when the support of your men is essential to the success of the battle.

General Alexander M. Patch

Men grow only in proportion to the service they render their fellow men and women.

Captain Edward V. Rickenbacker
Rickenbacker, 1967

To some generations much is given. Of others much is expected. This generation of Americans has a rendezvous with destiny.

Franklin D. Roosevelt
Presidential nomination acceptance speech, 1936

The first requisite of a good citizen in this republic of ours is that he shall be able and willing to pull his weight.

Theodore Roosevelt
Address at New York City, 11 November 1902

Far and away the best prize that life offers is the chance to work hard at work worth doing.

Theodore Roosevelt
Labor Day address in Syracuse, New York, 1903

There is no higher religion than human service. To work for the common good is the greatest creed.

Albert Schweitzer

The general who advances without coveting fame and retreats without fearing disgrace, whose only thought is to protect his country and do good service for his sovereign, is the jewel of the kingdom.

Sun-Tzu
The Art of War, circa fourth century B.C.

The badge of rank which an officer wears on his coat is really a symbol of servitude to his men.

General Maxwell D. Taylor
The Field Artillery Journal, January/February 1947

Whoever serves his country well has no need of ancestors.

Voltaire
Mérope, 1743

There is something better, if possible, that a man can give his life. That is his living spirit to a service that is not easy, to resist counsels that are hard to resist, to stand against purposes that are difficult to stand against.

Woodrow Wilson
30 May 1919

The Soldier

Old soldiers never die;
They simply fade away.

Anonymous
(British soldiers' song
popular in World War I)

Modern weapons have not altered this country's primary reliance on ground forces in case of war.

Wilbur M. Brucker

I believe the Army is an indispensable component of our national security. Nothing has occurred on the world scene that diminishes the fundamental role of land forces.

Wilbur M. Brucker

When a staff officer does not understand soldiers and does not understand the environment of the battlefield, he can be very dangerous to the troops.

General Bruce C. Clarke

The time to start reenlisting a good man is when he first joins your unit.

General Bruce C. Clarke

The most precious commodity with which the Army deals is the individual soldier who is the heart and soul of our combat forces.

General J. Lawton Collins

Men, they are the first and best instruments of war.

General Mikhail Ivanovich Dragomirov

Technical means of mutual annihilation have focused world attention away from the one incalculable secret weapon—man. In our haste to achieve weapons superiority over our potential enemy, there is a constant danger that we may overlook the ability of small groups of determined men to decide great issues by bold exploit.

Major Burton F. Hood

Every citizen should be a soldier. This was the case with the Greeks and the Romans, and must be that of every free state.

Thomas Jefferson
Letter to U.S. President James Monroe, 1813

Arms alone are not enough to keep the peace. It must be kept by men.

John F. Kennedy
State of the Union Message, January 1963

A soldier has a hard life, and but little consideration.

General Robert E. Lee

For who ought to be more faithful than a man that is entrusted with the safety of his country, and has sworn to defend it to the last drop of his blood? Who ought to be fonder of peace than those that suffer by nothing but war?

Niccolò di Bernardo Machiavelli
Arte Della Guèrra, 1520

Contrary to the general opinion, the sinews of war are not gold, but good soldiers; for gold alone will not produce good soldiers, but good soldiers will always procure gold.

Niccolò di Bernardo Machiavelli
Discorsi, 1531

No human being knows how sweet sleep is but a soldier.
                                        Colonel John S. Mosby

Man, not men, is the most important consideration.
                                        Napoleon Bonaparte

Soldiers generally win battles; generals generally get credit for them.
                                        Napoleon Bonaparte
                        To General Gaspard Gouraud, St. Helena, 1815

    The muffled drum's sad roll has beat
        The soldier's last tattoo;
    No more on life's parade shall meet
        That brave and fallen few.

    On Fame's eternal camping ground
        Their silent tents are spread,
    And glory guards, with solemn round,
        The bivouac of the dead.
                                        Theodore O'Hara
                                "The Bivouac of the Dead," 1847
                                (Commemorating the American dead
                                    at the Battle of Buena Vista, 1847)
                                (Required by nineteenth century congressional act
                                    to be displayed in every national cemetery)

Man is the foremost instrument of combat.
                                        Ardant du Picq
                                        Battle Studies, 1880

And is there anything more important than that the work of the soldier
should be well done?
                                        Plato

I do, however, believe that it is vitally important to remember that
wars are won by the achievement of domination over human beings,
and the territory they inhabit, and that only land forces can achieve
and maintain such domination.
                                        General Matthew B. Ridgway

An Army needs more than weapons. It needs the bold and competent leadership of men who are proud of their profession. It must have sufficient numbers of trained, courageous men. For in the last analysis, man is the only ultimate weapon, and upon his determination, his courage, his stamina, and his skill, rests the issue of victory or defeat.

General Matthew B. Ridgway
Soldier: The Memoirs of Matthew B. Ridgway, 1956

Therefore, the more we improve the fire-arm the more will be the necessity for good organization, good discipline and intelligence on the part of the individual soldier and officer.

General William Tecumseh Sherman

Ours is an Army that looks to the resourcefulness and brains of the individual American soldier to counter the threat of a potential enemy whose great advantage lies in abundant manpower and a ruthless control over that manpower.

Robert T. Stevens

I know of no startling advances or marvelous breakthroughs on the keystone of our national security—our superb American fighting man. He must still push forward against any odds; he must still help to keep the peace or win success in battle through his own courage, skill, experience, resourcefulness, and fighting heart, but we must use him more effectively with all the resources at our command if he has to fight.

Lieutenant General Arthur G. Trudeau

Military men are not imperialists. They are not war mongers or savage killers. They are profound lovers of peace who believe that it can be obtained and maintained through an efficient military organization.

General Jonathan M. Wainwright
Hero of Bataan, 1981

What are the qualities of the good soldier, by the development of which we make the man war-worthy? . . . The following four—in whatever order you place them—pretty well cover the field: discipline, physical fitness, technical skill in the use of his weapons, battle-craft.

Field Marshal Sir Archibald P. Wavell

Standards

We must live by standards, and when a nation, society, or organization lowers its standards or output, it eventually fails, because others can do it better or cheaper as a result of their maintaining standards.

Admiral Arleigh A. Burke
Quoted in Karel Montor et al.,
Naval Leadership: Voices of Experience, 1987

You owe it to your men to require standards which are for their benefit even though they may not be popular at the moment.

General Bruce C. Clarke

Standards must be established and maintained in the most routine matters. Shaving, cleanliness, police of areas, and care of weapons may appear to be of minor importance, but laxness in these and other routine matters invariably leads to a breakdown in control and discipline. . . . Maintaining high standards requires persistent correction. In units that are weak or have problems, close scrutiny will usually show that the chain of command has lost the art of correcting the soldier.

Lieutenant General Arthur S. Collins, Jr.
Common Sense Training, 1978

The superior man is easy to serve and difficult to please.

Confucius
Analects, circa 500 B.C.

Never for an instant can you divest yourselves of the fact that you are officers. On the athletic field, at the club, in civilian clothes, or even at home on leave, the fact that you are a commissioned officer in the Army imposes a constant obligation to higher standards than might ordinarily seem normal or necessary for your personal guidance.

General George C. Marshall
Selected Speeches and Statements of General of the Army George C. Marshall, edited by Major H. A. DeWeerd, 1945

A military career cannot be fashioned in battle or on drill fields alone, but must meet the standards expected of soldiers wherever they go.

Major General Aubrey "Red" Newman
Follow Me, 1981

A commander must accustom his staff to a high tempo from the outset, and continuously keep them to it. If he once allows himself to be satisfied with norms, or anything less than an all-out effort, he gives up the race from the starting post, and will sooner or later be taught a bitter lesson.

Field Marshal Erwin Rommel

There may be justification, or even a definite need, to restate in strong and clear terms those principles of conduct which retain an unchallengeable relevance to the necessity of the. military profession and to which the officer corps will be expected to conform regardless of behavioral practices elsewhere.

General Maxwell D. Taylor

Stress

There are some instances when a man acts improperly under a strain greater than human nature can bear and which no one could endure. Yet, there are perhaps also acts which no man could possibly be compelled to do, but rather than to do them he would accept the most terrible suffering and death.

Aristotle
Nicomachean Ethics, circa 340 B.C.

Nobody knows what is in him until he tries to pull it out. If there's nothing, or very little, the shock can kill a man.

Ernest Hemingway

The military way is a long, hard road, and it makes extraordinary requirements of every individual. In war, particularly, it puts stresses upon men such as they have not known elsewhere, and the temptation to "get out from under" would be irresistible if their spirits had not been tempered to the ordeal.

Brigadier General S.L.A. Marshall
The Armed Forces Officer, 1950

The ultimate test of military training and of the military discipline that results therefrom is the capacity of troops to suffer losses without being turned aside from the task before them.

Major James W. McAndrew
The Infantry Journal Reader, November/December 1913

The first qualification of a general-in-chief is to possess a cool head, so that things may appear to him in their true proportions and as they really are. He should not suffer himself to be unduly affected by good or bad news.

There are some men who, from their physical and moral constitution, deck everything in the colors of imagination. With whatever knowledge, talents, courage or other good qualities these may be endowed, nature has not fitted them for command of armies and the direction of the great operations of war.

Napoleon Bonaparte
Maxims, LXXIII, 1831

One of the common ways that seniors induce self-defeating stress in their juniors is to over-supervise them. Another is to summon them repeatedly to report in person about inconsequential administrative details.

Major General Aubrey "Red" Newman
Follow Me, 1981

This means maneuver . . . that produces as realistically as possible, within the bounds of prudence, the actual conditions a soldier will encounter on the battlefield. Only so can you condition, not only the human body, but the human spirit, to face and survive the stresses and strains the soldier will encounter in battle. And in future battle, if it comes, these stresses and strains will be immeasurably greater.

General Matthew B. Ridgway

Professional soldiers are sentimental men, for all the harsh realities of their calling. In their wallets and in their memories they carry bits of philosophy, fragments of poetry, quotations from the Scriptures, which in times of stress and danger speak to them with great meaning.

General Matthew B. Ridgway

Stress is essential to leadership. Living with stress, knowing how to handle pressure, is necessary for survival. It is related to a man's ability to wrest control of his own destiny from the circumstances that surround him.

Vice Admiral James Bond Stockdale
Military Ethics,
"Education for Leadership and Survival," 1987

The general is dealing with men's lives, and must have a certain mental robustness to stand the strain of this responsibility.

Field Marshal Sir Archibald P. Wavell
"Lees Knowles Lectures,"
Trinity College, Cambridge, 1939

Subordinates

By people I do not mean personnel. . . . I mean living, breathing, serving human beings. They have needs and interests and desires. They have spirit and will, and strengths and abilities. They have weaknesses and faults; and they have means. They are at the heart of our preparedness . . . and this preparedness—as a nation and as an Army—depends upon the spirit of our soldiers. It is the spirit that gives the Army . . . life. Without it we cannot succeed.

General Creighton W. Abrams

There are no bad troops. There are only bad leaders.

Brigadier General S.L.A. Marshall

He is a man; he expects to be treated as an adult, not as a school boy. He has rights; they must be made known to him and thereafter respected. He has ambition; it must be stirred. He has a belief in fair play; it must be honored. He has the need of comradeship; it must be supplied. He has imagination; it must be stimulated. He has personal dignity; it must not be broken down. He has pride; it can be satisfied and made the cornerstone of his character, once he gains assurance that he is playing a useful and respected part in a superior and successful organization. To give individuals working as a group the feeling of great accomplishment together is the crowning achievement of inspired leadership.

Brigadier General S.L.A. Marshall
The Armed Forces Officer, 1950

There are no bad regiments; there are only bad colonels.

Attributed to Napoleon Bonaparte

The way one soldier is treated is viewed by others as a weather vane of the commander's judgment, fairness, and personal interest in his men.

Major General Aubrey "Red" Newman
Follow Me, 1981

The recipe for success is, first, [make] a reputation for creative genius; second, surround yourself with partners who are better than you are; third, leave them to get on with it.

David Olgilvie

Truly in war "Men are nothing; a man is everything."

Major George S. Patton, Jr.
The Infantry Journal Reader, "Success in War," 1931

No matter how fine its weapons, no matter how accurate its intelligence, in the final analysis, the Army is dependent upon the quality of its men.

General Matthew B. Ridgway

It is the chaps, not the charts, that get the job done.

Lieutenant General Walter Bedell Smith

Confront your soldiers with the deed itself; never let them know your design. When the outlook is bright, bring it before their eyes; but tell them nothing when the situation is gloomy.

Sun-Tzu
The Art of War, circa fourth century B.C.

American troops, in particular, resent any suggestion that they are without individuality, that they are ciphers and not people. They want to be known for themselves and will resist any attempt to mold them into an anonymous pattern.

General Maxwell D. Taylor
Speech to Citadel cadets, 21 January 1956

When dealing with your superiors and subordinates, assume they are like you: professionals.

Lieutenant General Walter F. Ulmer, Jr.

These men, as soon as enlisted, should be taught to work on entrenchments, to march in ranks, to carry heavy burdens, and to bear the sun and dust. Their meals should be coarse and moderate; they should be accustomed to lie sometimes in the open air and sometimes in tents. After this they should be instructed in the use of their arms. And if any long expedition is planned, they should be encamped as far as possible from the temptations of the city.

Vegetius
Dē Re Mīlĭtāri, Book I, 378

Tact

Folks who think they must always speak the truth often overlook another good choice—silence.

Anonymous

Before you give someone a piece of your mind—make sure you can spare it.

Anonymous

Silence is not always tact and it is tact that is golden, not silence.
Samuel Butler
Notebooks, 1912

Tact in audacity is knowing how far you can go without going too far.

Jean Cocteau
Le Rappel a l'ordre, 1926

If you don't say anything, you won't be called on to repeat it.
Calvin Coolidge

Coughlin's Law: Don't talk unless you can improve the silence.
Laurence C. Coughlin

Avoid victories over superiors.
Baltasar Gracián Y Morales

Tact [is the] ability to tell a man he's open-minded when he has a hole in his head.

F. G. Kernan

The value of "tact" can be over-emphasized in selecting officers for command; positive personality will evoke a greater response than negative pleasantness.

B. H. Liddell Hart
Thoughts on War, 1944

Tact is the ability to describe others as they see themselves.

Abraham Lincoln

Men should utter nothing for which they would not willingly be responsible through time and in eternity.

Abraham Lincoln
Address to Congress, 1 December 1861

I command—or I hold my tongue.

Napoleon Bonaparte
Political Aphorisms, 1848

There is no substitute for empathy—for understanding the viewpoints and situations of others—when deciding how direct you can be in your dealings with others.

Major General Aubrey "Red" Newman
Follow Me, 1981

When someone faces you directly with an unexpected issue that is disconcerting, keep in mind the old axiom: take no offense where none is meant.

Major General Aubrey "Red" Newman
Follow Me, 1981

Tact is the art of making a point without making an enemy.

Howard W. Newton

Admonish your friends in private; praise them in public.

Publilius Syrus
Sententiae, circa 50 B.C.

I have often regretted my speech, never my silence.

Publilius Syrus
Moral Sayings, circa first century B.C.

Long ago I had learned that in conversation with an irate senior, a junior should confine himself to the three remarks, "Yes, sir," "No, sir," and "Sorry, sir." Repeated in the proper sequence, they will get him through the most difficult interview with the minimum discomfort.

Field Marshal Sir William Slim
Unofficial History, 1959

I believe that you should not reprimand subordinates in front of their juniors or in front of their seniors. They should be reprimanded in private and praised in public. I think that tact embodies those terms.

General Louis H. Wilson
Quoted in Karel Montor et al.,
Naval Leadership: Voices of Experience, 1987

Teamwork

The teams and staffs through which the modern commander absorbs information and exercises his authority must be a beautifully interlocked, smooth-working mechanism. Ideally, the whole should be practically a single mind.

General Dwight D. Eisenhower
Crusade in Europe, 1948

Teamwork is built best through training. First the individual is trained to make sure he knows how to handle his skills; then the subunit is trained as a subunit; then the unit as a unit, and then the command as a whole. This is how people learn to work as a team, because they know that other people are doing the same thing they are.

Admiral James L. Holloway III
Quoted in Karel Montor et al.,
Naval Leadership: Voices of Experience, 1987

Discipline is willing obedience to attain the greatest good by the greatest number. It means [the] laying aside, for the time being, of ordinary everyday go-as-you-please and do-what-you-like. It means one for all and all for one—teamwork. It means a machine—not of inert metal, but one of living men—an integrated human machine in which each does his part and contributes his full share.

Admiral Ernest J. King

The real trick in building a team is to have 25 individual stars on it. Recognition should be given not only for team performance but to those "heroes" who did something special.

Tom Peters

Troops should not be encouraged to foster a spirit of jealousy and unjust detraction towards other arms of the service, where all are mutually dependent and mutually interested, with functions differing in character but not in importance.

Lieutenant General J.E.B. Stuart

Training

The object of teaching is to enable the young man or young woman to get along without their teachers. . . . To provide them an independence of mind and soul, without an arrogance of spirit or self-deceptive sophistication.

General Creighton W. Abrams

Soldiers can only be ready when they are trained for the job they are doing and doing the job they are trained for. To insure that our Army can perform as the nation deserves and expects, we must continually insure that they are assigned where their training, knowledge, and experience contribute to the Army's readiness.

General Creighton W. Abrams
Army, October 1973

Prepare and prevent instead of repair and repent.

Anonymous

A good teacher is one who drives the students to think.

Anonymous

Training is not done in a sterile environment of cold calculating management. Training has to be rooted in deep ideals and beliefs— something worth dying for. The warmth of service to those beliefs— love of country, pride and belief in each other—yes, duty, honor, country—that's the warrior ethic.

General Richard E. Cavazos

The more you sweat in peace, the less you bleed in war.

Chinese proverb

That you should have been able to preserve the art not only of creating mighty armies almost at the stroke of a wand—but of leading and guiding those armies upon a scale incomparably greater than anything that was prepared for or even dreamed of, constitutes a gift made by the officer corps of the United States to their Nation in time of trouble, which I earnestly hope will never be forgotten here. . . . I shall always urge that the tendency in the future should be to prolong the courses of instruction at the colleges rather than to abridge them and to equip our young officers with that special technical professional knowledge which soldiers have a right to expect from those who can give them orders, if necessary, to go to their deaths. Professional attainment, based upon prolonged study, and collective study at colleges, rank by rank, and age by age—those are the title deeds of the commanders of future armies, and the secret of future victories.

Sir Winston Churchill
Address to senior officers, 1946

The soldier who can and will shoot is essential to victory in battle.

General Bruce C. Clarke

Do essential things first. There is not enough time for the commander to do everything. Each commander will have to determine wisely what is essential, and assign responsibilities for accomplishment. He should spend the remaining time on near essentials. This is especially true of training. Nonessentials should not take up time for essentials.

General Bruce C. Clarke

A good commander and trainer never misses an opportunity to teach all those in a position of responsibility, especially the noncommissioned officers and junior officers, what to look for, how to correct the deficiencies they detect, and why it is important to do so.

Lieutenant General Arthur S. Collins, Jr.
Common Sense Training, 1978

I hear and I forget; I see and I remember; I do and I understand.

Confucius

To lead an untrained people to war is to throw them away.

Confucius
Analects, circa 500 B.C.

No speech of admonition can be so fine that it will at once make those who hear it good men if they are not good already; it would surely not make archers good if they had not had practice in shooting; neither could it make lancers good, nor horsemen; it cannot even make men able to endure bodily labour, unless they had been trained to it before.

Cyrus the Younger of Persia

All training must stress that every soldier regardless of assignment has as his primary duty the obligation to fight. Individual training has two purposes: first, to teach men to fight; and second, to teach men to instruct others to fight. Unit training has three purposes: first, to teach individuals how teamwork produces an effective combat unit; second, to develop cadres on which fighting units can be built; third, to produce smooth working units which are ready for combat in the minimum time.

General Jacob L. Devers
1949

Today's Leavenworth graduates—a national asset of incalculable value— are a prime force in shaping armies of the free world that may some day stand as civilization's last, but sure, defense.

General Dwight D. Eisenhower

Our defense must rest on trained manpower and its most economical and mobile use. A professional corps is the heart of any security organization.

General Dwight D. Eisenhower

Proceeding as we do, upon the possibility of war, it would certainly be unwise, if not foolish, to build defenses, cast cannon, devise projectiles, and then neglect in peace to teach those things in relation to the use of them which it will be too late to learn after the war begins.

Major General Winfield Scott Hancock
American Military Thought, 1878

The leader of fighting men must never lose sight of the continual training it takes to perfect his troops as individual fighters. He receives them well trained from the training center and then it's his job to perfect them. He must constantly see, during all of his units' training, that his troops form the fighting man's crafty habits. He must give them hours for special training in these things as they need it. He must take quick steps of criticism and even punishment to rid them of careless, over-confident, and unrealistic habits in training that would invite unnecessary death in battle. He must see that his unit grows into a fighting team made of Soldiers.

Editorial in *The Infantry Journal Reader*,
"The Battle-Wise Fighting Soldier," 1941

The battle wisdom of a soldier, his true basis for confidence, can only be gained through repeated, hardened practice. Dirty, tiring, but utterly necessary, livesaving work. The dirt of the ground is the soldier's friend in battle just as much as his weapon. The closer he can keep to the ground as he fights and advances, the more professional his fighting is and the more he will live to accomplish for his army, his country, and himself.

Editorial in *The Infantry Journal Reader*,
"The Battle-Wise Fighting Soldier," 1942

We must train and classify the whole of our male citizens, and make military instruction a regular part of collegiate education. We can never be safe until this is done.

Thomas Jefferson

They do not wait for war to begin before handling their arms, nor do they sit idle in peacetime and take action only when the emergency comes—but as if born ready armed they never have a truce from training or wait for war to be declared. Their battle-drills are no different from the real thing; every man works as hard at his daily training as if he was on active service. That is why they stand up so easily to the strain of battle; no indiscipline dislodges them from their regular formation, no panic incapacitates them, no toil wears them out; so victory over men not so trained follows as a matter of course. It would not be far from the truth to call their drills bloodless battles, their battles bloody drills.

Josephus
The Jewish Wars, circa A.D. 75

A government is the murderer of its citizens which sends them to the field uninformed and untaught, where they are to meet men of the same age and strength, mechanized by education and discipline for battle.

Major General Henry "Light Horse Harry" Lee

In no other profession are the penalties for employing untrained personnel so appalling or so irrevocable as in the military.

General Douglas MacArthur

Naval education and training lie at the foundation of naval success; and the power that neglects this essential element of strength will, when the battle is fought, find that its ships, however formidable, are but built for a more thoroughly trained and educated enemy.

Stephen R. Mallory
Report to Jefferson Davis, 1864

If we say (maybe in other words) that we love the soldier, and if this comes not from just our mouths but from down deep in our soul, then we really have no choice but to bend every effort, every resource, every activity, and every priority toward his *training*.

Colonel Dandridge M. "Mike" Malone

SKILL × WILL × DRILL = KILL

Colonel Dandridge M. "Mike" Malone

But now my boys, leave off, and list to me,
That mean to teach you rudiments of war.
I'll have you learn to sleep upon the ground,
March in your armor through watery fens,
Sustain the scorching heat and freezing cold,
Hunger and thirst, right adjuncts of the war.

Christopher Marlowe
Tamburlaine the Great, Act III, Scene ii, 1587

During peace, the Army's primary mission is deterrence—being so well-trained, equipped, and led that no potential adversary would mistake our nation's ability and resolve to defend our interests.

John O. Marsh, Jr.

The reality of past and present conflicts confirms there is no substitute for the well-trained soldier who is: physically tough and mentally conditioned; possesses the individual skills for combat and survival. We will always rely on the leadership of NCOs and officers who are professionally qualified, motivated and courageous.

John O. Marsh, Jr.

We cannot train without planning and we cannot teach without preparation.

General George C. Marshall

In the past we have jeopardized our future, penalized our leaders and sacrificed our men by training untrained troops on the battlefield.

General George C. Marshall
Selected Speeches and Statements of General of the Army
George C. Marshall, edited by Major H. A. DeWeerd, 1945

It is difficult to overemphasize the importance of the [field-army] maneuvers. . . . The present maneuvers are the closest peacetime approximation to actual fighting conditions that has ever been undertaken in this country. . . . As an insurance policy against whatever operations our troops might be called upon to perform, the cost of these maneuvers represents a trifling premium to pay. Tremendous sums of money have been spent on our national defense effort, but I know of no single investment which will give this country a greater return in security and in the saving of lives than the present maneuvers.

General George C. Marshall
Selected Speeches and Statements of General of the Army
George C. Marshall, edited by Major H. A. DeWeerd, 1945

The fundamental purpose of all training today is to develop the natural faculties and stimulate the brain of the individual rather than to treat him as a cog that has to be fitted into a great machine.

Brigadier General S.L.A. Marshall
The Armed Forces Officer, 1950

In any epoch, the difference between a rabble and an effective professional Army is training. No task is more important than training as we face this decade.

General Edward C. Meyer

It is not sufficient that the soldier must shoot; he must shoot well.

Napoleon Bonaparte

Nothing is stronger than habit.

Ovid
"Ămŏres," circa A.D. 5

For every day of training we undertake in peacetime, we may save weeks and months of war.

Robert P. Patterson

Practice those things in peacetime that you intend to do in war.

General George S. Patton, Jr.

A pint of sweat will save a gallon of blood.

General George S. Patton, Jr.
War as I Knew It, 1947
(Also as message to troops before landing
at Casablanca, 8 November 1942)

The psychology of the citizen as a cadet was that of the citizen soldier. Under training by one who understands him he can be quickly developed into a loyal and efficient fighting man. It would be an excellent thing if every officer in the army could have contact in this way with the youth which forms our citizenship in peace and our armies in war. It would broaden the officer's outlook and better fit him for his duties.

General of the Armies John J. Pershing

All a soldier needs to know is how to shoot and salute.

Attributed to General of the Armies John J. Pershing

Let such teach others who themselves excel.

Alexander Pope
"Essay on Criticism," 1711

Practice is the best of all instructors.

Publilius Syrus
Maxims, circa first century B.C.

Our job is to produce combat leaders who can train and lead units capable of executing missions under conditions of severe hardship, searing emotion, and extreme danger.

General William R. Richardson

The requirement upon all soldiers to master their profession—always of fundamental importance—has gained new emphasis with the advent of new weapons and the resultant greater capabilities and responsibilities of the Army.

General Matthew B. Ridgway

Only through high training requirements, rigidly enforced, can low casualty rates be possible. Only well-armed and equipped, adequately trained, and efficiently led forces can expect victory in future combat.

General Matthew B. Ridgway
21 May 1953

It makes no difference how fine your weapons are, nor how competent your leaders, if the men in the ranks are not physically hardened and highly skilled, you do not have an effective fighting force. Training takes time—not in the use of the individual weapon, but in making the best use possible of all the weapons available, in almost endless combinations. This must be more than theoretical training.

General Matthew B. Ridgway
Soldier: The Memoirs of Matthew B. Ridgway, 1956

Train in difficult, trackless, wooded terrain. War makes extremely heavy demands on the soldier's strength and nerves. For this reason make heavy demands on your men in peacetime exercises.

Field Marshal Erwin Rommel
Infantry Attacks, 1937

The commander must be at constant pains to keep his troops abreast of all the latest tactical experience and developments, and must insist on their practical application. He must see to it that his subordinates are trained in accordance with the latest requirements. The best form of "welfare" for the troops is first class training, for this saves unnecessary casualties.

Field Marshal Erwin Rommel
Rommel Papers, 1953

Good ships and good guns are simply good weapons, and the best weapons are useless save in the hands of men who know how to fight with them.

Theodore Roosevelt
Message to Congress, 3 December 1901

It cannot be too often repeated that in modern war, and especially in modern naval war, the chief factor in achieving triumph is what has been done in the way of thorough preparation and training before the beginning of war.

Theodore Roosevelt
Graduation address at the U.S. Naval Academy, June 1902

In a society and worthy to be free, teaching which produces a willingness to lead, as well as a willingness to follow, must be given to all.

William F. Russell

In such times as these, the Army must be well trained, well equipped and well led by men of courage and of vision if it is to provide security of the quality and degree which the situation requires.

General Maxwell D. Taylor

An army is engaged constantly in either training or fighting. In common with all who have had experience of war, professional soldiers hope that our country will never be called upon to fight again. But in any case, training never ends, and training is teaching. Every officer and man in the Army is a teacher or a pupil most of his service. The average officer spends more of his time as a trainer and a teacher than in any other capacity.

General Maxwell D. Taylor

Numbers alone do not produce military strength. Soldier quality is essential to our strength. This quality is achieved by good leadership and instruction.

General Maxwell D. Taylor

We must remember that one man is much the same as another, and that he is best who is trained in the severest school.

Thucydides
History of the Peloponnesian War, circa 404 B.C.

The American soldier demonstrated that, properly equipped, trained and led, he has no superior among all of the armies in the world.

Lieutenant General Lucian K. Truscott, Jr.
Command Missions, 1954

What is necessary to be performed in the heat of action should be constantly practiced in the leisure of peace.

Vegetius
Dē Re Mīlītāri, Book I, 378

The mediocre teacher tells. The good teacher explains. The superior teacher demonstrates. The great teacher inspires.

William Arthur Ward

If the exercise is subsequently discussed in the officers' mess, it was probably worth while; if there is argument over it in the sergeants' mess, it was a good exercise; while if it should be mentioned in the corporals' room, it was an undoubted success.

Field Marshal Sir Archibald P. Wavell
Journal of the Royal United Service Institution, May 1933

Trust

Put your trust in God, my boys, and keep your powder dry!
> Oliver Cromwell
> To his troops on 2 July 1644
> Quoted in Valentine Blacker's *Oliver Cromwell's Advice*

The man who trusts men will make fewer mistakes than he who distrusts them.
> Count di Camillo Cavour

Public office is a public trust.
> Grover Cleveland

You may be deceived if you trust too much, but you will live in torment if you do not trust enough.
> Frank Crane

An army fearful of its officers is never as good as one that trusts and confides in its leaders.
> General Dwight D. Eisenhower

The essence of genius is spontaneity and instinct. Trust thyself.
> Ralph Waldo Emerson

Trust men, and they will be true to you.

Ralph Waldo Emerson
Essays: First Series, "Prudence," 1841

Units will follow only leaders who have earned their trust through demonstrations of honor and willingness to sacrifice for the good of their men.

James Fallows
National Defense, 1981

Men trust their ears less than their eyes.

Herodotus
Histories, Book I, circa 444 B.C.

The traditional esteem of the average citizen for the military officer is a major ingredient, indeed a prerequisite, of the national security. The Armed Services have recognized this since the time of Valley Forge. That is why there is such extreme emphasis on the imperative of personal honor in the military officer; not only the future of our arms but the well-being of our people depend upon a constant reaffirmation and strengthening of public faith in the virtue and trustworthiness of the officer body. Should that faith flag and finally fail, the citizenry would be reluctant to commit its young people to any military endeavor, however grave the emergency. The works of goodwill by which leaders of our military seek to win the trust and approval of the people are in that direct sense a preservative of our American freedoms. By the same reasoning, high character in the military officer is a safeguard of the character of the Nation. Anything less than exemplary conduct is therefore unworthy of the commission.

Brigadier General S.L.A. Marshall
The Armed Forces Officer, 1950

Trust is a many-splendored thing which pervades human relations at all levels in the military service.

Major General Aubrey "Red" Newman
Follow Me, 1981

Trust everyone, but always cut the cards.

Ronald Reagan
8 December 1988

Out of the Army's long and varied service to our nation, tested and tempered through 200 years of peace and war, have emerged certain fundamental roles, principles and precepts which underlie the more transitory military organizations, strategies, tactics and technologies. . . . They constitute the Army's anchor in history, law and custom, suggesting the sources of its present strength and of the trust and confidence of the nation in the essential role of the Army.

General Bernard W. Rogers
U.S. Army Field Manual 100-1, *The Army,*
29 September 1978

Truth

In war, truth is the first casualty.

Aeschylus

Adversity is the first path to truth.

Lord George Noel Gordon Byron
Don Juan, 1818

I must speak the truth, and nothing but the truth.

Miguel de Cervantes
Don Quixote, 1615

Veracity does not consist in saying, but in the intention of communicating truth.

Samuel Taylor Coleridge
Biographia Literaria, 1817

The aim of the superior man is truth.

Confucius

God offers to every mind its choice between truth and repose.

Ralph Waldo Emerson
Essays: First Series, "Intellect," 1841

He who wishes to uphold the truth and has but one tongue, he will uphold it indeed.

Johann Wolfgang von Goethe
Faust: Part II, 1832

Truth is tough.

Oliver Wendell Holmes, Sr.
1860

Veracity is the heart of morality.

Thomas Henry Huxley
Universities, Actual and Ideal, 1874

He who permits himself to tell a lie often finds it much easier to do it a second and third time, till at length it becomes habitual; he tells lies without attending to it, and truths without the world's believing him. This falsehood of the tongue leads to that of the heart, and in time depraves all its good dispositions.

Thomas Jefferson
19 August 1785

The casualty when war comes is truth.

Attributed to Senator Hiram Johnson

I speak truth, not so much as I would, but as much as I dare; and I dare a little more as I grow older.

Michel Eyquem de Montaigne
Essays, 1580

To be persuasive, we must be believable;
To be believable, we must be credible;
To be credible, we must be truthful.

Edward R. Murrow

White lies always introduce others of a darker complexion.

William Paley
The Principles of Moral and Political Philosophy, 1785

Repetition does not transform a lie into a truth.

Franklin D. Roosevelt
Radio address, 26 October 1939

Time discovers truth.

Seneca
Moral Essays, circa first century A.D.

How dreadful knowledge of the truth can be when there's no help in truth.

Sophocles

Vērĭtās nōn ērŭbescit.
[Truth does not blush.]

Tertullian
Adversus Vălentinianos, circa third century

I never give them hell. I just tell the truth, and they think it's hell.

Harry S. Truman

When in doubt tell the truth.

Mark Twain
Pudd'nhead Wilson's New Calendar, 1894

There is nothing so powerful as truth—and often nothing so strange.

Daniel Webster
6 April 1830

Valor

Son, I would rather have the right to wear this [Medal of Honor] than be President of the United States.

General Dwight D. Eisenhower
Quoted in Bruce Jacobs' *Heros of the Army,* 1956

Heroism feels and never reasons and therefore is always right.

Ralph Waldo Emerson
Essays: First Series, "Prudence," 1841

So sensible were the Romans of the imperfections of valor without skill and practice that, in their language, the name of an Army was borrowed from the word which signified exercise.

Edward Gibbon
Decline and Fall of the Roman Empire, 1776

The valor that wins our battles is not the trained hardihood of veterans, but a native and spontaneous fire; and there is surely a chivalrous beauty in the devotion of the citizen soldiers to his country's cause which the man who makes arms his profession and is but doing his duty cannot pretend to rival.

Nathaniel Hawthorne

That pain may cease, he yields his flesh to pain.

Joyce Kilmer
The Peacemakers, 14 June 1918

299

Among the men who fought on Iwo Jima, uncommon valor was a common virtue.

Admiral Chester W. Nimitz
Tribute to U.S. Marines, U.S. Pacific Fleet Message,
March 1945

It is not always from valor that men are brave, nor from virtue that women are chaste.

François, Duc de La Rochefoucauld
Maximes, 1665

Perfect valor is to do unwitnessed what we should be capable of doing before all the world.

François, Duc de La Rochefoucauld
Maximes, 1665

The better part of valor is discretion.

William Shakespeare
Henry IV, Act V, Scene iv, 1598

In valor there is hope.

Tacitus
Annals, circa A.D. 90

Valor is superior to numbers.

Vegetius
Dē Re Mīlĭtāri, Book III, 378

Values

The person who stands neutral usually stands for nothing.

Anonymous

Stand fast, and hold the traditions which ye have been taught.

Bible, II Thessalonians 2:15

The officer cannot be a member of his profession without subscribing to the operating norms of his professional community as a whole. These norms are in fact a necessity for the success of the group in fulfilling its tasks. Without a collective sense of duty the military could not function and certainly could not be trusted. Military professionals must share a sense of duty to the nation. The professional officer . . . must have a deep normative sense of duty to do this. The rigorous demands made upon the profession by this sense of duty, and the tasks required of it, explain the premium placed upon other "soldierly" qualities. One cannot do his duty unless he has courage, selflessness and integrity. The military profession must have these group values as a functional necessity.

Zeb Bradford and Frederic Brown
The United States Army in Transition, 1973

We hold these truths to be self-evident; that all men are created equal; that they are endowed by their creator with certain unalienable rights; that among these are life, liberty, and the pursuit of happiness.

U.S. Declaration of Independence

Vital to combat operations and therefore a necessary part of traditional military professionalism is a set of values which are to some extent contrary to those held by liberal civilian society. Military organization is hierarchical, not egalitarian, and is oriented to the group rather than to the individual; it stresses discipline and obedience, not freedom of expression; it depends on confidence and trust, not *caveat emptor*. It requires immediate decision and prompt action, not thorough analysis and extensive debate; it relies on training, simplification and predictable behavior, not education, sophistication and empiricism. It offers austerity, not material comforts.

Major General Robert G. Gard
Foreign Affairs, "The Military in American Society," July 1971

The aim of education is the knowledge not of fact, but of values.

Dean William Ralph Inge

We face a dilemma that armies have always faced within a democratic society. The values necessary to defend that society are often at odds with the values of the society itself. To be an effective servant of the people, the Army must concentrate not on the values of a liberal society, but on the hard values of the battlefield. We must recognize that the military community differs from the civilian community from which it springs. The civilian community exists to promote the quality of life. The military community exists to fight and if need be to die in defense of that quality of life. We must not apologize for those differences. The American people are served by soldiers disciplined to obey the orders of their leaders, and hardened and conditioned to survive the rigors of the battlefield. We do neither our soldiers nor the American people any favors if we ignore those realities.

General Walter T. "Dutch" Kerwin
Soldier, "The Values of Today's Army," September 1978

Leaders are the custodians of a nation's ideals, of the beliefs it cherishes, of its permanent hopes, of the faith which makes a nation out of a mere aggregation of individuals.

Walter Lippmann

Duty—Honor—Country. Those three hallowed words reverently dictate what you ought to be, what you can be, what you will be. They are your rallying points: to build courage when courage seems to fail; to regain faith when there seems to be little cause for faith; to create hope when hope becomes forlorn.

General Douglas MacArthur
Address to U.S. Military Academy cadets and graduates,
12 May 1962

Of all the thousands of things that come under the heading of "Leadership," what is it that's *"most important"*? Simple . . . soldiers' values.

Colonel Dandridge M. "Mike" Malone
"Soldier Values and Soldier Discipline"

It is in the national interest that personnel serving in the Armed Forces be protected in the realization and development of moral, spiritual, and religious values consistent with the religious beliefs of the individuals concerned. To this end, it is the duty of commanding officers in every echelon to develop to the highest degree the conditions and influences calculated to promote the health, morals, and spiritual values of the personnel under their command.

General George C. Marshall

It should be perfectly clear that any institution must know what its ideals are before it can become coherent and confident, and that there must be present in the form of clearly available ideals an imaginative conception of the good at which the institution aims.

Brigadier General S.L.A. Marshall
The Armed Forces Officer, 1950

As we work toward a vision of an Army fully attuned to the national needs of this decade, preparing our units for war and seeking to develop our individual talents, we must stay in touch with this set of values keyed to the fulfillment of our constitutional obligations. The heart of that task is the support and defense of the Constitution, ergo, the preservation of our national values through preparation for war.

It is from the stark reality of the battlefield—where our lives and the lives of those about us may be hazard to shield the republic—that we must firmly establish the validity of our institutional standards.

General Edward C. Meyer

We are an institution strengthened by our values.

General Edward C. Meyer

Military professionalism must ultimately be grounded on the premise that military ethics converge with the ethical values of the larger society. A military system in a democratic society cannot long maintain its credibility and legitimacy if its ethical standards significantly differ from the civilian values of the larger society.

Sam Sarkesian and Thomas M. Gannon
American Behavioral Scientist,
"Professionalism," May/June 1976

In peacetime, we practice tactics, strategy, and weapons firing. We must do the same with our values. We must develop the candor to display the courage to make a commitment to real competence, now, today. We can afford to do no less, for the time is short and stakes are too high.

General Donn A. Starry

Loyalty, duty, selfless service and integrity are essential values for all soldiers. Together, they form the bedrock of our profession.

General John A. Wickham

Never before in this nation's experience have the values and expectations in society been more at variance with the values and expectations that are indispensable to a military establishment.

George Will

Victory, Winning

There is no king saved by the multitude of an host; a mighty man is not delivered by much strength.

Bible, Psalms 33:16

Victory at all costs, victory in spite of all terror, victory however long and hard the road may be; for without victory, there is no survival.

Sir Winston Churchill
Address to House of Commons, 13 May 1940

The problems of victory are more agreeable than those of defeat, but they are no less difficult.

Sir Winston Churchill
Speech to House of Commons, 11 November 1942

Nothing succeeds like success.

Alexandre Dumas

Along with success comes a reputation for wisdom.

Euripides

Victory is won by bits and scraps.

Marshal Ferdinand Foch

No victory is possible unless the commander be energetic, eager for responsibilities and bold undertakings; unless he possess and can impart to all the resolute will of seeing the thing through; unless he be capable of exerting a personal action composed of will, judgment, and freedom of mind in the midst of danger.

Marshal Ferdinand Foch
Precepts, 1919

The will to conquer is victory's first condition, and therefore every soldier's first duty.

Marshal Ferdinand Foch
Precepts, 1919

Success has ruined many a man.

Benjamin Franklin
Poor Richard's Almanac, 1738

All victories breed hate.

Baltasar Gracián Y Morales
The Art of Wordly Wisdom, 1647

The battle, sir, is not to the strong alone; it is to the vigilant, the active, the brave.

Patrick Henry
Address to the Virginia Convention, 23 March 1775

In war, only what is simple can succeed.

Field Marshal Paul von Hindenburg

In starting and waging war, it is not right that matters but victory.

Adolf Hitler

Victory often changes her side.

Homer
The Iliad, Book VI, circa 700 B.C.

Always mystify, mislead, and surprise the enemy, if possible; and when you strike and overcome him, never let up in the pursuit so long as your men have strength to follow; for an army routed, if hotly pursued, becomes panic-stricken, and can then be destroyed by half their number. The other rule is, never fight against heavy odds, if by any possible maneuvering you can hurl your own force on only a part, and that the weakest part, of your enemy and crush it. Such tactics will win every time, and a small army may thus destroy a large one in detail, and repeated victory will make it invincible.

General Thomas J. "Stonewall" Jackson
Quoted in Battles and Leaders of the Civil War
by Brigadier General (CSA) John D. Imboden, 1956

Victory has a thousand fathers, but defeat is an orphan.

John F. Kennedy

Demand a commitment to excellence and to victory.

Vince Lombardi

Winning isn't everything. It's the *only* thing.

Vince Lombardi

From the Far East I send you one single thought, one sole idea— written in red on every beachhead from Australia to Tokyo—There is no substitute for Victory!

General Douglas MacArthur

To the victor belong the spoils of the enemy.

William Learned Marcy
Speech to U.S. Senate, 1832

The nature of the ground is the fundamental factor in aiding the army to set up its victory.

Mei Yao-Ch'ên

Today is victory over yourself of yesterday; tomorrow is your victory over lesser men.

Miyamoto Musashi
A Book of Five Rings, circa 1643

All my care will be to gain victory with the least shedding of blood.

Napoleon Bonaparte

The first object which a general who gives battle should consider is the glory and honor of his arms; the safety and conservation of his men is but secondary; but it is also true that in audacity and obstinacy will be found the safety and conservation of the men. In a retreat, besides the honor of the army, a commander often loses more men than in two battles. This is why he should never despair so long as brave men remain with the colors. By such conduct he will obtain, and deserve to obtain, victory.

Napoleon Bonaparte
Maxims, XV, 1831

Almighty and most merciful Father we humbly beseech Thee, of Thy great goodness, to restrain these immoderate rains with which we have to contend. Grant us fair weather for battle. Graciously hearken to us as soldiers who call upon Thee that armed with Thy power, we may advance from victory to victory, crush the oppression and wickedness of our enemies, and establish Thy justice among men and nations. Amen.

Lieutenant General George S. Patton, Jr.
Prayer provided to soldiers of Third Army, December 1944

A good general not only sees the way to victory; he also knows when victory is impossible.

Polybius
Histories, circa 125 B.C.

There is no pain in the wound received in the moment of victory.

Publilius Syrus
Moral Sayings, circa first century B.C.

Show me a good and gracious loser, and I'll show you a failure.

Knute Rockne

Physical strength can never permanently withstand the impact of spiritual force.

Franklin D. Roosevelt
4 May 1941

There is a homely adage which runs: "Speak softly and carry a big stick; you will go far."

Theodore Roosevelt
Speech at Minnesota State Fair, 2 September 1901

A victory is twice itself when the achiever brings home full numbers.

William Shakespeare
Much Ado About Nothing, Act I, Scene i, 1598

A skilled commander seeks victory from the situation, and does not demand it from his subordinates.

Sun-Tzu
The Art of War, circa fourth century B.C.

The gods are on the side of the stronger.

Tacitus
Histories, circa A.D. 109

Victory in war does not depend entirely upon numbers or mere courage; only skill and discipline will insure it.

Vegetius
Dē Re Mīlītāri, Book I, 378

A handful of men, inured to war, proceed to certain victory, while on the contrary numerous armies of raw and undisciplined troops are but multitudes of men dragged to slaughter.

Vegetius
Dē Re Mīlītāri, Book I, 378

Whoever wants to keep alive must aim at victory. It is the winners who do the killing and the losers who get killed.

Xenophon
Speech to Greek army after defeat of Cyrus at Cunaxa,
401 B.C.

Virtue

Virtue is like a rich stone; best plain set.

> Sir Francis Bacon
> *Essays,* "Of Beauty," 1625

Whatsoever things are true, whatsoever things *are* honest, whatsoever things *are* just, whatsoever things *are* pure, whatsoever things *are* lovely, whatsoever things *are* of good report; if *there be* any virtue, and if *there be* any praise, think on these things.

> *Bible,* Philippians 4:8

Readiness, obedience, and a sense of humor are the virtues of a soldier.

> Brasidas of Sparta
> Speech to Lacadaemonian Army at the Battle of Amphipolis,
> 422 B.C.

There is no road or ready way to virtue.

> Sir Thomas Browne
> *Rěligǐo Mědǐci,* 1642

He that is valiant and dare fight, though drubbed, can lose no honor by't.

> Samuel Butler
> *Hudibras,* 1663

Caesar's wife must be above suspicion.

Attributed to Julius Caesar

Virtue is its own reward.

Marcus Tullius Cicero

Virtue is not left to stand alone. He who practices it will have neighbors.

Confucius
Analects, circa 500 B.C.

I have not seen a person who loved virtue, or one who hated what was not virtuous. He who loved virtue would esteem nothing above it.

Confucius
Analects, circa 500 B.C.

When a man's knowledge is sufficient to attain, and his virtue is not sufficient to enable him to hold, whatever he may have gained, he will lose again.

Confucius
Analects, circa 500 B.C.

Fine words and an insinuating appearance are seldom associated with true virtue.

Confucius
Analects, circa 500 B.C.

The spirit of man is more important than mere physical strength, and the spiritual fiber of a nation than its wealth.

General Dwight D. Eisenhower

The only reward of virtue is virtue.

Ralph Waldo Emerson
Essays: First Series, "Friendship," 1841

The essence of greatness is the perception that virtue is enough.

Ralph Waldo Emerson
Essays: First Series, "Heroism," 1841

The louder he talked of his honor, the faster we counted our spoons.

Ralph Waldo Emerson
Conduct of Life, "Worship," 1860

I have a lantern. You steal my lantern. What, then, is your honor worth no more to you than the price of my lantern?

Epictetus

What you have inherited from your fathers, earn over yourselves or it will not be yours.

Johann Wolfgang von Goethe

If you can keep your head when all about you
Are losing theirs and blaming it on you.
If you can trust yourself when all men doubt you
And make allowance for their doubting, too.

Rudyard Kipling
If, 1910

Virtue is harder to be got than knowledge of the world; and, if lost in a young man, is seldom recovered.

John Locke
Some Thoughts on Education, 1693

Democracy is the best system of government yet devised, but it suffers from one grave defect—it does not encourage those military virtues upon which, in an envious world, it must frequently depend for survival.

Major Guy du Maurier

When we are planning for posterity, we ought to remember that virtue is not hereditary.

Thomas Paine
Common Sense, "Of the Present Ability of America," 1776

War is the foundation of all the arts, because it is the foundation of all high virtues and faculties of men.

John Ruskin

Virtue is bold, and goodness never fearful.
William Shakespeare
Measure for Measure, Act III, Scene i, 1605

'Tis held that valor is the chiefest virtue and
Most dignifies the haver.
William Shakespeare
Coriolanus, Act II, Scene ii, 1608

Virtue must shape itself in deed.
Alfred, Lord Tennyson
1885

War

To win a war quickly takes long preparation.

Anonymous

A bayonet is a weapon with a worker at both ends.

Anonymous

The advantages of successful war are doubtful; the disadvantages of unsuccessful war are certain. Real security lies in the prevention of war—and today that hope can come only through adequate preparedness.

General Omar N. Bradley

The way to win an atomic war is to make certain it never starts.

General Omar N. Bradley

The notion that wars can be won by remote control—with push buttons—is a dangerous myth.

Wilbur M. Brucker

However absorbed a commander may be in the elaboration of his own thoughts, it is sometimes necessary to take the enemy into consideration.

Sir Winston Churchill

No one can guarantee success in war, but only deserve it.

Sir Winston Churchill
Their Finest Hour, 1949

To introduce into the philosophy of war a principle of moderation would be an absurdity. War is an act of violence pushed to its utmost bounds.

Karl von Clausewitz

The probable character and general shape of any war should mainly be assessed in the light of political factors and conditions.

Karl von Clausewitz
On War, 1832

Every age has its own kind of war, its own limiting conditions and its own peculiar preconceptions.

Karl von Clausewitz
On War, 1832

War is nothing more than the continuation of politics by other means.

Karl von Clausewitz
On War, 1832

War is not only chameleon-like in character, because it changes its colors in some degree in each particular case, but it is also, as a whole, in relation to the predominant tendencies that are in it, a wonderful trinity, composed of the original violence of its elements, hatred and animosity, which may be looked upon as blind instinct; of the play of probabilities and chance, which make it a free activity of the soul; and of the subordinate nature of a political instrument, by which it belongs purely to reason.

Karl von Clausewitz
On War, 1832

I detest war. It spoils armies.

Grand Duke Constantine of Russia

War is now utterly preposterous.

General Dwight D. Eisenhower
Speech in Rio de Janeiro, 24 February 1960

War educates the senses, calls into action the will, perfects the physical constitution, brings men into such swift and close collision in critical moments that man measures man.

Ralph Waldo Emerson
War, 1849

What I want to urge is that all men, common and uncommon, great and small . . . have been profoundly and unceasingly influenced by war. Our literature, our art and our architecture are stamped with the vestiges of war. Our very language has a thousand bellicose words and phrases woven into its fabric. And our material destinies, our social life and habits, our industry and trade, have assumed their present forms and characteristics largely as the result of war. . . . We are, all of us, indeed, the heirs of many wars.

Cyril B. Falls

War is a trade for the ignorant and a science for the expert.

Jean Charles Folard
Decouvertes sur la Guerre, 1724

There never was a good war or a bad peace.

Benjamin Franklin
Letter to Josiah Quincy, 11 September 1773

The art of war is simple enough. Find out where your enemy is. Get at him as soon as you can. Strike at him as hard as you can, and keep moving on.

General Ulysses Simpson Grant

Older men declare war. But it is the youth that must fight and die.

Herbert Hoover
Speech to Republican National Convention, 27 June 1944

To move swiftly, strike vigorously, and secure the fruits of victory is the secret of successful war.

General Thomas J. "Stonewall" Jackson
1863

War is as much a punishment to the punisher as to the sufferer.

Thomas Jefferson
Letter to Tench Coxe, May 1794

War is always to be conducted according to the great principles of the art; but great discretion must be exercised in the nature of the operations to be undertaken, which should depend upon the circumstances of the case.

Baron Henri de Jomini
Précis de l'Art de Guerre, 1838

Mankind must put an end to war—or war will put an end to mankind.

John F. Kennedy

Henceforth the adequacy of any military establishment will be tested by its ability to preserve the peace.

Henry Kissinger

It is well that war is so terrible—we would grow too fond of it.

General Robert E. Lee
Comment passed to General James Longstreet,
13 December 1862

War should be the only study of a prince. He should consider peace only as a breathing-time, which gives him leisure to contrive, and furnishes an ability to execute military plans.

Niccolò di Bernardo Machiavelli
The Prince, 1513

If the Free World should lose to communism, the loss would be total, final, and irrevocable. The citadel of freedom must be preserved because there is no road back to freedom for anyone if the citadel is lost.

Robert S. McNamara

War loses a great deal of its romance after a soldier has seen his first battle.

Colonel John S. Mosby
War Reminiscences, 1887

War alone brings all human energies to their highest tension, and sets a seal of nobility on the people who have the virtue to face it.

Benito Mussolini

All wars should be systematic, for every war should have an aim and be conducted in conformity with the principles and rules of the art. War should be undertaken with forces corresponding to the magnitude of the obstacles that are to be anticipated.

Napoleon Bonaparte
Maxims, V, 1831

One may dislike war just as one dislikes disease; but to decry the necessity for studying it . . . is no less absurd than it would be to minimize the need for medical investigation because one disliked cancer or tuberculosis.

Sir Charles Oman

It is the object only of war that makes it honorable.

Thomas Paine
The American Crisis, 21 March 1778

War is killing business. You've got to spill their blood, or they'll spill yours. Rip 'em up the belly, or shoot 'em in the guts.

General George S. Patton, Jr.

War is very simple, direct and ruthless. It takes a simple, direct, and ruthless man to wage war.

General George S. Patton, Jr.
Diary entry, 15 April 1943

War is an art and as such is not susceptible of explanation by fixed formula.

Major George S. Patton, Jr.
The Infantry Journal Reader, "Success in War," 1931

War is sweet to those who have never experienced it.

Pindar

War, as is becoming realized in the modern world, is more than a mere clash of arms. The development of armies and of their organization, and the narratives of campaign strategy and of operational tactics, which were formerly the military historian's exclusive concern, can be understood only in relation to developments in the world at large, in relation to advances in technology, and in relation to changes in political and economic organization.

Richard Preston

We are interested only in inflicting maximum casualties to the enemy with minimum casualties to ourselves. To do this we must wage a war of maneuver—slashing at the enemy when he withdraws and fighting delaying actions when he attacks.

General Matthew B. Ridgway

No triumph of peace is quite so great as the supreme triumphs of war. The courage of the soldier, the courage of the statesman who has to meet storms which can be quelled only by soldierly virtues— this stands higher than any quality called out merely in time of peace.

Theodore Roosevelt
Speech at the U.S. Naval War College, 2 June 1897

You cannot qualify war in harsher terms than I will. War is cruelty, and you cannot refine it.

General William Tecumseh Sherman
Letter to James C. Calhoun (Mayor of Atlanta),
12 September 1864

War is hell.

General William Tecumseh Sherman
Speech at Michigan Military Academy graduation, 1879

There is many a boy here today who looks on war as all glory, but, boys, it is all hell.

General William Tecumseh Sherman
Speech in Columbus, Ohio, 1880

War is, at best, a tragic necessity—an answer to aggression and oppression. It is, at worst, mankind's most cruel and destructive activity.

Roger L. Shinn
Military Ethics, 1987

Diplomacy has rarely been able to gain at the conference table what cannot be gained or held on the battlefield.

Lieutenant General Walter Bedell Smith
On return from Geneva Conference on Indo-China, 1954

War never slays a bad man in its course,
But the good always!

Sophocles
Philoctetes, 409 B.C.

All warfare is based on deception.

Sun-Tzu
The Art of War, circa fourth century B.C.

The deterrence of war is the primary objective of the armed forces.

General Maxwell D. Taylor
The Uncertain Trumpet, 1960

Men will always judge any war in which they are actually fighting to be the greatest at the time.

Thucydides
History of the Peloponnesian War, circa 404 B.C.

War is the unfolding of miscalculations.

Barbara Tuchman
The Guns of August, 1962

Where are the vaunts and the proud boasts with which you went forth? Where are your banners, and your bands of music, and your ropes to bring back your prisoners? Well, there isn't a band playing—and there isn't a flag but clings ashamed and lank to its staff.

Walt Whitman
After the Battle of First Bull Run, 21 July 1861

Only the dead have seen the end of war.

—Plato

PART TWO

Readings on Leadership

Principles
of Leadership

Principles provide the cornerstone for military doctrine. They are universal and are founded upon the unique requirements of combat. The Principles of Leadership were developed by seasoned combat veterans as a result of an in-depth study of military leadership in 1948 at the U.S. Army Command and General Staff College. The principles first appeared in a U.S. Army training circular later that year and were incorporated in the Army's first doctrinal leadership manual in 1951. As principles, these tenets are fundamental truths that have stood the test of time.

Be Technically and Tactically Proficient

This principle is paramount. Effective leaders know their profession. They are thoroughly competent in combat operations, training, and technical aspects of their basic branch—regardless of their current assignment. Leaders demonstrating technical and tactical competence inspire confidence in young soldiers. Combat won't allow for detailed preparation of leaders to assume new leadership positions. This principle entails staying abreast of current military doctrinal and policy developments through service school training, experience in units, exposure to senior leaders, and personal study. Leaders will never know everything; the key is to always keep striving for proficiency. This principle is related to the principle of "Know Yourself and Seek Self-Improvement" by the inherent requirement to be prepared to assume the duties and responsibilities of leading at the next higher echelon.

The list of principles first appeared in U.S. Army Training Circular No. 6, 19 July 1948; the discussion of each principle provided here is based on my input to Appendix A of U.S. Army Field Manual 22-103, *Leadership and Command at Senior Levels*, June 1987.

Know Yourself and Seek Self-Improvement

Professional development is a continuous process and is essential to understanding and leading young soldiers. Through self-evaluation a leader is able to recognize his strengths and weaknesses in order to determine his specific capabilities and limitations. Be honest in your assessment and have confidence in yourself even though you identify some weak areas. As a result, a leader can take actions tailored to his needs to further develop strengths and to work on correcting weaknesses. Profit from the lessons learned and mistakes of others. This process enhances a leader's self-confidence as well as facilitates his ability to effectively lead at increasingly higher levels of responsibility.

Seek Responsibility
and Take Responsibility for Your Actions

Military leadership means accepting responsibility and going after the tough, demanding challenges. While specific responsibility for portions of the organization's mission may be delegated to subordinates, ultimate responsibility for completion of the mission is borne by the leader. If the desired goal isn't reached, don't pass the buck. Accept responsibility, identify what went wrong, and fix the problem. Leaders cannot be omnipresent or omnipotent. Hence delegation of responsibility is a necessity. Leaders exercise initiative, resourcefulness, and imagination—and take risks. Leaders must be decisive and in times of crisis must not hesitate to make decisions or act to achieve success. Combat is dynamic and leaders must act in the absence of orders to take advantage of fleeting windows of opportunity. Leaders see problems as challenges rather than as obstacles. Leaders accept just criticism and admit mistakes; they encourage others to do likewise. This principle is related to a leader's self-confidence. Any effort to evade responsibility will destroy the bonds of loyalty and trust that are essential between leaders and those they lead. Seeking additional responsibility will assist in preparing for duties at higher levels of responsibility and is essential to operating within the senior commander's intent. Leaders adhere to what they believe is right and have the courage to act on their convictions.

Make Sound and Timely Decisions

Combat demands that leaders make rapid estimates of situations, arrive at sound decisions, and initiate actions to accomplish those decisions. Leaders must reach and control the decisive point on the battlefield at the crucial time. The leader who delays or attempts to avoid making a decision may cause unnecessary casualties as well as cause failure of the mission. The key to success is innovative, flexible leaders who can quickly grasp the situation, accurately read the battle, anticipate opposing force reactions, and rapidly execute actions. As you make decisions consider all available information (realizing that you can't achieve 100%) to include the immediate and follow-on impact that decisions will have on soldiers and the unit. Don't be afraid to seek the advice and counsel of subordinate leaders. Use the *"KISS"* principle. This principle is related to the Army's emphasis on maneuver and is consonant with taking responsibility for one's actions.

Set the Example

The power of example is great. Leaders win confidence and loyalty by their actions. Soldiers will emulate the behavior of their leaders. This principle entails demonstrating both moral and physical courage. Leaders influence their soldiers and their units by what they Be, Know, and Do. Leaders establish and maintain high, but yet attainable, goals and standards for their subordinates and units. Further, they ensure that their own performance is in consonance with those goals and standards. The key is that leaders must do the very best they can at all times. It is essential that leaders share the dangers and hardships of their soldiers. Leaders reflect their professionalism by everything they say and do or don't do. Leaders must embody and demonstrate professional attributes. This principle is related to all the other leadership Principles.

Know Your Soldiers
and Look Out for Their Well-Being

This principle focuses on instilling confidence and trust in soldiers. Confidence and trust develops and sustains loyalty and cohesion, thereby creating more effective units. This is key in that cohesive units are more successful than those which are not. Loyalty builds upon this confidence and is the foundation for motivating soldiers. Loyalty begins at the top—not at the bottom—and is a two-way function. Soldiers who respect their leaders will expend more effort to ensure their task is accomplished to the best of their abilities. Leaders must know their soldiers in order to motivate and influence them to accomplish the mission. Leaders must establish an environment that is open and honest and provides for the physical, emotional, and spiritual needs of their soldiers. This can be done by showing genuine concern for your soldiers and by ensuring that the needs of the soldier's family are met.

Keep Your Soldiers Informed

Success on the battlefield is founded upon actions taken in the absence of orders. Informing subordinates supports the ability of subordinate leaders to make decisions and execute actions within the context of the senior commander's intent. The more a subordinate leader or soldier knows, the more determined and resolute he will be. Information will also greatly reduce fears and rumors which severely affect the attitude and morale of soldiers. It is characteristic of soldiers to be inquisitive. Keeping your soldiers informed will enhance initiative, teamwork, cohesion, and morale. Make sure all subordinates understand their tasks and how their personal role relates to accomplishing the mission. It enhances the purposefulness, determination, and fortitude of your soldiers. This principle is directly related to establishing trust between the leader and those he leads.

Develop a Sense of Responsibility in Your Subordinates

The human emotions of pride and determination can be employed to develop a sense of responsibility through delegation. Effective units perform well in all situations—even in the absence of critical leaders. Assignment of tasks with commensurate resources develops subordinate leaders to assume leadership roles at succeeding higher levels. Recognize the good performance of young leaders. Leaders are teachers and are responsible for professionally developing subordinate leaders. Critique performances and (if possible) have subordinate leaders repeat accomplishing the mission if it is not done to standard. Establishing an environment where leaders will accept the honest mistakes of subordinate leaders will ensure capable leaders are developed.

Ensure the Task Is Understood, Supervised, and Accomplished

This principle is essential to accomplishing the mission and is a critical element of leadership. Understanding the task ensures that soldiers know what is to be accomplished, how and when it is to be accomplished, and who is to accomplish it. Since the battlefield is dynamic and characterized by change, this enhances the ability of soldiers to accomplish the task, even in the absence of detailed orders or when adjustments to the plan must be made because of unforeseen circumstances. Supervision must take place at the appropriate level and is essential to ensure that actions will be performed properly in combat. Care must be exercised in supervising, because oversupervising stifles subordinate leaders and insufficient supervising leads to not accomplishing the mission. Always put someone in charge of every facet of the operation—and make certain they know they are responsible for that particular portion. Then provide sufficient latitude to accomplish their mission. This principle is employed with the principles of "Developing a sense of responsibility in your subordinates" and "Keeping your soldiers informed."

Train Your Soldiers as a Team

Cohesion is essential on the battlefield. Soldiers will fight resolutely when they are well trained, when they respect and have confidence in their leaders and buddies, and when they know they are part of a good unit. Failure to foster a sense of teamwork will produce an ineffective unit. Soldiers must be proficient in fundamental skills and then trained to integrate those skills into effective team operations. Performance as a unit provides the foundation for effective performance at each succeedingly higher level. An all-prevailing unity of effort contributes to synchronization.

**Employ Your Unit
in Accordance with Its Capabilities**

This principle synthesizes all Leadership Principles and focuses on the precepts of accomplishing the mission while looking out for the well-being of soldiers. All units, regardless of size, have specific capabilities and limitations. While it is necessary for units to continually train on tough and challenging tasks and to strive for improved performance, tasks must be attainable. Otherwise, the unit begins to lose confidence in itself and in its leaders. Train to *WIN!* Don't over-commit your unit unless it is absolutely essential. Key is the necessity to expand a unit's capabilities through effective training.

Traits of Leadership

Traits facilitate effective leadership by providing the basis to implement the Principles of Leadership. These traits are not all inclusive; rather they serve as a guide for self-assessment and for self-improvement. Leadership Traits appeared with the Leadership Principles in the July 1948 U.S. Army Training Circular 6 and subsequently were incorporated in doctrinal manuals. The traits discussed below are considered traditional and first appeared in the December 1958 leadership manual, although the actual number of traits discussed in Army manuals has fluctuated from twelve in the 1948 training circular to ten in a December 1948 army pamphlet to nineteen in the Army's first leadership manual in 1951. Traits are discussed alphabetically; there is no priority assessed. (Traits included in previous manuals but not discussed include alertness, force, humility, humor, and sympathy.)

Bearing

As a leader, soldiers look to see how you behave. Your appearance and personal conduct have a tremendous influence on young soldiers. They must be of the highest standards. Leaders express competence and self-confidence by how they behave in situations. This translates to instilling confidence and exerting a firm and steadying influence over soldiers. Bearing is not superficial and means more than wearing a shiny belt buckle and pressed uniform. Frequent uncontrolled displays of emotion indicate to your soldiers that you do not have control over even yourself. Bearing also entails avoiding the unnecessary use of profanity. Perhaps the term which best typifies this trait is *dignity*.

The traits of leadership have appeared in various Army leadership publications for over forty years. Presented here is a discussion I wrote in 1988 about each of the traits listed.

Courage

Courage is an essential leader attribute and means both moral and physical courage. It is difficult to define and measure. Leaders must demonstrate the courage of their convictions; they stand up for what is right regardless of what others might think. Never quit, no matter how tough the situation or how low the odds of successfully completing the mission. Act calmly and firmly. Recognize and take acceptable risks. Understand that courage does not mean the absence of fear; everyone is afraid—the leader must recognize fear and overcome it so that his subordinates will follow. Don't be afraid of failure.

Decisiveness

Make decisions promptly and then articulate them in a clear, concise, and forceful manner. There are generally several equally correct ways to solve a problem—the point is to quickly gather the information, analyze the situation, decide on the best course of action, and then execute it. Perfect and complete information is seldom available. Don't worry on always being correct; just learn from your own mistakes and the lessons of others' decisions. A good plan executed quickly is better than a perfect plan executed late. Use common sense.

Dependability

Leaders must be relied upon to perform intelligently and willingly the commander's intent. Always do the best you can. Do what you say you were going to do and be where you say you are going to be. Don't take the easy way out; what is right and what is wrong is important. Attention to detail and seeing tasks through to completion are important.

Endurance

The military profession demands accomplishing physically challenging tasks, under difficult situations, and with extremely high standards. Stamina is essential. Once a task is started, stick to it and see it through, regardless of the obstacles. Leaders will always experience mental and/or physical strain—the point is to be aware of it, meet it, and then beat it.

Enthusiasm

Show interest in each and every task, determined to do a good job. It will become infectious to your soldiers. Enthusiasm breeds enthusiasm. It means the willing and vigorous accomplishment of tasks—no matter how difficult or undesirable. Sometimes this involves an inordinate amount of discipline and courage to overcome the elements or the situation, but it must be done. Be a positive example to your subordinates and encourage soldiers to perform to the best of their ability.

Initiative

Do what needs to be done and when it needs to be done, even without being told to do it. This is a time-honored characteristic of the American soldier. Be innovative and improvise if necessary. Consider the task and look for better ways to do things. Doing something is generally better than doing nothing. Think ahead and recognize what needs to be done, then initiate actions to accomplish it. Encourage subordinates to do likewise.

Integrity

A very special and essential leader attribute. Integrity is non-negotiable. Always tell the truth—to superiors and subordinates alike. Get the facts so that your statements are accurate; don't repeat hearsay. Encourage honest and candid communication.

Judgment

Apply common sense and experience in everything. No-one is perfect; the expectation is merely that the most appropriate or best possible decision is made. Think the situation and courses of action through, ascertain the second- and third-order effects, decide, and act with confidence. Judgment is primarily a product of technical and tactical proficiency.

Justice

Be impartial and consistent in exercising command, specifically the assessment of rewards and punishments. Judge each situation separately on its merits. Be cautious and keep perspective. Keep foremost mission accomplishment while considering the well-being of your soldiers.

Knowledge

Know your job and your soldiers. Be technically and tactically proficient. If you don't know something, don't fake it—your soldiers will know. Instead, study and learn it. Recognize and correct inadequate performance.

Loyalty

Loyalty is a two-sided issue. You have to give it in order to receive it. The profession demands loyalty both up and down. Provide full support to the task at hand—even though you might not personally agree with it.

Tact

Consider the result of your comments. A good approach is to follow the Golden Rule: "Do unto others as you would have them do unto you." Make criticism meaningful, not embarrassing or harmful. Consider the dignity of the soldier by realizing the impact of your comments. Respect for people is the key. Works both from top down and bottom up.

Unselfishness

This is the essence of the military profession and service to the Nation. Leaders do not take advantage of situations for personal pleasure, gain, or safety at the expense of the unit. Look out for your soldiers before you look out for yourself. Share danger, hardship, and discomfort with your soldiers. Total commitment to the profession is essential.

Cadet Prayers

United States Military Academy
Cadet Prayer

O God, our Father, Thou Searcher of Men's hearts, help us draw near to Thee in sincerity and truth. May our religion be filled with gladness and may our worship of Thee be natural.

Strengthen and increase our admiration for honest dealing and clean thinking, and suffer not our hatred of hypocrisy and pretense ever to diminish. Encourage us in our endeavor to live above the common level of life. Make us to choose the harder right instead of the easier wrong, and never to be content with a half truth when the whole can be won. Endow us with courage that is born of loyalty to all that is noble and worthy, that scorns to compromise with vice and injustice and knows no fear when truth and right are in jeopardy. Guard us against flippancy and irreverence in the sacred things of life. Grant us new ties of friendship and new opportunities of service. Kindle our hearts in fellowship with those of a cheerful countenance, and soften our hearts with sympathy for those who sorrow and suffer. Help us to maintain the honor of the Corps untarnished and unsullied and to show forth in our lives the ideals of West Point in doing our duty to Thee and to our Country. All of which we ask in the name of the Great Friend and Master of men. Amen.

The cadet prayers from the nation's three major military academies serve as a source of personal reflection and inspiration. All address common commitments to the enduring values of integrity, honor, selfless service, personal responsibility, and duty.

United States Naval Academy
Midshipman Prayer

Almighty God, whose way is in the sea, whose paths are in the great waters, whose command is over all and whose love never faileth: Let me be aware of Thy presence and obedient to Thy will. Keep me true to my best self, guarding me against dishonesty in purpose and in deed, and helping me so to live that I can stand unashamed and unafraid before my shipmates, my loved ones, and Thee. Protect those in whose love I live. Give me the will to do my best and to accept my share of responsibilities with a strong heart and a cheerful mind. Make me considerate of those entrusted to my leadership and faithful to the duties my country has entrusted in me. Let my uniform remind me daily of the traditions of the service of which I am a part. If I am inclined to doubt, steady my faith; if I am tempted, make me strong to resist; if I should miss the mark, give me courage to try again. Guide me with the light of truth and give me strength to faithfully serve thee, now and always. Amen.

United States Air Force Academy
Cadet Prayer

Lord, God of hosts, my life is a
    stewardship in Your sight.
Grant the light of Your wisdom to the path
    of my cadet days.
Instill within me an abiding awareness of
    my responsibility toward You, my country
    and my fellowman.

I ask true humility that, knowing self,
    I may rise above human frailty.
I ask courage that I may prove faithful
    to duty beyond self.
I ask unfailing devotion to personal
    integrity that I may
    ever remain honorable without
    compromise.

Make me an effective instrument of Your
    peace in the defense of the skies that
    canopy free nations.
So guide me daily in each thought, word
    and deed, that I may fulfill Your will.
May these graces abide with me, my
    loved ones, and all who share my
    country's trust. Amen.

The Will of
Marshal de Belle-Isle

Marshal de Belle-Isle gained prominence during the War of Austrian Succession, 1740–1748, and was active in reforming the French Army. The following is a letter he wrote to his son on the duties of a military commander after his son was selected to command a regiment.

The regiment which God has just given you is one of the best in the army; its lieutenant colonel is a soldier respected for his long and excellent service; all of its captains are older than you, and there is not a one of them who, if his personal services had been considered, would not have merited more than you being named colonel. However, it is you who will be their commander; let this first thought never leave your memory.

I will not tell you: seek to merit the esteem of the corps which you are going to command, for this maxim is too trivial. But I will tell you: seek to merit its love. Every colonel who has won this precious sentiment obtains things with ease, even the most difficult, while he who has not acquired it only obtains things with great difficulty, even the most simple. Make yourself loved therefore, my son, and the difficult role of colonel will become for you an easy game. You would deceive yourself greatly if you were to imagine that, in order to obtain the love of your regiment, you should let discipline slide or give in easily to the desires of each of your officers; this method would be neither certain nor glorious. You would also deceive yourself if you were to imagine that a sole virtue, however brilliant or fortunate it might be, can win this sentiment; as it is not only the eyes of a woman which captivate you, but

Translated by Major (U.S. Army) Larry J. Brown.

the totality, the sum of her traits, it is the same with the combination of virtues and knowledge, of which I will speak to you in this document, which will gain for you the love of your regiment.

Have therefore for your lieutenant colonel the greatest respect; give no order without consulting him. I have often given you this advice, this command; I will do so again each time I find the opportunity. If following the example of certain young commanders you lack respect or consideration for your lieutenant colonel, you would cause me to have the most unfavorable opinion of you, and you would soon become the victim of your imprudence. Your regiment, divided between you and him, would be easy prey for cliques and factions, and from then on, you could no longer hope to do it any good.

Have marked respect for the older captains, consult them frequently, show them friendship and confidence. Be the support, the friend, the father of the young officers; love the old sergeants and soldiers; speak to them often and always with good will, even seek their advice from time to time. A commander of troops will always profit from this popularity; it has often been useful to me.

Study and know profoundly all the officers of your regiment. Deprived of this knowledge, you would be deceived each day; you would confuse modesty with lack of talent, confidence which comes from the belief in one's strengths with vain conceit, desire for order with malicious criticism, love of good and justice with snooping and accusation, envy, or excessive ambition, moderation with apathy or indifference, and severity with inflexibility. You would take advice prompted by flattery or self-interest as if it were based on truth; you would believe yourself to be rewarding virtue, but these rewards would fall upon intrigue; thinking yourself to be favoring real talents, you would only be extolling apparent or artificial ones.

When, after having studied the officers of your regiment for a long time, you know them all, you will choose among the eldest two special friends in whom you will have recognized virtue, knowledge, love of truth and order. You will confide in them the important task of speaking freely to you of your faults, and of showing them to you clearly. Listen to these officers with attention and tractability; however, keep from giving them exclusive or blind confidence and from showing too clearly to the rest of the command the preference you give to these two officers. This knowledge could become the source of animosities.

I have shown you the genius and the character of the French people, their customs and prejudices. I have taught you the best way to repress them and to animate them, to reward them and to punish them. Therefore, I will not repeat for you here the lessons which I have given you on these subjects, but I will tell you never to employ with your soldiers heartless words, dishonorable oaths, and never use profanity or degrading language in their presence. The colonel who uses these expressions with his soldiers degrades himself, and if he is speaking to his officers, he commits an extremely evident blunder. Never forget that the officers of your regiment are men, French, your equals, and that you must, consequently, employ a tone and language when giving them orders which is suitable to those persons in whom honor is the motivating factor. Understand clearly, my son, that this method is the only good one, that only it can make your orders respected, make them acceptable, accelerate their execution, and inspire in the soldiers that confidence in their officers which is the key to good discipline and success.

Never use punishments which the law forbids or the national spirit condemns. When you must punish, let all the pain that you feel to be forced to take such extreme measures be visible on your face. Never miss the opportunity to render small services to officers of your command; in waiting for momentous occasions to oblige them, you risk never being of any service to them. As it is the small kindnesses which retain affection, look often and hard for chances to request medals for your officers, sergeants, and soldiers. The government may refuse your requests, but they will know your sincerity by the warmth that you put in your requests, and your regiment will love you the more for it.

Never lead on any of your subordinates with hopes that you have no possibility of fulfilling. When the persons who hold them see them dashed, they will accuse you of having neglected their interests.

I have accustomed you, over a long period of time, to rising at four in the morning. Keep this fortunate habit. You will never have a greater need of time, because you will never have so many studies to do and duties to execute. Having attained the grade of colonel very young, you will be, or so it appears, a general officer very soon. There is no better time, therefore, to devote yourself to the study of the great tactics of war. You must learn them now. But no matter whether you arrive at a grade higher than that which you now hold, believe me, my son, the duties of a colonel require the most varied and extended knowledge. Can you hope to judge the talents of your corporals if you do not know, as well as the most intelligent among them, the sequence that one must follow to train a recruit. Nor can you judge the knowledge and skill of your sergeants if you do not know the full extent of the duties with which they are charged. What I am telling you of the sergeant is equally applicable to the lieutenant, to the captain, to the major, to the lieutenant colonel; yes, my son, it is only by making yourself capable of filling all the different positions subordinate to your own that you can fill in a worthy fashion that which has been confided to you, and to force the others to carry out all their duties.

I will not recommend to you the study of military regulations, because you undertook that at an early age, but never deviate from what they prescribe. I will be the first to punish you or to request your punishment if I ever learn that you have permitted yourself to stray from them. The law is, in the eyes of every good citizen, of every good soldier, the most sacred subject. It is said, I know well, and in my youth I said it as well as did others: "The letter of the law kills and the spirit brings to life." But as I have always seen that, under the pretext of this theory the greatest transgressions have been permitted, I order you expressly to hold to the letter of the law. Also respect the customs which have been in effect for some time. If you find among them, however,

338

one which is abused, then it must be abolished, but proceed in so doing with care and wisdom. Prepare by your conduct and by your words the changes which you want to put into effect, and make their advantages felt. Never undertake the destruction of several abuses at once. Begin with the most significant, the most essential. If one attacks at once all portions of a structure one wishes to reconstruct, one always unsettles it and sometimes even topples [it]. Do not demolish without having prepared that which must be put in the place of what you wish to topple. Remember that one always does more harm than good when one proposes without consideration even the most advantageous changes, and when one uses violence to have them accepted. Consult the experienced officers concerning the reforms you want to undertake; they will bring, in the wake of their opinion, that of the entire command.

I will not speak to you at all here of the study of war. I have already demonstrated to you the advantages and the necessity of this in a memoir which preceded this one, and I indicated to you the plan you must follow in order to learn this science.

I will limit myself to reminding you that history is the source on which you must constantly draw. Do not read history to learn history, but to learn war, morals, and politics. History has been, ever since my childhood, the object of my study, and I owe to it all that I know. Do not neglect mathematics; I am displeased with myself for not having studied this subject enough. I learned it early, I liked it, I made progress, I owe much to the little I know of mathematics.

You are brave, you have proven it, but keep yourself from being so to excess. How many tears have cost me the bravery of someone who was so very dear to me. Let your bravery be less cruel to me. Bravery, which is the most important quality of a soldier must, in a colonel, be tempered by caution. However, I would much rather have to mourn your death and your glory than your honor.

Remember that those who advise you most often to spare yourself would be the first to blame you if you follow their advice.

Love your country, love your king; you must, my son, both because that is a duty imposed on all citizens, and because the medals which have been awarded me make it a law for you. These feelings are etched in your heart deeply enough that I can dispense with chiseling over them once more.

Love glory; let the desire to obtain it always be ardent. This passion for glory has sustained me in the difficult career that I have led. It made me forget that I was born of delicate health and frail body.

I will not speak to you of honesty, but I recommend to you that you watch over that of your troops. Some colonels are accused of selling positions in their regiments. I do not believe that this can be. They give them away, but their men sell them.

Have a regiment which is superior and better trained than the others, this vanity is permissible to a colonel, but do not seek to make it a thing of beauty or to overload it with ornaments. See that your companies are always full of men ready for war. Let no false pity allow you to permit your captains to receive the pay of the soldiers so that they have none. He who permits himself this embezzlement deceives the king and lacks honesty. You also lack it if you do not use the most exact fairness in the distribution of awards and if you do not insure that your subordinates are not making illicit profits at the expense of your soldiers. This attention, my son, is one of the principles which a colonel must have.

Never let yourself be driven by impatience or anger. One always regrets having followed the first dictates of his emotions. "If you wish to do something foolish, follow the counsel of your anger" correctly observed one of our poets. It is in heeding anger that a commander sometimes compromises his honor, sometimes his life, and even more often that of the men who serve under him.

Obey the laws and the men that the prince has chosen to carry them out. Insubordination is, in the first place, the greatest of military vices. It spreads like wildfire and it becomes stronger as it is diffused. Can any colonel who does not obey his superiors expect or hope to be obeyed by his subordinates?

Consider yourself the judge, the headmaster, the magistrate, and the father of your regiment. As judge and magistrate, you will watch over the maintenance of moral standards. Concern yourself particularly with this objective, always forgotten or too neglected by military commanders. Where there are high morals, laws are observed, and what is worth even more, they are respected. Look to purifying morals but do not think that they can be established through orders. They must be taught by example and inspiration. The power of the example is here, like almost everywhere, stronger than that of will. Vigilance would have us discover, in vain, vices in others with which we ourselves could be reproached. If your morals are pure, those of your regiment will be also, your temperament will be fortified, you will save much time, you will be sheltered from numerous ridiculous things, you will never be the victim of circumstances, and public esteem will compensate you for the deprivations you will have imposed upon yourself.

Avoid gambling, and especially games of chance. Banish them from your regiment. They are the ruin of many soldiers.

Keep yourself from developing a taste for wine, for it stupefies. Your mess should be well-prepared, but never delicate. Admit into it the officers of your corps, giving preference to general officers, colonels, and other commanders. In your mess, let the places be marked according to the degree of esteem that your table guests merit.

Reduce your trains to the bare essential. You must give the example of simplicity, of modesty, because you are the colonel and because you are my son. This moderation will be less difficult for you since I paid the greatest care to prepare you to avoid the excessive softness which transforms the majority of young soldiers into delicate women. I never allowed gold or silver to be placed on your horses, your mules, or the uniforms of your men. I hope that you will continue to practice this necessary simplicity.

The opulence which is so fitting of a man charged to represent a prince is dangerous to a soldier in general and fatal to a colonel. His command makes it a duty, an honor, to imitate him. I have never seen, without extreme indignation, the young commanders of your regiments dragging the luxury and the softness of court after them in camp and in garrison, seeking to make themselves distinguished by the richness and the brilliance of their trains, a horde of valets, the beauty of their horses, the delicacy of their mess. All these officers do is to rival one another in the art of sensual pleasures. Is this the ambition which should motivate military commanders? I have said enough. Bitterness would soon cause me to be carried way. In any case, my advice to you is less necessary on this point than on many others.

You have never seen a man suffer without strongly desiring to make his ills disappear or to lighten them. Keep, my son, this sensitivity. It may well cause you difficulties from time to time, but it will more often bring you pure pleasure. It is as much for your glory as for your honor that I recommend that you show yourself to be humane and generous. Humanity and liberality win and conserve for us the hearts of the men with whom we live and whom we command. Whatever it costs you to aid suffering humanity, I will provide it with joy. I prefer that they speak of your charity than of your skill at organizing celebrations. Let them be surprised at the number of people you make happy as opposed to the number of high and mighty ones that you try to entertain. The memory of a celebration that you have given leaves neither in the mind nor in the heart any agreeable trace; that of an unhappy person whom one has consoled leaves most delightful thoughts. I am not at all opposed to your distributing, on some important occasion, a general reward to the soldiers of your regiment. However, I would prefer that you spend the same amount of money on those who have been wounded, who have accomplished some feat of bravery, or whom, in fulfilling their duties, have suffered a loss which to them is significant. Never allow a single week to go by without visiting once or twice the sick of your regiment. Speak to them kindly, listen to their complaints and respond to them, hear the details of their injuries. This obligingness will contribute as much as medicine to hastening their healing. Visit often the prisoners of your regiment. A guilty man must be punished, but not locked up in an unhealthy place. I do not tell you to spare in war the blood and pain of your soldiers. He who exposes them to unnecessary perils, in order to advance his own reputation, is unworthy to be called a man. You should know also that the glory which one obtains at such a price is neither desirable nor lasting.

French colonels have long been renowned throughout all of Europe for their politeness. I am certain that you will not injure this reputation. Far from remaining below the level of your models, you will surpass them. The majority of colonels are only polite with women, their superiors, and their equals. You will be so with those below you. You will never speak to nor of the officers of your regiment with the imperial tone which certain commanders affect. I repeat, remember that many of your subordinates have earned more than you the right to command a regiment. Many have a more ancient and illustrious family than yours. The only thing they have lacked in not having been placed over you is a little wealth or good luck. Therefore, be accessible, affable, polite, considerate, but even more so towards your subordinates than towards your equals. Politeness with one's equals is often no more than skillful politics, while that which one exercises with his subordinates is proof of goodness of heart. The praise that I have received for never having caused the weight of my authority to be felt should encourage you to follow my example.

If you ever make any mistakes, be quick to admit and especially to correct them. While this manner of conducting one's self is totally natural and is not deserving of praise, it will however draw praise for you, will win you hearts and will allow you to pardon mistakes in others. I have often experienced this myself.

Pay special attention to the young officers of your regiment. Watch over their conduct yourself, as well as their training and their habits. Be, as I have told you, their father, their support, and if necessary, their teacher. Your regiment will be no better than the training of your officers nor its constant zeal for the service. Believe me when I say that you will only obtain these results by paying strict attention to the young officers and by making them acquire proper habits of conduct quickly. Act in such a manner that the old officers feel for the young the tenderness of a father for his children, or at least that a teacher has for his pupil. Insure that the young officers have the proper regard, respect, and condescension for the old officers, like well-raised children have for their father. Create and maintain unity in your regiment. Hasten to snuff out discord before it takes root, to rid it of animosities, or at least to head off their destructive effects. This is one of the prime and most essential obligations imposed on colonels.

Only have recourse to other eyes or to other hands when it is impossible for you to see everything, to do everything. Delve into all the details. One only knows things well when one knows their smallest parts. It is not for colonels to see only the big picture. However, do not look to take charge of those details which regulations have given to your subordinates. Content yourself to observe that each one of them is fulfilling his duty properly.

Finally, here is my last precept: Always remember, my son, that it was not for yourself that you were made a colonel, but for the good of the service and the regiment which has been confided to you. Let the glory of the nation thus be your primary preoccupation.

"Know Your Men—
Know Your Business—
Know Yourself"

C. A. Bach enlisted in the Thirteenth Minnesota Infantry Regiment of the Army National Guard and served as a sergeant with the regiment in the Philippines. Promoted to lieutenant in the Thirty-sixth U.S. Volunteer Infantry, he transferred to the regular Army as a first lieutenant in the Seventh Cavalry and advanced to the rank of major.

His analysis of how to be a leader—an address delivered to the graduating officers of the Second Training Camp at Fort Sheridan—so moved the reserve officers of his battalion that they besieged him for copies. The Waco (Texas) Daily Times Herald, *learning of the great interest the speech had aroused, obtained a copy and printed it verbatim on Sunday, 27 January 1918.*

In a short time each of you men will control the lives of a certain number of other men. You will have in your charge loyal but untrained citizens, who look to you for instruction and guidance.

Your word will be their law. Your most casual remark will be remembered. Your mannerisms will be aped. Your clothing, your carriage, your vocabulary, your manner of command will be imitated.

A copy of the speech was inserted in the *Congressional Record* by Senator Henrik Shipstead of Minnesota in November 1942 and printed as Congressional Document 289.

When you join your organization you will find there a willing body of men who ask from you nothing more than the qualities that will command their respect, their loyalty, and their obedience.

They are perfectly ready and eager to follow you so long as you can convince them that you have those qualities. When the time comes that they are satisfied you do not possess them you might as well kiss yourself good-bye. Your usefulness in that organization is at an end.

From the standpoint of society, the world may be divided into leaders and followers. The professions have their leaders, the financial world has its leaders. We have religious leaders, and political leaders, and society leaders. In all this leadership it is difficult, if not impossible, to separate from the element of pure leadership that selfish element of personal gain or advantage to the individual, without which such leadership would lose its value.

It is in the military service only, where men freely sacrifice their lives for a faith, where men are willing to suffer and die for the right or the prevention of a great wrong, that we can hope to realize leadership in its most exalted and disinterested sense. Therefore, when I say leadership, I mean military leadership.

In a few days the great mass of you men will receive commissions as officers. These commissions will not make you leaders; they will merely make you officers. They will place you in a position where you can become leaders if you possess the proper attributes. But you must make good—not so much with the men over you as with the men under you.

Men must and will follow into battle officers who are not leaders, but the driving power behind these men is not enthusiasm but discipline. They go with doubt and trembling, and with an awful fear tugging at their heartstrings that prompts the unspoken question, "What will he do next?"

Such men obey the letter of their orders but no more. Of devotion to their commander, of exalted enthusiasm which scorns personal risk, of their self-sacrifice to ensure his personal safety, they know nothing. Their legs carry them forward because their brain and their training tell them they must go. Their spirit does not go with them.

Great results are not achieved by cold, passive, unresponsive soldiers. They don't go very far and they stop as soon as they can. Leadership not only demands but receives the willing, unhesitating, unfaltering obedience and loyalty of other men; and a devotion that will cause them, when the time comes, to follow their uncrowned king to hell and back again if necessary.

You will ask yourselves: "Of just what, then, does leadership consist? What must I do to become a leader? What are the attributes of leadership and how can I cultivate them?"

Leadership is a composite of a number of qualities. Among the most important I would list self-confidence, moral ascendancy, self-sacrifice, paternalism, fairness, initiative, decision, dignity, courage.

Let me discuss these with you in detail.

Self-confidence results, first, from exact knowledge; second, the ability to impart that knowledge; and third, the feeling of superiority over others that naturally follows. All these give the officer poise.

To lead, you must know—you may bluff all your men some of the time, but you can't do it all the time. Men will not have confidence in an officer unless he knows his business, and he must know it from the ground up.

The officer should know more about paper work than his first sergeant and company clerk put together; he should know more about messing than his mess sergeant; more about diseases of the horse than his troop farrier. He should be at least as good a shot as any man in his company.

If the officer does not know, and demonstrates the fact that he does not know, it is entirely human for the soldier to say to himself, "To hell with him. He doesn't know as much about this as I do," and calmly disregard the instructions received.

There is no substitute for accurate knowledge. Become so well informed that men will hunt you up to ask questions—that your brother officers will say to one another, "Ask Smith—he knows."

And not only should each officer know thoroughly the duties of his own grade, but he should study those of the two grades next above him. A twofold benefit attaches to this. He prepares himself for duties which may fall to his lot at any time during battle; he further gains a broader viewpoint which enables him to appreciate the necessity for the issuance of orders and join more intelligently in their execution.

Not only must the officer know, but he must be able to put what he knows into grammatical, interesting, forceful English. He must learn to stand on his feet and speak without embarrassment.

I am told that in British training camps student officers are required to deliver ten-minute talks on any subject they may choose. This is excellent practice. For to speak clearly one must think clearly, and clear, logical thinking expresses itself in definite, positive orders.

While self-confidence is the result of knowing more than your men, moral ascendancy over them is based upon your belief that you are the better man. To gain and maintain this ascendancy you must have self-control, physical vitality and endurance and moral force.

You must have yourself so well in hand that, even though in battle you be scared stiff, you will never show fear. For if you by so much as a hurried movement or a trembling of the hand, or a change of expression, or a hasty order hastily revoked, indicate your mental condition it will be reflected in your men in a far greater degree.

In garrison or camp many instances will arise to try your temper and wreck the sweetness of your disposition. If at such times you "fly off the handle" you have not business to be in charge of men. For men in anger say and do things that they almost invariably regret afterward.

An officer should never apologize to his men; also an officer should never be guilty of an act for which his sense of justice tells him he should apologize.

Another element in gaining moral ascendancy lies in the possession of enough physical vitality and endurance to withstand the hardships to which you and your men are subjected, and a dauntless spirit that enables you not only to accept them cheerfully but to minimize their magnitude.

Make light of your troubles, belittle your trials, and you will help vitally to build up within your organization an esprit whose value in time of stress cannot be measured.

Moral force is the third element in gaining moral ascendancy. To exert moral force you must live clean, you must have sufficient brain power to see the right and the will to do right.

Be an example to your men. An officer can be a power for good or a power for evil. Don't preach to them—that will be worse than useless. Live the kind of life you would have them lead, and you will be surprised to see the number that will imitate you.

A loud-mouthed, profane captain who is careless of his personal appearance will have a loud-mouthed, profane dirty company. Remember what I tell you. Your company will be the reflection of yourself. If you have a rotten company it will be because you are a rotten captain.

Self-sacrifice is essential to leadership. You will give, give all the time. You will give of yourself physically for the longest hours; the hardest work and the greatest responsibility is the lot of the captain. He is the first man up in the morning and the last man in at night. He works while others sleep.

You will give of yourself mentally, in sympathy and appreciation for the troubles of men in your charge. This one's mother has died, and that one has lost all his savings in a bank failure. They may desire help, but more than anything else they desire sympathy.

Don't make the mistake of turning such men down with the statement that you have troubles of your own, for every time that you do you move a stone out of the foundation of your house.

Your men are your foundation, and your house of leadership will tumble about your ears unless it rests securely upon them.

Finally, you will give of your own slender financial resources. You will frequently spend your money to conserve the health and well-being of your men or to assist them when in trouble. Generally you get your money back. Very infrequently you must charge it to profit and loss.

When I say that paternalism is essential to leadership I use the term in its better sense. I do not now refer to that form of paternalism which robs men of initiative, self-reliance and self-respect. I refer to the paternalism that manifests itself in a watchful care for the comfort and welfare of those in your charge.

Soldiers are like children. You must see that they have shelter, food, and clothing, the best that your utmost efforts can provide. You must be far more solicitous of their comfort than of your own. You must see that they have food to eat before you think of your own; that they each have as good a bed as can be provided before you consider where you will sleep. You must look after their health. You must conserve their strength by not demanding needless exertion or useless labor.

And by doing all these things you are breathing life into what would be otherwise a mere machine. You are creating a soul in your organization that will make the mass respond to you as though it were one man. And that is esprit.

And when your organization has this esprit you will wake up some morning and discover that the tables have been turned; that instead of your constantly looking out for them they have, without even a hint from you, taken up the task of looking out for you. You will find that a detail is always there to see that your tent, if you have one, is promptly pitched; that the most and the cleanest bedding is brought to your tent; that from some mysterious source two eggs have been added to your supper when no one else has any; that an extra man is helping your men give your horse a supergrooming; that your wishes are anticipated; that every man is Johnny-on-the-spot. And then you have arrived.

Fairness is another element without which leadership can neither be built up nor maintained. There must be first that fairness which treats all men justly. I do not say alike, for you cannot treat all men alike—that would be assuming that all men are cut from the same piece; that there is no such thing as individuality or a personal equation.

You cannot treat all men alike; a punishment that would be dismissed by one man with a shrug of the shoulders is mental anguish for another. A company commander who for a given offense has a standard punishment that applies to all is either too indolent or too stupid to study the personality of his men. In his case justice is certainly blind.

Study your men as carefully as a surgeon studies a difficult case. And when you are sure of your diagnosis apply the remedy. And remember that you apply the remedy to affect a cure, not merely to see the victim squirm. It may be necessary to cut deep, but when you are satisfied as to your diagnosis don't be divided from your purpose by any false sympathy for the patient.

Hand in hand with fairness in awarding punishment walks fairness in giving credit. Everybody hates a human hog.

When one of your men has accomplished an especially creditable piece of work, see that he gets the proper reward. Turn heaven and earth upside down to get it for him. Don't try to take it away from him and have it for yourself. You may do this and get away with it, but you have lost the respect and loyalty of your men. Sooner or later your brother officers will hear of it and shun you like a leper. In war there is glory enough for all. Give the man under you his due. The man who always takes and never gives is not a leader. He is a parasite.

There is another kind of fairness—that which will prevent an officer from abusing the privilege of his rank. When you exact respect from soldiers be sure you treat them with equal respect. Build up their manhood and self-respect. Don't try to pull it down.

For an officer to be overbearing and insulting in the treatment of enlisted men is the act of a coward. He ties the man to a tree with the ropes of discipline and then strikes him in the face, knowing full well that the man cannot strike back.

Consideration, courtesy, and respect from officers toward enlisted men are not compatible with discipline. They are parts of our discipline. Without initiative and decision no man can expect to lead.

In maneuvers you will frequently see when an emergency arises, certain men calmly give instant orders which later, on analysis, prove to be, if not exactly the right thing, very nearly the right thing to have done. You will see other men in emergency become badly rattled; their brains refuse to work, or they give a hasty order, revoke it, give another, revoke that; in short, show every indication of being in a blue funk.

Regarding the first man you may say: "That man is a genius. He hasn't had time to reason this thing out. He acts intuitively." Forget it. "Genius is merely the capacity for taking infinite pains." The man who was ready is the man who has prepared himself. He has studied before-hand the possible situations that might arise, he has made tentative plans covering such situations. When he is confronted by the emergency he is ready to meet it.

He must have sufficient mental alertness to appreciate the problem that confronts him and the power of quick reasoning to determine what changes are necessary in his already formulated plan. He must have also the decision to order the execution and stick to his orders.

Any reasonable order in an emergency is better than no order. The situation is there. Meet it. It is better to do something and do the wrong thing than to hesitate, hunt around for the right thing to do and wind up by doing nothing at all. And, having decided on a line of action, stick to it. Don't vacillate. Men have no confidence in an officer who doesn't know his own mind.

Occasionally you will be called upon to meet a situation which no reasonable human being could anticipate. If you have prepared yourself to meet other emergencies which you could anticipate, the mental training you have thereby gained will enable you to act promptly and with calmness.

You must frequently act without order from higher authority. Time will not permit you to wait for them. Here again enters the importance of studying the work of officers above you. If you have a comprehensive grasp of the entire situation and can form an idea of the general plan of your superiors, that and your previous emergency training will enable you to determine that the responsibility is yours and to issue the necessary orders without delay.

The element of personal dignity is important in military leadership. Be the friend of your men, but do not become their intimate. Your men should stand in awe of you—not fear. If your men presume to become familiar it is your fault, not theirs. Your actions have encouraged them to do so.

And, above all things, don't cheapen yourself by courting their friendship or currying their favor. They will despise you for it. If you are worthy of their loyalty and respect and devotion they will surely give all these without asking. If you are not, nothing that you can do will win them.

And then I would mention courage. Moral courage you need as well as physical courage—that kind of moral courage which enables you to adhere without faltering to a determined course of action which your judgment has indicated as the one best suited to secure the desired results.

Every time you change your orders without obvious reason you weaken your authority and impair the confidence of your men. Have the moral courage to stand by your order and see it through.

Moral courage further demands that you assume the responsibility for your own acts. If your subordinates have loyally carried out your orders and the movement you directed is a failure, the failure is yours, not theirs. Yours would have been the honor had it been successful. Take the blame if it results in disaster. Don't try to shift it to a subordinate and make him the goat. That is a cowardly act.

Furthermore, you will need moral courage to determine the fate of those under you. You will frequently be called upon for recommendations for the promotion or demotion of officers and noncommissioned officers in your immediate command.

Keep clearly in mind your personal integrity and the duty you owe your country. Do not let yourself be deflected from a strict sense of justice by feelings of personal friendship. If your own brother is your second lieutenant, and you find him unfit to hold his commission, eliminate him. If you don't, your lack of moral courage may result in the loss of valuable lives.

If, on the other hand, you are called upon for a recommendation concerning a man whom, for personal reasons you thoroughly dislike, do not fail to do him full justice. Remember that your aim is the general good, not the satisfaction of an individual grudge.

I am taking it for granted that you have physical courage. I need not tell you how necessary that is. Courage is more than bravery. Bravery is fear-lessness—the absence of fear. The merest dolt may be brave, because he lacks the mentality to appreciate his danger; he doesn't know enough to be afraid.

Courage, however, is that firmness of spirit, that moral backbone, which, while fully appreciating the danger involved, nevertheless goes on with the undertaking. Bravery is physical; courage is mental and moral. You may be cold all over; your hands may tremble; your legs may quake; your knees be ready to give away—that is fear. If, nevertheless, you go to lead your men against the enemy, you have courage. The physical manifestations of fear will pass away. You may never experience them but once. They are the "buck fever" of the hunter who tries to shoot his first deer. You must not give way to them.

A number of years ago, while taking a course in demolitions, the class of which I was a member was handling dynamite. The instructor said regarding its manipulation: "I must caution you gentlemen to be careful in the use of these explosives. One man has but one accident." And so I would caution you. If you give way to the fear that will doubtless beset you in your first action, if you show the white feather, if you let your men go forward while you hunt a shell crater, you will never again have the opportunity of leading those men.

Use judgment in calling on your men for display of physical courage or bravery. Don't ask any man to go where you would not go yourself. If your common sense tells you that the place is too dangerous for you to venture into, then it is too dangerous for him. You know his life is as valuable to him as yours is to you.

Occasionally some of your men must be exposed to danger which you cannot share. A message must be taken across a fire-swept zone. You call for volunteers. If your men know you and know that you are "right" you will never lack volunteers, for they will know your heart is in your work, that you are giving your country the best you have, that you would willingly carry the message yourself if you could. Your example and enthusiasm will have inspired them.

And lastly, if you aspire to leadership, I would urge you to study men.

Get under their skins and find out what is inside. Some men are quite different from what they appear to be on the surface. Determine the workings of their minds.

Much of General Robert E. Lee's success as a leader may be ascribed to his ability as a psychologist. He knew most of his opponents from West Point days, knew the workings of their minds, and he believed that they would do certain things under certain circumstances. In nearly every case he was able to anticipate their movements and block the execution.

You do not know your opponent in the same way. But you can know your own men. You can study each to determine wherein lies his strength and his weakness; which men can be relied upon to the last grasp and which cannot.

Know your men, know your business, know yourself.

"Duty, Honor, Country"

This is the text of General MacArthur's address at the U.S. Military Academy, West Point, on presentation of the Sylvanus Thayer Medal by the Association of Graduates, 12 May 1962. The Sylvanus Thayer Medal was first awarded in 1958 and is awarded annually to U.S. citizens whose records of service to their country, accomplishments in national interest, and personal achievements exemplify outstanding devotion to the principles of the motto of the U.S. Military Academy— "Duty, Honor, Country."

General Westmoreland, General Groves, distinguished guests, and gentlemen of the corps.

As I was leaving the hotel this morning, a doorman asked me, "Where are you bound for, General?" and when I replied, "West Point," he remarked, "Beautiful place, have you ever been there before?"

No human being could fail to be deeply moved by such a tribute as this. Coming from a profession I have served so long, and a people I have loved so well, it fills me with an emotion I cannot express. But this award is not intended primarily to honor a personality, but to symbolize a great moral code—the code of conduct and chivalry of those who guard this beloved land of culture and ancient descent. That is the meaning of this medallion. For all eyes and for all time, it is an expression of the ethics of the American soldier. That I should be integrated in this way with so noble an ideal arouses a sense of pride and yet of humility which will be with me always.

Duty—Honor—Country. Those three hallowed words reverently dictate what you ought to be, what you can be, what you will be. They are your rallying points: to build courage when courage seems to fail; to create hope

Reprinted from *Bugle Notes* (West Point, N.Y.: United States Military Academy, 1967), pp. 101–109.

when hope becomes forlorn. Unhappily, I possess neither the eloquence of diction, that poetry of imagination, nor that brilliance of metaphor to tell you all that they mean. The unbelievers will say they are but words, but a slogan, but a flamboyant phrase. Every pendant, every demagogue, every cynic, every hypocrite, every troublemaker, and, I am sorry to say, some others of an entirely different character, will try to downgrade them even to the extent of mockery and ridicule. But here are some of the things they do. They build your basic character, they mold you for your future roles as the custodians of the nation's defense, they make you strong enough to know when you are weak, and brave enough to face yourself when you are afraid. They teach you to be proud and unbending in honest failure, but humble and gentle in success; not to substitute words for actions, nor to seek the path of comfort, but to face the stress and spur of difficulty and challenge; to learn to stand up in the storm but to have compassion on those who fall; to master yourself before you seek to master others; to have a heart that is clean, a goal that is high; to learn to laugh yet never forget how to weep; to reach into the future yet never neglect the past; to be serious yet never to take yourself too seriously; to be modest so that you will remember the simplicity of true greatness, the open mind of true wisdom, the meekness of true strength. They give you a temper of the will, a quality of the imagination, a vigor of the emotions, a freshness of the deep springs of life, a temperamental predominance of courage over timidity, an appetite for adventure over love of ease. They create in your heart the sense of wonder, the unfailing hope of what next, and the joy and inspiration of life. They teach you in this way to be an officer and a gentleman.

And what sort of soldiers are those you are to lead? Are they reliable, are they brave, are they capable of victory? Their story is known to all of you; it is the story of the American man-at-arms. My estimate of him was formed on the battlefield many, many years ago, and has never changed. I regarded him then as I regard him now—as one of the world's noblest figures, not only as one of the finest military characters but also as one of the most stainless. His name and fame are the birthright of every American citizen. In his youth and strength, his love and loyalty he gave—all that mortality can give. He needs no eulogy from me or from any other man. He has written his own history and written it in red on his enemy's breast. But when I think of his patience under adversity, of his courage under fire, and his modesty in victory, I am filled with an emotion of admiration I cannot put into words. He belongs to history as furnishing one of the greatest examples of successful patriotism; he belongs to posterity as the instructor of future generations in the principles of liberty and freedom; he belongs to the present, to us, by his virtues and by his achievements. In 20 campaigns, on a hundred battlefields, around a thousand campfires, I have witnessed that enduring fortitude, that patriotic self-abnegation, and that invincible determination which have carved his statue in the hearts of his people. From one end of the world to the other he has drained deep the chalice of courage.

As I listened to those songs of the glee club, in memory's eye I could see those staggering columns of the First World War, bending under soggy packs, on many a weary march from dripping dusk to drizzling dawn, slogging ankle-deep through the mire of shell-shocked roads to form grimly for the attack, blue-lipped, covered with sludge and mud, chilled by the wind and rain; driving home to their objective, and, for many, to the judgment seat of God. I do not know the dignity of their birth but I do know the glory of their death. They died unquestioning, uncomplaining, with faith in their hearts and on their lips the hope that we would go on to victory. Always for them, Duty—Honor—Country; always their blood and sweat and tears as we sought the way and the light and the truth.

And twenty years after, on the other side of the globe, again the filth of murky foxholes, the stench of ghostly trenches, the slime of dripping dugouts; those boiling suns of relentless heat, those torrential rains of devastating storms; the loneliness and utter desolation of jungle trails, the bitterness of long separation from those they loved and cherished, the deadly pestilence of tropical disease, the horror of stricken areas of war; their resolute and determined defense, their swift and sure attack, their indomitable purpose, their complete and decisive victory—always victory. Always through the bloody haze of their last reverberating shot, the vision of gaunt, ghastly men reverently following your password of Duty—Honor—Country.

The code which those words perpetuate embraces the highest moral laws and will stand the test of any ethics or philosophies ever promulgated for the uplift of mankind. Its requirements are for the things that are right, and its restraints are from the things that are wrong. The soldier, above all other men, is required to practice the greatest act of religious training—sacrifice. In battle and in the face of danger and death, he discloses those divine attributes which his Maker gave when He created man in His own image. No physical courage and no brute instinct can take the place of the Divine help which alone can sustain him. However horrible the incidents of war be, the soldier who is called upon to offer and to give his life for his country, is the noblest development of mankind.

You now face a new world—a world of change. The thrust into outer space of the satellite, spheres, and missiles marked the beginning of another epoch in the long story of mankind—the chapter of the space age. In the five or more billions of years of development of the human race, there has never been a greater, a more abrupt or staggering evolution. We deal now not with things of this world alone, but with the illimitable distances and as yet unfathomed mysteries of the universe. We are reaching out for a new and boundless frontier. We speak in strange terms: of harnessing the cosmic energy; of making winds and tides work for us; of creating unheard synthetic materials to supplement or even replace our old standard basics; of purifying sea water for our drink; of mining ocean floors for new fields of wealth and food; of disease preventatives to expand life into the hundred of years; of controlling the weather for a more equitable distribution of heat and cold, of rain and shine; of space ships to the moon; of the primary target in war, no longer limited to the armed forces of an enemy, but instead to include his civil population; of ultimate conflict between a united human race and the sinister forces of some other planetary galaxy; of such dreams and fantasies as to make life the most exciting of all time.

And through all this welter of change and development, your mission remains fixed, determined, inviolable—it is to win our wars. Everything else in your professional career is but corollary to this vital dedication. All other public purposes, all other public projects, all other public needs, great or small, will find others for their accomplishment; but you are the ones who are trained to fight; yours is the profession of arms—the will to win, the sure knowledge that in war there is no substitute for victory; that if you lose, the nation will be destroyed; that the very obsession of your public service must be Duty—Honor—Country. Others will debate the controversial issues, national and international, which divide men's minds; but serene, calm, aloof, you stand as the nation's war-guardian, as its lifeguard from the raging tides of international conflict, as its gladiator in the arena of battle. For a century and a half you have defended, guarded, and protected its hallowed traditions of liberty and freedom, of right and justice. Let civilian voices argue the merits or demerits of our processes of government; whether our strength is being sapped by deficit financing, indulged in too long, by federal paternalism grown too mighty, by power groups grown too arrogant, by politics grown too corrupt, by extremists grown too rampant, by morals grown too low, by taxes grown too high, by extremists grown too violent; whether our personal liberties are as thorough and complete as they should be. These great national problems are not for your professional participation or military solution. Your guidepost stands out like a ten-fold beacon in the night: Duty—Honor—Country.

You are the leaven which binds together the entire fabric of our national system of defense. From your ranks come the great captains who hold the nation's destiny in their hands the moment the war tocsin sounds. The Long Gray Line has never failed us. Were you to do so, a million ghosts in olive drab, in brown khaki, in blue and gray, would rise from their white crosses thundering those magic words, Duty—Honor—Country.

This does not mean that you are war mongers. On the contrary, the soldier, above all other people, prays for peace, for he must suffer and bear the deepest wounds and scars of war. But always in our ears ring the ominous words of Plato, that wisest of all philosophers, "Only the dead have seen the end of war."

The shadows are lengthening for me. The twilight is here. My days of old have vanished tone and tint; they have gone glimmering through the dreams of things that were. Their memory is one of wondrous beauty, watered by tears, and coaxed and caressed by the smiles of yesterday. I listen vainly for the witching melody of faint bugles blowing reveille, of far drums beating the long roll. In my dreams I hear again the crash of guns, the rattle of musketry, the strange, mournful mutter of the battlefield.

But in the evening of my memory, always I come back to West Point. Always there echoes and re-echoes Duty—Honor—Country.

Today marks my final roll call with you, but I want you to know that when I cross the river my last conscious thoughts will be of The Corps, and The Corps, and The Corps.

I bid you farewell.

General Clarke's Guidelines

General Bruce C. Clarke was commissioned in 1925 after graduating from the U.S. Military Academy. He established an outstanding combat commander record during World War II and subsequently served at the highest levels of the Army. Throughout his active career and after his retirement, he was an active voice in how the Army can develop leaders and commanders.

What Soldiers Have a Right to Expect from Leaders

1. Honest, just, and fair treatment.
2. Consideration due them as mature, professional soldiers.
3. Personal interest taken in them as individuals.
4. Loyalty.
5. Shielding from harassment from "higher up."
6. The best in leadership.
7. That their needs be anticipated and provided for.
8. All the comforts and privileges practicable.
9. To be kept oriented and told the "reason why."
10. A well-thought-out program of training, work and recreation.
11. Clear-cut and positive decisions and orders which are not constantly changing.

Reprinted from General Bruce C. Clarke, *Thoughts on Leadership* (Ft. Belvoir, Va.: U.S. Army Engineer School, n.d.).

12. Demands on them commensurate with their capabilities—not too small, not too great.
13. That their good work be recognized, and publicized when appropriate.

What Commanders Have a Right to Expect from Higher Commanders

1. That their honest errors be pointed out but be underwritten at least once in the interests of developing initiative and leadership.
2. To be responsible for and be allowed to develop their own units with only the essential guidance from above.
3. A helpful attitude toward their problems.
4. Loyalty.
5. That they not be subject to the needling of unproductive "statistics" competitions between like units.
6. The best in commandership.
7. That the needs of their units be anticipated and provided for.
8. To be kept oriented as to the missions and situation in the unit above.
9. A well-thought-out program of training, work and recreation.
10. To receive timely, clear-cut, and positive orders and decisions which are not constantly changed.
11. That the integrity of their tactical units be maintained in assigning essential tasks.
12. That their success be measured by the overall ability of a unit to perform its whole mission and not by the performance of one or two factors.
13. That good works by their units be recognized and rewarded in such a way as to motivate the greatest number to do well and to seek further improvement.

Thirteen Mistakes

Brigadier General S.L.A. Marshall was a military writer, journalist, and historian. He pioneered combat history techniques as a result of his exposure to small unit engagements in the Pacific Theater of World War II and helped record the Army's European campaigns. His best-known and perhaps most-controversial work was Men Against Fire.

1. To attempt to set up your own standard of right and wrong.
2. To try to measure the enjoyment of others by your own.
3. To expect uniformity of opinions in the world.
4. To fail to make allowance for inexperience.
5. To endeavor to mold all dispositions alike.
6. Not to yield on unimportant trifles.
7. To look for perfection in our own actions.
8. To worry ourselves and others about what can't be remedied.
9. Not to help everybody wherever, however, whenever we can.
10. To consider impossible what we cannot ourselves perform.
11. To believe only what our finite minds can grasp.
12. Not to make allowances for the weaknesses of others.
13. To estimate by some outside quality, when it is that within which makes the man.

Reprinted from *The Officer as a Leader* by Brigadier General S.L.A. Marshall with permission of Stackpole Books.

Robert Rogers' Standing Orders

Major Robert Rogers fought for the British against the French in the mid-1750s. Through his expertise and skill in wilderness fighting, coupled with his dynamic leadership, he established an elite unit of fighters. Though he was a pioneer in the early development of ranger training and tactics, his rules remain applicable today.

- Don't forget nothing.
- Have your musket clean as a whistle, hatchet scoured, 60 rounds powder and ball, and be ready to march at a minute's warning.
- When you're on the march, act the way you would if you was sneaking up on a deer. See the enemy first.
- Tell the truth about what you see and what you do. There is an army depending on us for correct information. You can lie all you please when you tell other folks about the Rangers, but don't never lie to a Ranger or officer.
- Don't never take a chance you don't have to.
- When we're on the march, we march single file, far enough apart so one shot can't go through two men.
- If we strike swamps, or soft ground, we spread out abreast, so it's hard to track us.
- When we march, we keep moving till dark, so as to give the enemy the least possible chance at us.
- When we camp, half the party stays awake while the other half sleeps.

Source: "Major Robert Rogers' Famous Ranging Rules," Appendix D, U.S. Army Field Manual 7-85, *Ranger Unit Operations,* June 1987.

- If we take prisoners, we keep 'em separate till we have had time to examine them.
- Don't ever march home the same way. Take a different route so you won't be ambushed.
- No matter whether we travel in big parties or little ones, each party has to keep a secure 20 yards ahead, 20 yards in the rear, so the main body can't be surprised and wiped out.
- Every night you'll be told where to meet if surrounded by a superior force.
- Don't sit down to eat without posting sentries.
- Don't sleep beyond dawn. Dawn's when the French and Indians attack.
- Don't cross a river by a regular ford.
- If somebody's trailing you, make a circle, come back onto your own tracks, and ambush the folks that aim to ambush you.
- Don't stand up when the enemy's coming against you. Kneel down, lie down, hide behind a tree.
- Let the enemy come till he's almost close enough to touch. Then let him have it and jump out and finish him up with your hatchet.

Index of Authors

The following abbreviations are used in this index: USA = United States Army; USN = United States Navy; USMC = United States Marine Corps; USAF = United States Air Force; CSA = Confederate States of America. The term "floruit" indicates "is known to have lived at that time."

peace, 218
praise, 233
stress, 272
AUGUSTINE, Saint (Aurelius Augustinus)
[354–430]: Italian philosopher
duty, 89

BACH, C. A., Major (USA) [floruit 1917]:
American soldier
courage, 59
decision making, 74
knowledge, wisdom, intelligence, 140
"Know Your Men" speech, 343
military ethics, 163
responsibility, 246
BACON, Francis, Viscount St. Albans [1561–
1626]: English philosopher and essayist
adversity, 6
ambition, 13
fear, 109
honor, 116
knowledge, wisdom, intelligence, 140
virtue, 310
BAKER, Milton G., Lieutenant General (USA)
[1896–1976]: American soldier
duty, 89
BAKER, Newton Diehl [1871–1937]: American
Secretary of War (1916–1921)
military ethics, 164
BARNETT, Correlli [1927–]: American writer
faith, 106
military ethics, 164
BARROW, Robert H., General (USMC)
[1922–]: American marine and
Commandant of U.S. Marine Corps
(1979–1983)
creativity, imagination, innovation, 68
judgment, 132
BARTLETT, Gerald T., Lieutenant General
(USA) [1936–]: American soldier
military leadership, 180
BAUDOUIN I [1930–]: King of Belgium
peace, 218
BEE, Bernard Elliott, Brigadier General (CSA)
[1824–1861]: American soldier
military history, 169
BEECHER, Henry Ward [1813–1887]:
American writer
ambition, 13
humor, 124
military ethics, 164
BELISARIUS [505–565]: Byzantine soldier
peace, 218
BELLAMY, Francis [1856–1931]: American
editor and writer
patriotism (Pledge of Allegiance), 210
BELLE-ISLE, Charles-Louis-Auguste Fouquet,
Marshal de (French Army) [1684–1761]:
French soldier
advice, 11
discipline, 78
emotion, 96
military ethics, 164
military history, 169

mistakes, 185
motivation, 196
will of, 336
BENNIS, Warren [1925–]: American scholar
and writer
communication, 46
leadership, 147
mistakes, 185
BIBLE: Authorized King James Version (1611)
advice (Proverbs 19:20/Proverbs 20:18), 11
ambition (Matthew 7:20/Mark 8:36), 13
boldness, audacity (Matthew 7:7), 23
caring (Luke 6:31), 28
character (Proverbs 22:1/Ecclesiastes 6:1),
33
commander's intent (I Corinthians 14:8), 43
confidence (Isaiah 30:15), 55
emotion (Proverbs 16:32/Ephesians 4:26/
James 1:19), 96
faith (Mark 9:23/John 20:29/II Corinthians
5:7), 106
integrity (Psalms 25:21), 129
just, justice (Mark 4:24/II Samuel 23:3),
137
knowledge, wisdom, intelligence (Proverbs
17:27), 140
leadership (Matthew 8:9), 147
loyalty (Matthew 6:24), 153
pride (Proverbs 16:18), 236
responsibility (Luke 12:48), 246
role modeling, leadership by example (I
Timothy 4:12), 254
second-, third-order effects (James 3:5), 259
service (Matthew 22:14), 261
values (II Thessalonians 2:15), 301
victory, winning (Psalms 33:16), 305
virtue (Philippians 4:8), 310
BIERCE, Ambrose Gwinett [1842–circa 1914]:
American journalist and poet
emotion, 97
BISMARCK-SCHÖNHAUSEN, Otto Eduard
Leopold von, Prince [1815–1898]: Prussian
statesman and first Chancellor of German
Empire
experience, 101
BLACKER, Valentine, Lieutenant Colonel
(Royal British Army) [1778–1823]: British
soldier
trust, 293
BOHN, Henry George [1796–1884]: English
writer
character, 33
mistakes, 185
BOK, Derek C. [1930–]: American scholar and
President of Harvard (1971–)
military ethics, 164
BRADFORD, Zeb Boyce, Jr., Brigadier
General (USA) [1933–]: American soldier
values, 301
BRADLEY, Omar Nelson, General (USA)
[1893–1981]: American soldier and
General of the Army; Army Chief of Staff
(1948–1949); first Chairman, Joint Chiefs
of Staff (1949–1953)

CHAPIN, George [1826–1880]
courage, 59
CHARRON, Pierre [1541–1603]: French
philosopher and theologian
caring, 28
CHARLES, Karl Ludwig Johann [1771–1847]:
Archduke of Austria and Duke of Teschen
experience, 101
CH'ÊN HAO [floruit 700]: Chinese
philosopher and commentator
second-, third-order effects, 259
CHESTERFIELD, Earl of (Philip Dormer
Stanhope) [1694–1773]: English statesman
and scholar
advice, 12
human nature, 118
CHURCHILL, John, Duke of Marlborough
[1650–1722]: British soldier and statesman
role modeling, leadership by example, 254
CHURCHILL, Winston Leonard Spencer, Sir
[1874–1965]: British statesman and writer;
Prime Minister of Great Britain (1940–
1945 and 1951–1955)
adversity, 7
communication, 46
competence, 50, 51
courage, 60
discipline, 79
duty, 89
emotion, 97
fear, 109
judgment, 133
loyalty, 153
luck, fate, 155
military history, 169
military leadership, 180
moral courage, will, 188
peace, 218
perseverance, determination, 221
training, 284
victory, winning, 305
war, 314, 315
CICERO, Marcus Tullius [106–43 B.C.]: Roman
orator, statesman, and scholar
ambition, 13
duty, 89
just, justice, 137
mistakes, 185
obedience, 202
praise, 233
virtue, 311
CLARKE, Bruce Cooper, General (USA)
[1901–1988]: American soldier and writer
caring, 28
cohesion, 39
commander's intent, 43
communication, 46
guidelines, 355
initiative, 126
management, 160
mentor, 162
military history, 169
mistakes, 185
morale, 191

motivation, 196
NCO corps, 199
officer corps, 205
physical presence, 225
physical stamina, 230
pride, 236
problem solving, 238
reflection, 240
respect, 242
responsibility, 247
service, 261
the soldier, 266
standards, 270
training, 284
CLARKE, James Freeman [1810–1898]:
American theologian
faith, 106
CLAUSEWITZ, Karl Maria von [1780–1831]:
Prussian and Russian soldier and military
writer
attributes, 16
boldness, audacity, 23, 24
cohesion, 39
communication, 46
danger, 72
judgment, 133
knowledge, wisdom, intelligence, 140
luck, fate, 155
military ethics, 165
military history, 170
military leadership, 180–181
moral courage, will, 188
obedience, 202
war, 315
CLEON OF ATHENS [died 422 B.C.]: Greek
soldier and leader
decision making, 74
CLEVELAND, Grover Stephen [1837–1908]:
American President (1885–1889 and
1893–1897)
trust, 293
COCTEAU, Jean [1891–1963]: French novelist,
poet, and playwright
tact, 278
COLERIDGE, Samuel Taylor [1772–1834]:
English poet and essayist
experience, 101
truth, 296
COLLINS, Arthur S., Jr., Lieutenant General
(USA) [1915–1984]: American soldier,
trainer, and writer
leadership, 148
standards, 270
training, 284
COLLINS, John Churton [1848–1908]: English
critic
pride, 236
COLLINS, Joseph Lawton, General (USA)
[1896–1987]: American soldier and Army
Chief of Staff (1949–1953)
the soldier, 267
CONFUCIUS [551–479 B.C.]: Chinese
philosopher
boldness, audacity, 24

DRAKE, Francis, Sir [circa 1540–1596]:
British explorer and naval officer
motivation, 197
perseverance, determination, 221
DRAKE, Joseph Rodman [1795–1820]:
American poet
patriotism, 211
DRUCKER, Peter Ferdinand [1909–]:
American scholar and management expert
judgment, 133
DUMAS, Alexandre [1824–1895]: French
playwright
victory, winning, 305
DUTOURD, Jean [1920–]: French novelist and
satirist
discipline, 79
duty, 90
leadership, 149
risk, 250

EDISON, Thomas Alva [1847–1931]:
American inventor
motivation, 197
EINSTEIN, Albert [1879–1955]: German-
Swiss-American scientist
commander's intent, 43
creativity, imagination, innovation, 68
human nature, 118
EISENHOWER, Dwight David, General (USA)
[1890–1969]: American soldier, General of
the Army, and President (1953–1961)
ability, 3
attributes, 17
commander's intent, 43
creativity, imagination, innovation, 68
leadership, 149
luck, fate, 155
mistakes, 186
morale, 191, 192
patriotism, 211
perseverance, determination, 221
praise, 234
teamwork, 281
training, 285
trust, 293
valor, 299
virtue, 311
war, 316
ELLER, Ernest N., Rear Admiral (USN)
[1903–]: American naval officer
boldness, audacity, 24
EMERSON, Ralph Waldo [1803–1882]:
American philosopher, essayist, and poet
ability, 3
advice, 12
ambition, 14
character, 34
courage, 60
duty, 90
just, justice, 137
knowledge, wisdom, intelligence, 141
military history, 170
motivation, 197
peace, 219

second-, third-order effects, 260
service, 262
trust, 293, 294
truth, 296
valor, 299
virtue, 311, 312
war, 316
EPICTETUS [circa A.D. 50–120]: Greek
philosopher
adversity, 7
ambition, 14
fear, 109
perseverance, determination, 222
respect, 242
virtue, 312
ERASMUS, Desiderius [1465–1536]: Dutch
scholar and philosopher
boldness, audacity, 24
EURIPIDES [circa 485–406 B.C.]: Greek
playwright
ability, 3
authority, 21
boldness, audacity, 24
danger, 72
judgment, 133
just, justice, 137
knowledge, wisdom, intelligence, 141
leadership, 149
luck, fate, 155
perseverance, determination, 222
second, third order effects, 260
victory, winning, 305

FALLQWS, James [1949–]: American
journalist and writer
trust, 294
FALLS, Cyril Bentham [1888–1971]: British
military historian
war, 316
FARRAGUT, David Glasgow, Admiral (USN)
[1801–1870]: American naval officer; most
successful Union Admiral in Civil War
boldness, audacity, 24
duty, 90
human nature, 119
FEHRENBACH, Theodore Reed [1925–]:
American military writer
military leadership, 181
FISH, Hamilton [1808–1893]: American
Secretary of State (1869–1877)
patriotism, 211
FITTON, Robert Arthur, Lieutenant Colonel
(USA) [1949–]: American soldier
principles of leadership, 325
traits of leadership, 330
FLANAGAN, Edward Michael, Jr., Lieutenant
General (USA) [1921–]: American soldier
and writer
military ethics, 165
military leadership, 181
problem solving, 239
FOCH, Ferdinand, Marshal (French Army)
[1851–1929]: French soldier
commander's intent, 44

knowledge, wisdom, intelligence, 141
military history, 170
perseverance, determination, 222
second-, third-order effects, 260
victory, winning, 305, 305–306, 306
FOLARD, Jean Charles de, Chevalier [1669–
1752]: French writer and military theorist
war, 316
FORD, Henry [1863–1947]: American inventor
and businessman
creativity, imagination, innovation, 69
safety, 257
FORGY, Howell Maurice, Chaplain (USN)
[1908–?]: American naval officer and
military chaplain
military history, 171
FORMAN, Robert H., Lieutenant General
(USA) [1930–]: American soldier
ambition, 14
perseverance, determination, 222
FOSDICK, Harry Emerson [1878–1969]:
American clergyman
patriotism, 212
FOSTER, John Watson [1836–1917]: American
Secretary of State (1892–1893)
duty, 90
FRANKLIN, Benjamin [1706–1790]:
American statesman, writer, and scientist
experience, 101
just, justice, 138
patriotism, 212
praise, 234
victory, winning, 306
war, 316
FREDERICK THE GREAT [1712–1786]:
Prussian soldier and King of Prussia
(1740–1786)
caring, 29
creativity, imagination, innovation, 69
discipline, 79
esprit, 99
fear, 109
flexibility, change, 114
human nature, 119
knowledge, wisdom, intelligence, 141
luck, fate, 156
military history, 171
motivation, 197
NCO corps, 200
physical presence, 225
reflection, 240
FREEMAN, Douglas Southall [1886–1953]:
American historian and writer
military history, 171
FRENCH ARMY FIELD REGULATIONS
morale, 192
FROST, Holloway Halstead [1889–1935]:
American naval officer
risk, 251
FRY, James Clyde, Major General (USA)
[1897–1982]: American soldier
competence, 51
FULBRIGHT, James William [1905–]:
American statesman

military ethics, 165
FULLER, James Frederick Charles, Major-
General (Royal British Army) [1878–
1966]: British soldier
attributes, 17
creativity, imagination, innovation, 69
danger, 72
human nature, 119
physical presence, 225
FULLER, Thomas [1654–1734]: English
physician and writer
competence, 51
emotion, 97
failure, 104
humor, 124
just, justice, 138
knowledge, wisdom, intelligence, 142
luck, fate, 156
military leadership, 181
praise, 234
risk, 251

GABRIEL, Richard A. [1942–]: American
writer
responsibility, 247
GALLIGAN, Francis Bernard, Jr., Major
(USA) [1944–1980]: American soldier
officer corps, 206
GANNON, Thomas Michael [1936–]:
American theologian, sociologist, and
writer
values, 304
GARD, Robert Gibbons, Jr., Major General
(USA) [1928–]: American soldier
values, 302
GERMAN ARMY LEADERSHIP MANUAL
(Truppenführung)
decision making, 75
GIBBON, Edward [1737–1794]: English
historian
competence, 51
valor, 299
GIDEON [floruit 1249 B.C.]: Biblical Jewish
leader and soldier
role modeling, leadership by example, 255
GLADIATOR SALUTE
duty, 90
GLASGOW, Arnold H. [floruit 1970]:
American scholar
leadership, 149
GLOVER, James Malcolm, General Sir (Royal
British Army) [1929–]: British soldier
character, 34
GOETHE, Johann Wolfgang von [1749–1832]:
German novelist and poet
adversity, 7
boldness, audacity, 24, 25
caring, 29
danger, 73
initiative, 126
mistakes, 186
motivation, 197
respect, 242
service, 262

LAO-TZU [circa 604–531 B.C.]: Chinese
philosopher
discipline, 80
knowledge, wisdom, intelligence, 142
military leadership, 182
LAWRENCE, James, Admiral (USN) [1781–
1813]: American naval officer
perseverance, determination, 223
LAWRENCE, Thomas Edward (Lawrence of
Arabia) [1888–1936]: British soldier and
archeologist
discipline, 80
judgment, 133
knowledge, wisdom, intelligence, 143
reflection, 241
LEDRU-ROLLIN, Alexandre Auguste [1807–
1874]: French political leader
leadership, 149
LEE, Henry "Light Horse Harry," Major
General (USA) [1756–1818]: American
soldier
training, 287
LEE, Robert Edward, General (CSA) [1807–
1870]: American soldier; Superintendent,
U.S. Military Academy (1852–1855);
commanded Army of Northern Virginia
during Civil War
competence, 52
confidence, 57
discipline, 80
duty, 91
obedience, 203
safety, 257
the soldier, 267
war, 317
LEJEUNE, John A., General (USMC) [1867–
1942]: American marine and Commandant
of U.S. Marine Corps (1920–1929)
attributes, 17
discipline, 80
mentor, 162
LE MAY, Curtis Emerson, General (USAF)
[1906–]: American airman and Air Force
Chief of Staff (1961–1965)
discipline, 81
LEMNITZER, Lyman Louis, General (USA)
[1899–1988]: American soldier and Army
Chief of Staff (1959–1960); Chairman,
Joint Chiefs of Staff (1960–1962);
Supreme Allied Commander, Europe
(1963–1969)
competence, 52
initiative, 127
judgment, 134
service, 262
LEWAL, Jules Lewis [1823–1908]: French
philosopher
flexibility, change, 114
LIDDELL HART, Basil Henry, Captain Sir
(Royal British Army) [1895–1970]: British
military historian, theorist, and soldier
boldness, audacity, 25
character, 35
creativity, imagination, innovation, 70

decision making, 75
discipline, 81
faith, 106–107
fear, 110
human nature, 119
judgment, 134
luck, fate, 156
military history, 172
moral courage, will, 189
perseverance, determination, 223
risk, 251
tact, 279
LIDDY, George Gordon Battle [1930–]:
American lawyer, writer, and government
official
patriotism, 213
LINCOLN, Abraham [1809–1865]: American
President (1861–1865)
character, 35
commander's intent, 44
communication, 47
duty, 92
human nature, 119
respect, 243
tact, 279
LINCOLN, James F. [1916–]: American lawyer
and writer
creativity, imagination, innovation, 70
leadership, 149
LIPPMANN, Walter [1889–1974]: American
journalist and scholar
creativity, imagination, innovation, 71
honor, 117
leadership, 150
values, 302
LIVSEY, William J., General (USA) [1931–]:
American soldier
caring, 29
LIVY (Titus Livius) [59 B.C.–A.D. 17]: Roman
historian
luck, fate, 157
safety, 257
LOCKE, John [1632–1704]: English
philosopher
virtue, 312
LOMBARDI, Vince [1913–1970]: American
football coach
duty, 92
emotion, 97
failure, 104
leadership, 150
motivation, 197
physical stamina, 231
victory, winning, 307
LONGFELLOW, Henry Wadsworth [1807–
1882]: American poet
role modeling, leadership by example, 255
LOTT, Arnold Samuel, Lieutenant
Commander (USN) [1912–]: American
naval officer and writer
respect, 243

MacARTHUR, Douglas, General (USA)
[1880–1965]: American soldier and

General of the Army, awarded Medal of
Honor; Superintendent, U.S. Military
Academy (1919–1922)
boldness, audacity, 25
creativity, imagination, innovation, 71
duty, 92
"Duty, Honor, Country" address, 351
failure, 104–105
military history, 172, 173
moral courage, will, 189
morale, 193
perseverance, determination, 223
physical presence, 226
reflection, 241
service, 263
training, 287
values, 302–303
victory, winning, 307
MACAULAY, Thomas Babington, Lord [1800–
1859]: English statesman, poet, historian,
and essayist
character, 35
knowledge, wisdom, intelligence, 143
MACHIAVELLI, Niccolò di Bernardo [1469–
1527]: Italian statesman and philosopher
adversity, 8
boldness, audacity, 25
confidence, 57
courage, 62
discipline, 81
knowledge, wisdom, intelligence, 143
obedience, 203
the soldier, 267
war, 317
MacINTIRE, John, Lieutenant (Royal
Marines) [floruit 1763]: British marine
discipline, 81
MacMANUS, Seumas [1869–1960]: Irish
scholar and writer
integrity, 130
MAGEE, William Connor, Bishop [1821–1891]:
Irish prelate
mistakes, 186
MAHAN, Alfred Thayer, Rear Admiral (USN)
[1840–1914]: American naval officer,
historian, and strategic theorist
management, 160
obedience, 203
perseverance, determination, 224
MALLORY, Stephen Russell [1813–1873]:
Confederate States' Secretary of the Navy
(1861–1865)
training, 287
MALONE, Dandridge M. "Mike," Colonel
(USA) [1930–]: American soldier and
writer
leadership, 150
military leadership, 182
training, 287
values, 303
MANN, Thomas [1875–1955]: German
novelist and essayist
peace, 219

MARCUS AURELIUS ANTONINUS [121–
180]: Roman emperor and philosopher
ambition, 14
character, 36
reflection, 241
MARCY, William Learned [1786–1857]:
American Secretary of War (1845–1849);
Secretary of State (1853–1857)
victory, winning, 307
MARINE CORPS MOTTO
duty, 92
faith, 107
MARLOWE, Christopher [1564–1593]: English
playwright and poet
training, 287
MARQUESS OF HALIFAX (Sir George
Savile) [1633–1695]: English statesman,
orator, and writer
risk, 251
MARRYAT, Frederick [1792–1848]: British
naval officer and novelist
service, 263
MARSH, John O., Jr. [1926–]: American
Secretary of the Army (1981–1989)
competence, 52
patriotism, 213
risk, 251
training, 287, 288
MARSHALL, George Catlett, General (USA)
[1880–1959]: American soldier and Army
Chief of Staff (1939–1945); Secretary of
State (1945–1949); Secretary of Defense
(1949–1950)
adversity, 8
boldness, audacity, 26
character, 36
discipline, 81–82
knowledge, wisdom, intelligence, 143
morale, 193, 193–194
patriotism, 214
physical stamina, 231
problem solving, 239
standards, 271
training, 288
values, 303
MARSHALL, Samuel Lyman Atwood,
Brigadier General (USA) [1900–1977]:
American soldier, military writer, and
journalist
caring, 29
character, 36
cohesion, 40, 41
communication, 47, 48
confidence, 57
courage, 62
creativity, imagination, innovation, 71
danger, 73
discipline, 82
esprit, 99
fear, 110
human nature, 120
initiative, 127
integrity, 130
knowledge, wisdom, intelligence, 143

authority, 21–22
knowledge, wisdom, intelligence, 144
MORAN, Charles McMoran Wilson, Lord
[1882–1977]: British physician and
historian
character, 37
moral courage, will, 189
MORE, Hannah [1745–1833]: English writer
and philanthropist
duty, 92
MOSBY, John Singleton, Colonel (CSA) [1833–
1916]: American soldier
the soldier, 268
war, 318
MURROW, Edward Roscoe [1908–1965]:
American journalist
patriotism, 214
truth, 297
MUSASHI, Miyamoto [1584–1645]: Japanese
samurai
victory, winning, 307
MUSSOLINI, Benito [1883–1945]: Italian
dictator (1924–1945)
war, 318

NAPIER, Charles, Admiral Sir (Royal British
Navy) [1786–1860]: British naval officer
knowledge, wisdom, intelligence, 144
obedience, 203
officer corps, 206
NAPIER, William Francis Patrick, General Sir
(Royal British Army) [1785–1860]: British
soldier
decision making, 76
military leadership, 183
NAPOLÉON BONAPARTE [1769–1821]:
French soldier; First Consul of France
(1799–1804); and Emperor of France
(1804–1815)
adversity, 8
attributes, 17, 17–18
boldness, audacity, 26
commander's intent, 44
competence, 52
confidence, 57
courage, 63
decision making, 76
failure, 105
fear, 110
flexibility, change, 115
judgment, 134
knowledge, wisdom, intelligence, 144
leadership, 150
luck, fate, 157
military history, 173
military leadership, 183
mistakes, 186
moral courage, will, 189
morale, 194
motivation, 197
patriotism, 214
praise, 234
risk, 252
safety, 258

service, 263
the soldier, 268
stress, 273
subordinates, 276
tact, 279
training, 289
victory, winning, 307, 308
war, 318
NELSON, Horatio, Lord Admiral (Royal
British Navy) [1758–1805]: British naval
officer
duty, 92, 93
luck, fate, 157
officer corps, 206
NEWCOMB, Arthur W.
leadership, 150
NEWMAN, Aubrey Strode "Red," Major
General (USA) [1903–]: American soldier
and writer
courage, 63
danger, 73
decision making, 76
discipline, 82
duty, 93
experience, 102
flexibility, change, 115
human nature, 121
humor, 125
judgment, 134, 135
knowledge, wisdom, intelligence, 144
loyalty, 154
military leadership, 183
NCO corps, 200
physical presence, 226
praise, 235
respect, 244
responsibility, 248
safety, 258
standards, 271
stress, 273
subordinates, 276
tact, 279
trust, 294
NEWTON, Howard W.
failure, 105
tact, 279
NEW YORK TIMES
confidence, 58
human nature, 120
NICHOLAS I OF RUSSIA [1796–1855]: Czar
of Russia (1825–1855)
military history, 173
NIETZSCHE, Friedrich Wilhelm [1844–1900]:
German philosopher
ability, 4
adversity, 8
knowledge, wisdom, intelligence, 144
military leadership, 183
NIMITZ, Chester W., Admiral (USN) [1885–
1966]: American naval officer
courage, 63
valor, 300
NIXON, Richard Milhous [1913–]: American
President (1969–1974).

failure, 105
patriotism, 214

O'DANIEL, John Wilson, Lieutenant General
(USA) [1894–1952]: American soldier
courage, 63
O'HARA, Theodore, Colonel (CSA) [1820–
1867]: American soldier and poet
the soldier, 268
OLGILVIE, David
subordinates, 276
OMAN, Charles William Chadwick, Sir [1860–
1946]: English historian
war, 318
OVID (Publius Ovidius Naso) [43 B.C.–circa
A.D. 18]: Roman poet
adversity, 8
flexibility, change, 115
training, 289

PAINE, Thomas [1737–1809]: American
patriot and essayist
character, 37
military ethics, 166
patriotism, 215
virtue, 312
war, 318
PALEY, William [1743–1805]: English
philosopher and theologian
truth, 297
PATCH, Alexander McCarrell, General (USA)
[1889–1945]: American soldier
caring, 29–30
character, 37
courage, 63
integrity, 130
service, 263
PATTERSON, Robert Porter [1891–1952]:
American Secretary of War (1945–1947)
training, 289
PATTON, George Smith, Jr., General (USA)
[1885–1945]: American soldier
attributes, 18
boldness, audacity, 26
communication, 48
confidence, 58
courage, 63, 64
decision making, 77
discipline, 82, 82–83, 83, 83–84
duty, 93
esprit, 99, 100
fear, 111
flexibility, change, 115
human nature, 121
initiative, 127
loyalty, 154
military history, 173–174
officer corps, 206–207, 207
perseverance, determination, 224
physical presence, 227
praise, 235
pride, 236
risk, 252
subordinates, 276

training, 289
victory, winning, 308
war, 318
PENN, William [1644–1718]: English Quaker
adversity, 8
discipline, 84
PERICLES [circa 495–429 B.C.]: Greek soldier,
statesman, and orator
patriotism, 215
PERRY, Oliver Hazard, Admiral (USN) [1785–
1819]: American naval officer
perseverance, determination, 224
PERSHING, John Joseph, General of the
Armies (USA) [1860–1948]: American
soldier
competence, 52
respect, 244
training, 289
PÉTAIN, Henri-Philippe Benoni Omer Joseph,
Marshal (French Army) [1856–1951]:
French soldier
military history, 174
PETERS, Thomas J. [1942–]: American writer
caring, 30
creativity, imagination, innovation, 71
motivation, 198
teamwork, 282
PETRONIUS ARBITER (Petronius Gaius)
[died A.D. 66]: Roman writer
cohesion, 41
PHILIP, John W., Captain (USN) [1840–1900]:
American naval officer
military history, 174
PHILIP OF MACEDONIA [382–336 B.C.]:
King of Macedon and military tactician
fear, 111
PHILLIPS, Wendell [1811–1884]: American
politician and orator
moral courage, will, 189
PHORMIO OF ATHENS [floruit 429 B.C.]:
Greek soldier and leader
fear, 111
DU PICQ, Ardant, Colonel (French Army)
[1821–1870]: French soldier
ability, 4
cohesion, 41, 42
courage, 64
discipline, 84
fear, 111
human nature, 121
knowledge, wisdom, intelligence, 144
military history, 174
moral courage, will, 190
morale, 194
physical presence, 227
the soldier, 268
PINCKNEY, Charles Cotesworth [1746–1825]:
American soldier and Minister to France
(1796–1797)
praise, 235
PINDAR [518–438 B.C.]: Greek poet
ability, 4
competence, 52
war, 319

PLATO [circa 428–348 B.C.]: Greek
    philosopher and writer
just, justice, 138
patriotism, 215
the soldier, 268
PLINY THE ELDER (Gaius Plinius Secundus)
    [A.D. 23–79]: Roman writer and scholar
knowledge, wisdom, intelligence, 145
PLINY THE YOUNGER (Gaius Plinius
    Secundus) [circa A.D. 61–114]: Roman
    orator, scholar, and statesman
praise, 235
POLYBIUS [circa 208–125 B.C.]: Greek
    historian
knowledge, wisdom, intelligence, 145
luck, fate, 158
victory, winning, 308
POPE, Alexander [1688–1744]: British poet
training, 289
PRESCOTT, William [1726–1795]: American
    patriot and soldier
military history, 174
PRESTON, Richard [1868–1850]: English legal
    writer
war, 319
PROVERB
British (advice, 11)
Chinese (military ethics, 165; training, 284)
English (ability, 3)
French (risk, 250)
German (advice, 12; ambition, 14;
    competence, 51; perseverance,
    determination, 222)
Greek (knowledge, wisdom, intelligence, 142)
Italian (creativity, imagination, innovation,
    70)
U.S. Marine Corps (duty, 92)
PUBLILIUS SYRUS [floruit 43 B.C.]: Roman
    writer
adversity, 8, 9
advice, 12
ambition, 14
boldness, audacity, 26
character, 37
competence, 53
confidence, 58
discipline, 84
emotion, 98
experience, 103
honor, 117
judgment, 135
pride, 237
tact, 280
training, 289
victory, winning, 308
PULLER, Lewis Burwell "Chesty," General
    (USMC) [1898–1971]: American marine
competence, 53
PUTNAM, Israel, Major General (USA)
    [1718–1790]: American soldier
military history, 174

QUINTUS CURTIUS RUFUS [floruit second
    century]: Roman historian

fear, 111

REAGAN, Ronald Wilson [1911–]: American
    President (1981–1989)
patriotism, 215
trust, 294
REEVES, Joseph Mason, Admiral (USN)
    [1872–1948]: American naval officer
military leadership, 183
REYNOLDS, John J. [1788–1865]: American
    historian and politician
emotion, 98
RICHARDSON, William Rowland, General
    (USA) [1929–]: American soldier
training, 290
RICHTER, Johann Paul Friedrich (Jean Paul)
    [1763–1825]: German novelist
courage, 64
RICKENBACKER, Edward Veron, Captain
    (U.S. Army Air Corps) [1890–1973]:
    American airman and pioneer aviator,
    awarded Medal of Honor
faith, 107
service, 264
RICKOVER, Hyman George, Admiral (USN)
    [1900–1986]: American naval officer
military ethics, 167
mistakes, 186
RIDGWAY, Matthew Bunker, General (USA)
    [1895–]: American soldier and Army
    Chief of Staff (1953–1955)
boldness, audacity, 26
caring, 30
character, 37
competence, 53
courage, 64, 64–65
decision making, 77
discipline, 84
fear, 112
integrity, 130
moral courage, will, 190
officer corps, 207
physical presence, 227
physical stamina, 231
the soldier, 268, 269
stress, 273
subordinates, 276
training, 290
war, 319
RIOUX, M., Captain (Royal Canadian Army):
    Canadian soldier
knowledge, wisdom, intelligence, 145
luck, fate, 158
ROBERTSON, James Logie [1846–1922]:
    Scottish writer
communication, 48
ROCHEFOUCAULD, François, Duc de la
    [1613–1680]: French writer
advice, 12
courage, 65
danger, 73
fear, 112
human nature, 121
humor, 125

judgment, 135
luck, fate, 158
pride, 237
valor, 300
ROCKNE, Knute [1888–1931]: American
    football coach
victory, winning, 308
ROGERS, Bernard William, General (USA)
    [1921–]: American soldier; Commandant
    of Cadets, U.S. Military Academy (1967–
    1969); Army Chief of Staff (1976–1979);
    Supreme Allied Commander, Europe
    (1979–1987)
trust, 295
ROGERS, Robert, Lieutenant Colonel (Royal
    British Army) [1731–1795]: American-born
    British soldier
standing orders, 358
ROGERS, Will [1879–1935]: American
    humorist
initiative, 127
ROMMEL, Erwin, Field Marshal (German
    Army) [1891–1944]: German soldier
authority, 22
decision making, 77
military ethics, 167
physical presence, 228
role modeling, leadership by example, 255
standards, 271
training, 290
ROOSEVELT, Anna Eleanor [1884–1962]:
    American humanitarian
fear, 112
peace, 219
ROOSEVELT, Franklin Delano [1882–1945]:
    American President (1933–1945)
fear, 112
leadership, 150
luck, fate, 158
military history, 175
peace, 219
service, 264
truth, 298
victory, winning, 308
ROOSEVELT, Theodore [1858–1919]:
    American soldier, awarded Medal of
    Honor; President (1901–1909)
ability, 4
character, 37
duty, 93
knowledge, wisdom, intelligence, 145
moral courage, will, 190
patriotism, 215–216
physical stamina, 232
risk, 253
service, 264
training, 291
victory, winning, 309
war, 319
RUSKIN, John [1819–1900]: English writer
character, 38
duty, 94
leadership, 151
virtue, 312

RUSSELL, Bertrand Arthur William [1872–
    1970]: British philosopher
competence, 53
military history, 175
RUSSELL, William Fletcher [1890–1956]:
    American scholar and President of
    Columbia University (1949–1956)
training, 291
RYAN, John D., General (USAF) [1915–1983]:
    American airman and Air Force Chief of
    Staff (1969–1973)
integrity, 130

SANDUSKY, R. M.
motivation, 198
SANTAYANA, George [1863–1952]:
    American philosopher, novelist, and poet
military history, 175
SARKESIAN, Samuel Charles [1927–]:
    American political science scholar
values, 304
SASSOON, Siegfried Lorraine [1866–1967]:
    British poet
second-, third-order effects, 260
SAVILE, George, Sir (Marquess of Halifax)
    [1633–1695]: English statesman, orator,
    and writer
risk, 251
SAXE, Maurice (Moritz), Marshal Comte de
    (French Army) [1696–1750]: French
    soldier and Count of Saxony
attributes, 18
competence, 53
danger, 73
discipline, 84
esprit, 100
faith, 107
human nature, 121, 122
just, justice, 138
luck, fate, 158
physical stamina, 232
praise, 235
pride, 237
SCHELL, Adolf von, Captain (German Army)
    [floruit 1917–1933]: German soldier
communication, 48–49
SCHOFIELD, John McAllister, Major General
    (USA) [1831–1906]: American soldier,
    awarded Medal of Honor; Secretary of
    War (1868–1869); Superintendent, U.S.
    Military Academy (1876–1881)
discipline, 84–85
respect, 244
SCHULENBURG, Johann Matthias von, Field
    Marshal (Prussian Army) [1661–1747]:
    Prussian soldier
obedience, 203
SCHURZ, Carl [1829–1906]: American
    politician
patriotism, 216
SCHWEITZER, Albert [1875–1965]: French
    philosopher, theologian, and doctor
responsibility, 248
service, 264

SOPHOCLES [circa 495–405 B.C.]: Greek
playwright
adversity, 9
advice, 12
attributes, 18
confidence, 58
courage, 66
failure, 105
human nature, 122
knowledge, wisdom, intelligence, 145, 146
luck, fate, 159
military leadership, 184
truth, 298
war, 320
SOUTHEY, Robert [1774–1843]: English poet
and scholar
communication, 49
SOVIET ARMY FIELD SERVICE
REGULATIONS
commander's intent, 45
STALIN, Josif (Josif Vissarionovich
Dzhugashvili) [1879–1953]: Dictator of
Soviet Union (1929–1953)
military history, 175
STANHOPE, Philip Dormer (Earl of
Chesterfield) [1694–1773]: English
statesman and scholar
advice, 12
human nature, 118
STARRY, Donn Albert, General (USA)
[1925–]: American soldier
values, 304
STEFFENS, Lincoln [1866–1936]: American
political writer
ambition, 15
STEUBEN, Frederic Wilhelm Ludolf Gerhard
Augustin, Major General, Baron von
[1730–1794]: Prussian and American
soldier
NCO corps, 200–201
obedience, 204
STEVENS, Robert Ten Broeck [1899–]:
American Secretary of the Army (1953–
1955)
attributes, 18
authority, 22
integrity, 131
the soldier, 269
STEVENSON, Adlai Ewing [1900–1965]:
American statesman
motivation, 198
patriotism, 216
peace, 219
role modeling, leadership by example, 255
STEVENSON, Robert Louis Balfour [1850–
1894]: Scottish novelist, poet, and essayist
fear, 113
officer corps, 208
STILWELL, Joseph Warren, General (USA)
[1883–1946]: American soldier
character, 38
STOCKDALE, James Bond, Vice Admiral
(USN) [1923–]: American naval officer,

scholar, and President of Citadel (1979–
1980); awarded Medal of Honor
attributes, 18
authority, 22
experience, 103
failure, 105
leadership, 151
military history, 175
military leadership, 184
patriotism, 216–217
stress, 273
STRAUSS, Franz-Joseph [1915–]: German
statesman
management, 161
STUART, James Ewell Brown, Lieutenant
General (CSA) [1833–1864]: American
soldier
teamwork, 282
STURGIS, Samuel D., General (USA) [1897–
1964]: American soldier
attributes, 18
SUMMERALL, Charles Pelot, General (USA)
[1867–1955]: American soldier
mentor, 162
SUN-TZU [400–320 B.C.]: Chinese soldier and
historian
ability, 5
attributes, 19
boldness, audacity, 26
competence, 53
courage, 66
creativity, imagination, innovation, 71
decision making, 77
discipline, 85, 85–86
fear, 113
knowledge, wisdom, intelligence, 146
military leadership, 184
moral courage, will, 190
officer corps, 208
respect, 244
service, 264
subordinates, 276
victory, winning, 309
war, 320
SWIFT, Eben French, Major (USA) [1854–
1938]: American soldier
military history, 175

TACITUS, Caius Cornelius [circa A.D. 55–
117]: Roman historian
fear, 113
judgment, 135
military history, 175
safety, 258
valor, 300
victory, winning, 309
TAYLOR, Maxwell Davenport, General (USA)
[1901–1987]: American soldier;
Superintendent, U.S. Military Academy
(1945–1949); Army Chief of Staff (1955–
1959); Chairman, Joint Chiefs of Staff
(1962–1964); Ambassador to Vietnam
(1965)
caring, 30–31, 31

379

VANDEGRIFT, Alexander Archer, General
(USMC) [1887–1973]: American marine,
awarded Medal of Honor; Commandant of
U.S. Marine Corps (1943–1947)
boldness, audacity, 26
VAUGHAN, Bill [1915–]: American columnist
failure, 105
VEGETIUS (Flavius Vegetius Renatius) [floruit
378]: Roman historian and soldier
boldness, audacity, 27
courage, 66
discipline, 86, 87
fear, 113
judgment, 135
knowledge, wisdom, intelligence, 146
luck, fate, 159
NCO corps, 201
peace, 220
physical stamina, 232
subordinates, 277
training, 292
valor, 300
victory, winning, 309
VIOTTI, Paul R., Colonel (USAF) [1944–]:
American airman and U.S. Air Force
Academy Professor of political science
attributes, 19
VIRGIL (Publius Vergilius Maro) [70–19 B.C.]:
Roman poet
boldness, audacity, 27
confidence, 58
VOLTAIRE (François Marie Arouet) [1694–
1778]: French philosopher, essayist, and
historian
human nature, 122
knowledge, wisdom, intelligence, 146
military history, 176
mistakes, 187
service, 264

WAINWRIGHT, Jonathan Mayhew, General
(USA) [1883–1953]: American soldier,
awarded Medal of Honor
patriotism, 217
the soldier, 269
WALPOLE, Hugh Seymour, Sir [1884–1941]:
British writer
safety, 258
WARD, Orlando, Major General (USA) [1891–
1972]: American soldier
esprit, 100
WARD, William Arthur [1921–]: American
writer and soldier
training, 292
WASHINGTON, Booker Taliaferro [1856–
1915]: American writer and scholar
responsibility, 249
WASHINGTON, George, General (USA)
[1732–1799]: American soldier and
President (1789–1797)
character, 38
competence, 54
courage, 66
discipline, 87, 88

faith, 107
honor, 117
integrity, 131
obedience, 204
officer corps, 208
peace, 220
WAVELL, Archibald Percival, Field Marshal
Sir (Royal British Army) [1883–1950]:
British soldier
ability, 5
adversity, 10
attributes, 19, 20
boldness, audacity, 27
courage, 67
discipline, 88
human nature, 122
management, 161
military history, 176
military leadership, 184
moral courage, will, 190
motivation, 198
officer corps, 208–209
physical presence, 229
safety, 258
the soldier, 269
stress, 274
training, 292
WEBSTER, Daniel [1782–1852]: American
statesman and Secretary of State (1841–
1843)
military ethics, 167
patriotism, 217
truth, 298
WEBSTER, Noah [1758–1843]: American
scholar and writer
perseverance, determination, 224
WELLESLEY, Arthur, Field Marshal (Royal
British Army) [1769–1852]: British soldier
and statesman, first Duke of Wellington
decision making, 77
fear, 113
judgment, 135–136
military history, 177
physical presence, 229
WESLEY, John [1703–1791]: English
theologian
perseverance, determination, 224
WESTMORELAND, William C., General
(USA) [1914–]: American soldier;
Superintendent, U.S. Military Academy
(1960–1963); Army Chief of Staff (1968–
1972); Chairman, Joint Chiefs of Staff
(1968–1972)
military ethics, 168
WHITMAN, Walt [1819–1892]: American
poet and essayist
war, 320
WHITTIER, John Greenleaf [1807–1892]:
American poet
duty, 94
faith, 108
peace, 220
WICKHAM, John Adams, Jr., General (USA)